Employment of Blacks in the South

A Perspective on the 1960s

Edited by Ray Marshall and
Virgil L. Christian, Jr.

University of Texas Press, Austin and London

The material in this book was prepared under Contract No. 81-46-70-24 from the Manpower Administration, United States Department of Labor, under the authority of Title I of the Manpower Development and Training Act of 1962, as amended. Researchers undertaking such projects under government sponsorship are encouraged to express freely their professional judgment. Therefore, points of view or opinions stated in this book do not necessarily represent the official position or policy of the Department of Labor.

Library of Congress Cataloging in Publication Data
Main entry under title:
Employment of Blacks in the South.
Results of a study conducted by the Center for the Study of Human Resources, University of Texas at Austin.
Includes index.
1. Afro-Americans–Employment–Southern States –Addresses, essays, lectures. 2. Southern States –Economic conditions–1945–
I. Marshall, F. Ray. II. Christian, Virgil L., 1922– III. Texas. University at Austin. Center for the Study of Human Resources.
E185.92E46 331.6'96073075 78-7331
ISBN 0-292-72024-6

Printed in the United States of America

Contents

Preface

This volume is the result of a study entitled "Negro Employment in the South" by the Center for the Study of Human Resources, University of Texas at Austin. The research was principally funded by the Office of Research and Development, Employment and Training Administration, U.S. Department of Labor, and was supplemented by a grant from the Equal Opportunity Commission. The Commission also provided invaluable data from EEO-1 forms filed by employers in compliance with Title VII of the Civil Rights Act of 1964. The research reflects the continuing interest of the Employment and Training Administration in uncovering the nature and causes of employment disadvantage of minorities in the labor markets of this country and in particular of blacks in the large metropolitan areas of the South. The study had three objectives:

1. To determine the status of employment of blacks in the South
2. To examine various questions concerning the forces that influence employment of blacks in the South
3. To suggest remedial programs that might improve patterns of black employment in the South

The first objective in itself was important to the overall picture of the employment trends in the United States. And, because employment of blacks in rural jobs is most concentrated in the South, researchers focused attention on that area. But a bonus, a side benefit, surfaced: the study provided a benchmark against which to measure changes in the economic conditions of southern blacks at a time of significant advances in legal measures (especially the Civil Rights Act of 1964) to combat discrimination.

As for the second objective, although other researchers had advanced a number of hypotheses (some general and historical, some specific and contemporary) to account for the then-current job positions of blacks, for our researchers to put into proper order the relative importance of these factors in many settings (i.e., different cities; and within cities, different industries; and within industries, different occupations) was crucial to the identification of pervasive patterns of institutional and labor market discrimination. Blacks in the South had historically faced staggering and, for them, insurmountable obstacles in finding employment:

1. Their origin in slavery and subsequent second-class citizenship following Reconstruction
2. Their concentration in agriculture until the recent past, which disadvantaged them immensely in the transition to a more urban industrial society
3. The segregated and inferior schools they attended, both in the rural South and in the urban ghettos of the South and elsewhere
4. The generally unfavorable conditions and poor environment available to those in their income class, which led to poor health, high mortality, and low-level aspirations
5. The inadequate vocational training provided those who reached the labor market without salable skills (displaced agricultural laborers, for example)
6. The concept of "Negro" jobs, rooted in widely held notions about the blacks' "place," which dead-ended in low-paying jobs and low social status
7. Employer discrimination in hiring, in seniority, and in promotion
8. Segregated housing, concentrated in the inner city, remote from expanding suburban industry
9. The impact of unions on black entry into unionized labor markets
10. The effect of union agreements on occupational upgrading
11. The relationship of the black labor force to sources of job information and in particular to government employment service
12. The effects of tight labor markets

Examining the forces that influence employment of blacks in the South required the specification of a conceptual framework which made it possible to separate the important from the unimportant causes.

The third objective was clearly dependent upon the first two because only they could identify the locales, the industries, and the firms where large numbers of disadvantaged blacks could be found. But the third objective would attempt to isolate the various factors that caused blacks to be disadvantaged and would assign relative weights to these factors. (It would then become possible, it was hoped, to attack the ills with remedies aimed at specific problems.)

Because of the large concentration of blacks in the South, thirteen southern states were chosen for detailed analysis of the labor market: Alabama, Arkansas, Florida, Georgia, Kentucky, Louisiana, Mississippi, North Carolina, Oklahoma, South Carolina, Tennessee, Texas, and Virginia. (In some instances, West Virginia data were employed to round out the information.) In addition, six standard metropolitan statistical areas (SMSAs) were studied in great detail: Atlanta, Birmingham, Houston, Louisville, Memphis, and Miami.

Researchers were anxious to develop an insight into the structure of black jobs in the South through detailed analyses of the labor markets in these areas, supplemented by studies of agricultural and government employment and the problems and status of black contractors in Atlanta and Houston. Nearly 55 percent of the southern black farm labor force is in metropolitan areas, and it was expected that the SMSAs that were covered would reflect the total picture.

Special interest was given to the agricultural study, since agriculture is still by a sizable margin the largest employer of southern black men. Moreover, many problems that blacks face–social, political, legal, economic–can be traced to the rural South, where plantation agriculture, poor health, discrimination, low productivity, and poor educational systems perpetuated poverty and caused blacks (and some whites) to be ill-prepared for nonfarm jobs when they were forced to leave the farms during the 1950s and 1960s.

A by-product of the agricultural study was another bonus. The study permitted estimation of the number and qualifications of rural southern blacks who were feeding the manpower pool in the nonagricultural sectors–for the farm labor force continued to shrink slowly, and the net reproduction rate for the rural black population was found to be high enough to yield a surplus of several thousand a year over agricultural replacement needs (even at present levels). Government employment, too, was found to be important–not only because it is a growth industry but also because government employers were in a position to influence public policies affecting black employment patterns.

The purpose of the study required the preparation and use of a sizable volume of data to exhibit and analyze the structure of employment of blacks. The data came mostly from federal government sources: the Bureau of the Census; the Departments of Agriculture, Commerce, and Labor; the Equal Employment Opportunity Commission; and the Social Security Administration. (See references at the end of each chapter.)

In addition, other data sources were employed (reports to federal commissions; books by demographers, historians, and economists; and articles in journals) to buttress information obtained by the researchers through extensive interviewing of employers, employees, employment agencies, government officials, and civil rights groups. These interviews attempted to clarify, to correct, and to update information from statistical sources.

The techniques of data analyses range in sophistication from the construction of simple tables to economic models designed to measure the strength of association among variables of interest. Many of the authors of the city studies used multiple-regression techniques to examine the hypotheses set forth earlier. If we take the occupational position of blacks in comparison to that of whites as the dependent variable, we find that these behavioral models examine the causal significance of such factors as education, industry skill requirements, proximity of black housing to job concentration, tightness of the labor market, growth rate of employment in the SMSAs, and degree of market control by the employer. In other sections of the study, where specific statistical techniques could not be used, an attempt was made to reinforce theoretical arguments with supporting data.

We must emphasize that the data and statistics in this volume are not to be regarded as ends in themselves; rather, they are a means for exhibiting the structure of black employment and for providing a basis for explaining it. They reveal, to a degree, the magnitude of the problem, the numbers of people involved, and the outlines of the causal system. On the other hand, there are important causal variables–discrimination, for example–which are difficult to quantify and which must be represented by proxies in the set of explanatory factors, if indeed they can be adequately represented at all. Consequently, in the reports of the study, descriptions and verbal analyses are relied upon to at least as great an extent as statistical analyses.

In preparing the study, we have attempted, first, to give the reader an appropriate chronology for understanding the position of blacks in southern employment, past and present. Chapter 1 details racial employment patterns in its analysis of the old South and the new, its outline of the development of racial employment patterns in the South, and its discussion of aspects of the southern economy which influence black employment patterns.

Chapters 2 and 3 analyze the position of blacks in southern agriculture. Chapter 4 contains an analysis of black employment in state and local governments; and chapter 5 analyzes black employment in the federal government. Chapter 6 discusses the status of black contractors in the construction industry in Atlanta and Houston; and chapter 7 compares black employment in the South with patterns in the non-South.

Chapter 8 reviews some theoretical and empirical studies of employment discrimination. It seeks primarily to contrast the neoclassical economic model of discrimination in employment with a broader behavioral-conceptual framework that we have found to be more useful. These theoretical concepts are significant because they shaped our thinking about important and unimportant things to look for in the studies in this project. Moreover, an understanding of the basic causal forces influencing racial employment patterns is essential to the prescription of effective policy solutions.

The statistical material in this report came primarily from the 1960s, complemented by detailed field interviews during the 1960s and early 1970s. The last half of the 1960s was a particularly important time for racial employment patterns because of the impact of the civil rights legislation and ferment of those years.

Although we do not have later data, the evidence is very strong that rising unemployment, economic stagnation, and benign neglect of civil rights issues caused very little change during the first half of the 1970s. We feel, therefore, that the period of the 1960s provides valuable insight into what probably was the most active period in black employment advance in the South.

Ray Marshall
Virgil L. Christian, Jr.

Acknowledgments

The study owes a great debt to several people in the Employment and Training Administration, and a few should be singled out. Howard Rosen, in particular, is due special recognition, for he has been interested in the employment problems of minorities for some time, and he provided much of the initial thrust in getting the project off the ground. Ellen Sehgal monitored the project and supplied steady liaison between the research team and the Labor Department, keeping us informed of ongoing research at other institutions and aware of new data sources as they became available. She, along with Mary Bedell and Herman Travis, edited preliminary versions of the city study manuscripts and corrected numerous errors. Richard Fogarty took care of the tedious but important budgeting problems.

Several people on the staff of the Equal Employment Opportunity Commission were invaluable at various stages of the study. The project was initiated and encouraged by Phyllis Wallace, who made many valuable suggestions on the initial project design. Jerolyn Lyle and Al Golub helped conceptualize the investigation in such a way that it would benefit from use of the EEO-1 data provided by the Commission, and Herb Hammerman took care of packing the data on tapes. Although Malcolm Liggett joined the Commission long after the study had begun, he pointed out gaps in the research design and suggested ways to plug them.

Several members of the research team itself should be mentioned, including all who conducted the city studies: Vernon Briggs, Houston; Arvil Van Adams, Memphis; John Mead, Louisville; Brian Rungeling and George Ignatin, Birmingham; Dale Truett, Miami; and James Hefner, Atlanta. Each was responsible for a particular SMSA; collectively they provided valuable insights into the entire project and made suggestions that strengthened the work of others. (Inquiries regarding the availability of these city case studies should be directed to the Center for the Study of Human Resources, University of Texas at Austin, 78712.) Arvil Van Adams, a graduate student at the University of Kentucky when the project began, made a pilot SMSA study that served, at least to a degree, as a model for the later city studies. He later filled the role of coordinator for these studies. On his own initiative, he made an intercity comparison built on the work of all the others.

Professor Adamantios Pepelasis gave form to the study of black employment in agriculture and pointed out the many links between agricultural and urban labor markets, and Dr. C. C. Erwin developed useful data on the continuing important role of blacks in southern agriculture. Andy Batts, Randy Merris, and Jim Nelson spent untold hours in the library collecting mountains of numbers from the *Census of Population* and the *Census of Agriculture* series, and Mr. Batts joined Nancy Gostomski in taking care of the necessary computer work.

Finally, we owe an enormous debt to Barbara Howenstine and Susie Turner, who functioned as administrative assistants at the University of Kentucky and the University of Texas, respectively. They performed all the tasks ordinarily associated with secretarial work and also functioned as accountants, office managers, and editors. The project might still be in a state of limbo had it not been for them.

Despite our obligation to others, the basic responsibility for the design of the study and for errors of fact and analysis must lie with the directors of the research. The interpretations of the data, the conclusions drawn from them, and the recommendations based on those conclusions are our own and do not necessarily reflect the views of the Employment and Training Administration or the Equal Employment Opportunity Commission.

Employment of Blacks in the South

A Perspective on the 1960s

1

The Old South and the New

Ray Marshall

It is difficult for nonsoutherners to fully understand trends and patterns of racial employment in today's South without first understanding past developments which have influenced these patterns. Traditionally, the employment of southern blacks has reflected ingrained racism that has permeated the region's political and social institutions. In agriculture (after slavery), blacks were primarily sharecroppers, agricultural wage workers, and small-farm owners. Segregated educational institutions; discrimination in the sale of land, in access to credit, and in technical assistance from governmental agencies; and disfranchisement made it difficult for southern blacks to improve their condition.

During the nineteenth century, the South became a distinctive region culturally and statistically. By 1900 southern states could be distinguished from others by such quantitative measures as fewer numbers of foreign born in their population, higher proportions of blacks to total population, lower levels of education, high fertility rates, higher proportions of Protestants in the total population and of agricultural to nonagricultural workers in the labor force, smaller acreage per farm, and lower amounts of horsepower per agricultural worker (Marshall, 1967, chap. 1).

The South's unique characteristics–and many of its economic development and race problems–resulted from the plantation system. Although the region was industrializing before 1840, thereafter the solidification of the plantation system, based at first on slavery and later on sharecropping, produced an economy that was relatively static at a time when other regions were advancing. Plantation agriculture did little to advance the productivity of slaves or free labor. Since the plantation was largely a self-contained economic unit, few towns grew up to promote nonagricultural pursuits and diversify the economy.

Moreover, immigrants generally avoided the South, where they would have to compete directly and indirectly with slaves, causing the region to miss the stimulation given to other areas by skilled immigrants. The South was also largely avoided by nonagricultural entrepreneurs because the agricultural creed that buttressed slavery and the plantation system was more than somewhat hostile to commercial and manufacturing undertakings–indeed, people like John C. Calhoun evolved fairly elaborate philosophies to defend slavery and the agricultural system as a means of avoiding the class conflicts which they saw as the inevitable consequences of industrialization.

Emancipation did not destroy the plantation system, because slavery was replaced by sharecropping, which also provided little incentive for technological or human resource development. After a period of social ferment following Reconstruction, when it appeared that workers and farmers might organize themselves on an interracial basis, institutionalized segregation became firmly entrenched and blacks were relegated to an inferior economic and social status.

Thus, while the North was industrializing and its political and social institutions were responding to a changing economic base, the institutions of the South continued to reflect the relatively static agricultural system upon which they were based. Conflict over slavery and race consumed an inordinate amount of the region's leadership energies; ideological conformity on matters of slavery and race stifled criticism and debate. The South's tradition also was a barrier to economic development in other ways: the rigid social structure made it difficult for the rural and urban poor to use political processes to solve their problems, and racial antagonisms made it difficult to adopt educational and training programs to advance the productivity of the region's people.[1]

As in other traditional societies, industrialization tended to erode the agricultural system and to remake the South more in the image of the rest of the United States. Statistics show that per capita incomes and other quantitative indicators listed above diverged from the national averages during the first half of the nineteenth century but began to converge around 1900. Per capita incomes in the South, compared to the national average, were little higher in 1880 than they had been in 1840, but there was a sharp increase in relative per capita incomes around 1900, associated with a period of rapid industrial growth.

Industrialization

The so-called new South is usually defined in terms of the resurgence of manufacturing around 1880 (Easterlin, 1960, pp. 138–140; Williamson, 1964). By that time, the economic vicissitudes of the plantation system and cotton culture had convinced many southerners that the region's economic salvation lay in industrialization. While there were some who lamented the passing of the agrarian way of life, the drive to industrialize the South assumed almost religious proportions by the 1920s. The number of manufacturing wage earners increased by 109 percent between 1880 and 1890, while the value of manufactures increased by 111 percent. Although the number of manufacturing workers did not increase so spectacularly in subsequent decades, it increased steadily until the Depression in the 1930s, when manufacturing employment was virtually constant. Decades of particularly marked increase in manufacturing employment were 1899 to 1909 (56%) and 1890 to 1899 (36%). The South's economy was also greatly stimulated by the first and second world wars (U.S. Department of Labor, 1946, p. 5).

As has been true of other traditional societies, industrialization and urbanization have had a profound impact on the South's social and economic relations. The region's traditional racial caste system and one-party political tradition were incompatible with the dynamism and rationalism required by an industrial society. As Kerr and others demonstrate, "the industrial society tends to be an open society, inconsistent with the assignment of workers to occupations or to jobs by traditional caste, racial groups, by sex or family status" (1960, p. 35). These authors emphasize that industrialism requires rational planning which tends to destroy static societies, even though traditional institutions usually slow down the rate of transformation and leave their marks on the emerging society. Economic efficiency becomes important, and industrializers tend to value people more for their individual abilities than for their race or social status.

An industrial society requires an increasingly highly qualified work force. Thus, the role of education changes from the promotion of tradition to preparation for the future, and agriculture becomes simply another industry, not a way of life. Industrial societies also tend to be pluralistic, producing such organizations as labor unions, farmers' movements, and business organizations to represent the emerging economic interests. In the South, the one-party political tradition was eroded by this process. Thus, although many of the region's traditional institutions have left their mark, there can be little doubt that industrialization and urbanization have caused a convergence of institutions between the South and the rest of the country.

Conditions of Black Workers

The traditional nonagricultural employment pattern for blacks in the South was to be restricted to menial or otherwise disagreeable jobs, except for some professional and skilled positions in black communities. There were few exceptions where blacks were able to penetrate better jobs (such as bricklaying in the construction industry) because they had learned these occupations as slaves, and techniques were sufficiently stable that whites could not freeze them out by monopolizing the latest technology–as they did with such occupations as electricians, locomotive engineers, plumbers, and sheet metal workers.

In manufacturing, blacks were generally relegated to laborer positions regardless of their qualifications. When industrial unions entered southern manufacturing industries for the first time on a significant scale during the 1930s and World War II, they usually formalized occupational segregation by seniority systems which continued to restrict blacks to laborer positions. Blacks, therefore, were disadvantaged not only by inferior educational systems but also by job segregation that denied them equal access to on-the-job training–which is probably the most important manner in which skills are acquired.

A number of developments have slowly undermined job segregation. The migration of blacks from the rural South into urban areas brought them into competition with white workers for jobs. Many employers hired blacks for nontraditional jobs when whites were not available (as strikebreakers or because they would do the same work for lower wages than whites). The employment of black workers, therefore, threatened white workers and their unions, requiring the latter to open their ranks or find their own positions weakened. The development of public policies favoring collective bargaining, first with railroads and then with other industries, weakened union discrimination by giving black workers votes in government-conducted representation elections. Blacks usually have had the greatest difficulty penetrating white occupations and unions where their numbers are not large enough to threaten white workers' jobs.

The migration of black workers from rural areas also increased their political power because their greater unity and economic independence in urban areas made it more difficult to deny them the vote. Black political clout was strengthened when blacks migrated to areas where political forces were fairly evenly balanced and they could become the balance of power.

Rising black political muscle and the impact of urbanization and industrialization on white attitudes toward racism gradually produced public policies which outlawed overt racism in employment and public facilities. The Voting Rights Act of 1965 and voter registration drives increased the importance of the black vote. Despite the decline in overt discrimination, however, the more subtle and powerful influences of institutionalized discrimination remain.

As the following chapters reveal, broad racial employment patterns were relatively stable between the 1920s and the 1960s. There have been some significant changes since 1966, but it is too early to see if these changes result from trends or merely short-run fluctuations. The remainder of this chapter deals with some aspects of the southern economy. Subsequent chapters attempt to account for the patterns and changes in racial employment practices.

Industrial Structure

Since the South's employment has been concentrated disproportionately in low-wage, slow-growth industries, it is instructive to examine the extent to which industrial composition changed in the last decade. The southern industries exhibiting the most rapid employment rates of growth from 1959 to 1969 were:

Electrical equipment and supplies (131.4%)
Machinery, except electrical (109%)
Transportation equipment (92.7%)
Fabricated metal products (80.3%)
Apparel and other textile products (70.6%)
Services (66.7%)
State and local government (64.4%)

However, the southern industries showing the largest absolute growth in employment over the period were:

Wholesale and retail trade (998,400)
State and local government (919,300)
Services (914,600)
Contract construction (295,500)
Finance, insurance and real estate (266,300)
Apparel and other textile products (212,000)
Transportation and public utilities (195,000)
Federal government (188,100)

This group of southern growth industries contains some which are nationally characterized as high wage and rapid growth, but it also contains some which are low wage and slow growth.

Several measures have been attempted to consider the question of whether the South's employment is increasing or decreasing in comparison to industries in the rest of the United States. The rank correlation between southern industry growth rates and national weekly earnings for 1969 is not statistically significant. Moreover, the South had exactly 43.6 percent of its employment in the thirteen highest paying sectors in 1959 and 1969, indicating no improvement in the region's industrial structure. However, a relative index of industrial wage structure (a ratio calculated by summing the percentage of southern employment in each industry weighted by national average weekly earnings in relation to the same calculation for the United States) would relate the region's structure to that of the nation. Thus, the index is calculated by the following formula:

$$RI_W S_W = \frac{\sum_{i=1}^{26} (\text{Percentage of southern employment in industry } i \times \text{national average weekly earnings in industry } i)}{\sum_{i=1}^{26} (\text{Percentage of national employment in industry } i \times \text{national average weekly earnings in industry } i)}$$

This measure was 0.9758 in 1959 and 0.9831 in 1969, indicating some improvement in the South's industrial structure in comparison to that of the entire United States.

It is also instructive to look at the changing industrial structure of the South in terms of growth rates. If the percentage rates of change (1959 to 1969) for the twenty-six sectors in the South and the nation are ranked by rates of growth, the rank correlation between the South's and the nation's industry increases is +0.613, indicating that the South's rapid relative growth industries have largely been national growth industries also, although this is a weak test as to whether the industrial structure was actually improving. A better test is accorded by noting the change in the percentage of southern employment in the thirteen nationally ranked above-average growth sectors. In 1969 the South had 69.7 percent of its employment in the more rapid growth sectors, as opposed to 64.8 percent in 1959, indicating a clear improvement.

The most comprehensive and unambiguous way to explore this question is to construct an index of industrial structure, using national sector growth rates. The summation of the percentage of southern employment in each sector multiplied by the respective national sector growth rates produces a weighted average expected growth rate for nonagricultural employment. In 1969 the expected growth rate (for ten years) for the South was 32 percent, as compared to 29 percent in 1959, a clear indication that the South's industrial structure was improving and providing a stronger base for future growth. But since the question of whether the South's industrial structure is improving is usually taken to mean in comparison to the rest of the nation, the appropriate measure is to divide the South's expected growth rate by the nation's. Thus:

26 (Percentage of southern industry, industry i, × national growth
$i = 1$ rate, industry i)

26 (Percentage of national industry, industry i, × national growth
$i = 1$ rate, industry i)

The growth rate will be greater than, equal to, or less than one, as the South's industrial structure is greater than, equal to, or less than the nation's for a given year. In 1969 the index was 0.9207, an improvement over the 1959 index of 0.9107, indicating that, even though the South's industrial structure was still heavily weighted with slower growth sectors, the South was improving at an even faster rate than the nation as a whole.

Thus, it is clear that the South's industrial structure, in terms of national wage levels and growth rates, has been improving in the past decade and converging toward that of the rest of the nation. That this convergence is also in terms of actual wage rates is evident from average weekly earnings of production workers on manufacturing payrolls between 1960 and 1969. State wages as a percentage of national wages improved for ten of the thirteen states (with the two significant declines in Texas and Oklahoma, which were already comparatively high-wage states), indicating that the improvements have been widely dispersed throughout the South.

Changes in the Rural South

As subsequent chapters demonstrate in greater detail, some of the most significant forces at work in the southern economy relate to long-run trends in the rural South. Many of the basic employment problems of blacks derive from their concentration in agriculture, which in 1970 was still a more important source of employment for southern blacks than any four manufacturing industries. Moreover, the manner in which blacks have been displaced from agriculture has had important implications for their nonagricultural employment. Unfortunately, public policy in the United States, beginning with the Emancipation Proclamation, has done little to prepare blacks for nonfarm jobs. During the 1950s, southern blacks were displaced from farming at an unprecedented rate because of technological changes and U.S. agricultural policy, with little effort by public policy to prepare them for nonfarm employment. As a consequence, the combined effects of their agricultural heritage–with almost no thought for human resource development–and institutionalized racism have seriously handicapped their ability to adjust to nonfarm employment.

It is important to emphasize the distinction between the rural population, which is about constant absolutely, and the agricultural population, which is declining absolutely and relatively. In 1960, for example, the rural population of the South was 21,777,269, compared to 21,184,407 in 1970. At the same time the agricultural work force declined from 2,994,000 in 1960 to 1,863,000 in 1969. These rural trends will be explored more fully in chapters 3 and 4.

In addition, labor force data reflect these population movements. The labor force expanded from 15.7 million in 1950 to 22.8 million in 1970, and nonagricultural employment rose by more than 6.5 million jobs. Simultaneously, the agricultural labor force fell by nearly 2.7 million–from more than 4.5 million to a little less than 2 million. Thus, not all displaced agricultural labor (within the South) found work outside that sector. Migration relieved some of the pressure but not all, and a pool of surplus low-skill labor built up in the region, with blacks disproportionately represented.

Since southern urban labor markets have been somewhat tight–and characterized by the importation of high-skill workers to staff the region's growth industries–it is reasonable to infer that the surplus labor is backed up in rural nonfarm areas, where it stands as a barrier to the absorption of further displaced agricultural labor into nonagricultural employment, primarily because those displaced from agriculture (*a*) do not have the necessary skills for nonfarm employment, (*b*) elect to remain in rural areas, or (*c*) face impediments in moving to nonfarm jobs.

Incomes and Poverty

The best overall indicators of the economic welfare of the South's people are their per capita incomes, which are below those of the rest of the United States, despite a long-run tendency for regional income gaps to narrow. In 1940, for example, per capita income in the South was 60 percent of that for the United States, but it was about 80 percent in 1969. There is, however, considerable variation among southern states. In 1969, for instance, per capita income was $3,680 in the United States but ranged from $3,427 in Florida to $2,192 in Mississippi.

Table 1-1 shows that the incidence of poverty was roughly 50 percent higher in the census South than in the nation in 1973. It was 9.3 percent for southern black families, compared with 7.1 percent nationally, and 34.8 percent for southern blacks, compared with a national rate of 29.0 percent. In 1969 the South had 46 percent of all the nation's poor persons, almost the same proportion as in 1968 (Table 1-2), indicating that, even though the region's poverty is being eradicated at approximately the same rate as in the rest of the nation, the South is improving only slightly in relation to other areas.

The incidence of poverty is particularly high among southern blacks, who are more than three times as likely to be poor as southern whites (see Table 1-1). Moreover, southern poor blacks are likely to be poorer than poor whites. The median *income deficit* (the income transfer needed to bring a family to the poverty threshold) is $1,375 for poor southern blacks, as compared to $925 for poor southern whites. In 1970 median incomes for southern blacks were only 57 percent of those of southern whites, a big improvement from 46 percent in 1959 but still a long way from the 77 percent ratio of the West.

TABLE 1-1. Families and Unrelated Individuals Below the
(By region; in thousands)

Residence	All Races Total	No.	%
Families			
South	17,275	2,314	13.4
North and West	37,098	2,761	7.4
United States	54,373	5,075	9.3
Unrelated individuals			
South	4,655	1,637	35.2
North and West	12,156	3,246	26.7
United States	16,811	4,883	29.0

Source: U.S. Department of Commerce, Bureau of the

*As of March 1973.

TABLE 1-2. Distribution of Persons Below the Poverty Level
(Selected Years)

Race and Year	United States (millions)	(%) South	(%) Northeast	(%) North Central	(%) West
All Races					
1959	38.8	48.0	16.0	25.0	11.0
1968	25.4	47.0	18.0	21.0	13.0
1969	24.3	46.0	54.0	54.0	54.0
White					
1959	28.3	40.0	18.0	29.0	13.0
1968	17.4	39.0	20.0	25.0	16.0
1969	16.7	37.0	63.0	63.0	63.0
Black					
1959	9.9	75.0	9.0	12.0	4.0
1968	7.6	69.0	13.0	14.0	4.0
1969	7.2	68.0	32.0	32.0	32.0

Source: U.S. Department of Commerce, Bureau of the Census, 1970 <u>a</u>, p. 5; and 1970 <u>b</u>, p. 72.

Low-Income Level in 1972*

White			Black		
Total	No.	%	Total	No.	%
14,508	1,350	9.3	2,676	931	34.8
33,968	2,091	6.2	2,589	598	23.1
48,476	3,441	7.1	5,265	1,529	29.0
3,663	1,143	31.2	956	489	51.2
10,832	2,792	25.8	1,072	380	35.5
14,495	3,935	27.1	2,028	860	42.9

Census, 1973, p.7.

Although the relative racial income gap is closing, the absolute gap between blacks and whites *increased* between 1959 and 1969 in both the South (from $3,321 to $3,776) and the United States ($2,918 to $3,796), as shown in Table 1-3.

To some extent, the lower median incomes of blacks are due to differences in family structure and occupations as well as lower earnings. If we compare craftworker and operative families with husband and wife present (controlling in a rough way for family status and occupation), the nonwhite/white ratio rises to 63 percent in the South and 82 percent elsewhere in 1970. Moreover, the median incomes of nonwhites increased faster absolutely and relatively in the South between 1960 and 1970 than they did in the non-South ($1,704 and 56% for the South, compared to $1,677 and 30% for the non-South).

Despite the heavier incidence of poverty among blacks, there were many more poor whites (6,166,000) than poor blacks (4,928,000) in the South in 1970. Moreover, about equal proportions of the black (65.3%) and white (62.9%) poor in the South were in nonmetropolitan areas. Outside the South, 93.8 percent of the black poor and 56.3 percent of the white poor were in metropolitan areas. Thus, poverty in the South is much more a rural phenomenon than it is in the North and West. Similarly, a study of the rural poor by Bowles and others

TABLE 1-3. Craftworkers and Operatives: Median Annual

Area	1960	
	White	Nonwhite
United States total	$6,408	$4,213
South total	5,546	3,054
In metropolitan South	6,266	3,551
Central cities	5,954	3,620
Outside central cities	6,491	*
Outside metropolitan South	4,730	2,394
Urban	5,198	2,609
Rural	4,478	2,224
Non-South total	6,616	5,565
In metropolitan non-South	6,838	5,546
Central cities	6,603	5,495
Outside central cities	7,033	5,773
Outside metropolitan non-South	6,068	*
Urban	6,217	*
Rural	5,917	*

Source: Adapted from U.S. Department of Commerce,

*Blank spaces are because the base is less than 75,000.

shows 2,810,000 poor whites seventeen years of age and over and 1,417,000 poor blacks, even though the incidence of poverty among whites was only 22 percent as compared with 59.4 percent of blacks (1973).

Of course southern incomes are nearer the national average in real than in monetary terms because the cost of living is substantially lower in the South than elsewhere. A more detailed analysis by Watts, which considers city size as well as regions, suggests even larger cost-of-living differentials between the rural South and other regions and

Income of Husband (Selected Years)

1970		Change from 1960 to 1970			
White	Nonwhite	White		Nonwhite	
$8,025	$5,979	$1,617	25%	$1,766	42%
7,070	4,758	1,524	28	1,704	56
7,830	5,525	1,564	25	1,974	56
7,152	5,427	1,198	20	1,807	50
8,198	5,778	1,707	26	*	*
6,411	4,012	1,681	36	1,618	68
6,546	4,099	1,348	26	1,490	57
6,373	3,977	1,893	42	1,755	79
8,402	7,242	1,786	27	1,677	30
8,806	7,286	1,968	29	1,740	31
8,341	7,117	1,738	26	1,622	32
9,063	7,759	2,030	29	1,986	30
7,616	*	1,548	26	*	*
7,775	*	1,558	25	*	*
7,492	*	1,575	27	*	*

Bureau of the Census, 1970c.

sizable cost-of-living differentials between rural and urban places in the South (1964).

One of the most disturbing trends in southern agriculture was the tendency for the racial income gap to widen between 1960 and 1965 (as revealed by Social Security data which give a constant identification of individuals through time). Although the incomes of black male farm operators averaged only about half those of others in 1960, the average increased 39.7 percent for others but only 6.5 percent for blacks between 1960 and 1965. All black farm operators gained only

$76 in income ($1,371 to $1,447) between 1960 and 1965, as compared with a gain of $1,025 for others ($2,734 to $3,759). The racial gap widened for operators, even though black farm operators earned less than half as much as others in 1960.

Summary and Conclusions

This chapter has outlined some of the main characteristics of the South's economy. It was noted that the traditional political, social, and economic institutions in the South were not conducive to improving individual or regional productivity. The agrarian system, racism, undemocratic political traditions, and low investments in human resources have been among the most important traditional impediments to improvements in the region's per capita incomes.

However, industrialization and urbanization have eroded the South's traditional institutions and caused most economic and social indicators to converge with their national averages. Industrial societies tend to be pluralistic and open, to require higher levels of education and skills, and to place greater emphasis on rational conduct and individual merit, all of which are incompatible with many aspects of the South's traditional institutions. It has been demonstrated that the South's economic structure is improving in terms of high-wage and growth industries. Industrialization and urbanization, therefore, have tended to unify the South with the rest of the nation, even though the traditional influences remain, especially in the rural South and in discrimination against blacks.

These traditional general influences manifest themselves as particular problems. The statistics show two of these lingering problems to be (*a*) limited investments in education and skills for blacks and whites, but especially blacks, and (*b*) surplus labor in rural areas, where many who work have been displaced by innovations, are underemployed, or have very low productivity because their agricultural work experiences and rural educations have not prepared them for high-wage nonfarm work.

For purposes of black employment patterns, the most pervasive and important development of the traditional South was institutionalized discrimination, which has permeated all aspects of life, especially preparation for work and access to job opportunities.

Notes

1. For a convincing discussion of the barriers of southern tradition to the economic development of the South, see Nicholls, 1960.

References

Bowles, Gladys, et al. 1973. *Poverty Dimensions of Rural-to-Urban Migration.* Joint study by U.S. Department of Agriculture, University of Georgia, and Office of Economic Opportunity. Washington, D.C.: U.S. Government Printing Office.

Easterlin, Richard A. 1960. "Interregional Differences in Per Capita Income, Population, and Total Income, 1840–1950." In *Trends in the American Economy in the Nineteenth Century.* Washington, D.C.: National Bureau of Economic Research Studies in Income and Wealth.

Kerr, Clark, et al. 1960. *Industrialization and Industrial Man.* Cambridge, Mass.: Harvard University Press.

Marshall, Ray. 1967. *Labor in the South.* Cambridge, Mass.: Harvard University Press.

Nicholls, W. H. 1960. *Southern Tradition and Regional Progress.* Chapel Hill: University of North Carolina Press.

U.S. Department of Commerce, Bureau of Census. 1970*a*. *Current Population Reports.* Series P-60, no. 76 (December).

———. 1970*b*. *Current Population Reports.* Series P-23, no. 30 (September).

———. 1970*c*. "Occupations and Earnings of Family Heads in 1969, 1965, and 1959." In *Current Population Reports.* Series P-60, no. 73 (September 30).

———. 1973. "Consumer Income." In *Current Population Reports.* Series P-60, no. 88 (June).

U.S. Department of Labor, Bureau of Labor Statistics. 1946. *Labor in the South.* Bulletin no. 898. Washington, D.C.: U.S. Government Printing Office.

Watts, Harold W. 1964. *The Measure of Poverty.* Reprint no. 42. Madison: University of Wisconsin, Institute for Research on Poverty.

Williamson, Jeffrey G. 1964. "National Economic Development and Interregional Inequality." Paper presented at a symposium on approaches to regional analysis, University of Texas at Austin, April 27–28.

2

Rural Problems

Virgil L. Christian, Jr., and
Adamantios Pepelasis

The twentieth century brought dramatic changes in American agriculture and agricultural labor. The farm labor force declined from 11.5 million to 8.2 million between 1910 and 1940, and to 5.1 million by 1960 (Hiestand, 1964, pp. 7–9). Labor displacement in the South paralleled the national trend until World War II, then accelerated, with the agricultural labor force falling by 1969 to a third of what it had been in 1950. (Mechanization of cotton accounted for much of the acceleration. The proportion of cotton harvested by hand fell from 92 to 11 percent between 1950 and 1966.) Blacks were disproportionately involved in these movements because they were concentrated in the region with the strongest agricultural orientation and were, in that region, intensely identified with the cotton industry.

At the beginning of the century, about 90 percent of the American black population lived in the South, and more than 80 percent of this population lived in rural regions. Six decades later the South contained only 60 percent of all blacks, with but 43 percent of these inhabiting its rural areas (Hayes, 1962, pp. 1356–1365; Kaun, 1970). This implies a great exodus from southern agriculture: more than half a million blacks currently in the nonagricultural labor force were at one time farm workers in the South. Yet agriculture still remains to southern blacks a sizable source of employment. In 1969 it absorbed more black labor than any four nonagricultural industries in the region, aggregated at the two-digit standard industrial code (SIC) level, and black farm ownership actually increased between 1950 and 1959.

The reduction of the farm labor force, on the one hand, and the continuing importance of farming to southern blacks, on the other, suggest that there are several facets to the study of black employment in agriculture:

1. The changing role of agriculture within the regional economy and the changing position of blacks within agriculture
2. The capacity of the secondary and tertiary sectors in the region to absorb displaced agricultural labor and the ability of such labor to meet manpower needs outside the primary sectors
3. The adequacy and the plasticity of the institutional framework to facilitate the transition from farm employment to employment in urban markets–both in industry and in services

Agricultural Labor Displacement since 1950

Farm productivity, measured by output per unit of labor input, continued to rise considerably throughout the decades of the 1950s and the 1960s (U.S. Department of Agriculture, 1969). This was particularly true in the southern crop that most involved blacks–cotton. Increased productivity was caused primarily by the introduction of improved technology in the form of more capital-intensive methods. USDA standard estimates of labor requirements–units of labor required to produce a given amount of output–show a consistent decline in the face of increasing agricultural output. Inevitably, the size of the agricultural labor force–farm operators, family workers, hired workers–followed the downward trend of the labor requirements. Tables 2-1 and 2-2 summarize these data: the first showing the reduction in labor requirements in southern agriculture in terms of man-hours of standard homogeneous labor units and the second showing the actual decline in farm labor for 1950 through 1973.

Incidentally, it is important to note that the concept of labor requirements is a noneconomic technological notion which does not allow for a range of possibilities of varying factor proportions in agriculture. Regional requirements were derived by extending labor requirements of the "average" farm to the entire region and making all farming activity conform to that of the average type. Obviously, the requirements do not constitute in any sense a demand for labor, inasmuch as demand for labor would vary with the return per unit of output (Desai and Muzumdar, 1970, pp. 39–40). Interpreted in this light, the data of Table 2-1 reflect technological changes which must have generated a considerable volume of surplus agricultural labor and precipitated the displacement of farm families in the South. (Surplus labor may be defined as the difference between labor available–the labor time that the agricultural population can provide under full employment–and

TABLE 2-1. Labor Requirements in Southern Agriculture (1951-1968)

Year	Man-Hours (millions)	Index
1951	6,976	100.0
1952	6,562	94.1
1953	6,286	90.1
1954	5,773	82.8
1955	5,561	79.7
1956	5,110	73.3
1957	4,460	63.9
1958	4,244	60.8
1959	4,253	61.0
1960	4,034	57.8
1961	3,904	56.0
1962	3,704	53.1
1963	3,609	51.7
1964	3,360	48.2
1965	3,148	45.1
1966	2,933	42.0
1967	2,909	41.7
1968	2,778	39.8

Source: U.S. Department of Agriculture, 1969.

labor required, given the area under cultivation, capital, technology, and the volume of output produced. Thus, the concept of chronic surplus labor refers to that part of the labor force which could be removed without a decrease in total farm output–given the level of technology applied. Operationally, labor becomes surplus and is pushed out of agriculture when its marginal product falls below the family subsistence level. The technology of agriculture has changed so rapidly, and become so much more capital intensive, that a significant proportion of labor used profitably one year becomes surplus the next.)

Not only did the farm labor force decline, but also falling labor requirements and an associated downward shift in the demand for farm

TABLE 2-2. Farm Labor in the South: Number of Workers and Man-Years of Work (1950-1973; thousands)

Year	Total Farm Labor	Index	Total Man-Years	Index
1950	4,550		2,501	
1951	4,329	100.0	2,315	100.0
1952	4,069	94.0	2,105	90.9
1953	3,901	90.1	1,946	84.1
1954	3,790	87.5	1,817	78.5
1955	3,674	84.9	1,704	73.6
1956	3,379	78.1	1,504	65.0
1957	3,262	75.4	1,375	59.4
1958	3,182	73.5	1,309	56.5
1959	3,146	72.7	1,248	53.9
1960	2,994	69.2	1,146	49.5
1961	2,945	68.0	1,017	43.9
1962	2,825	65.3	1,003	43.3
1963	2,771	64.0	955	41.3
1964	2,562	59.2	878	37.9
1965	2,331	53.8	789	34.1
1966	2,134	49.3	736	31.8
1967	2,031	46.9	713	30.8
1968	1,951	45.1	686	29.6
1969	1,863	43.0	663	28.6
1970	1,830	42.3	NA	NA
1971	1,777	41.0	NA	NA
1972	1,738	40.1	NA	NA
1973	1,738	40.1	NA	NA

Source: Data are from the following publications of the U.S. Department of Agriculture: for 1950-1969, Farm Employment (August 1963), Number of Farms: 1910-1959 (June 1962), and Farm Labor (1963-1969); for 1970-1971, Agricultural Statistics, Table 644 (1972); and for 1972-1973, Farm Labor (January 14, 1974). Operator and family worker data from Number of Farms were combined with hired worker data from Farm Employment and Farm Labor to arrive at the totals. Data reduction to full-time equivalents (man-years) came from the Census of Agriculture of the U.S. Department of Agriculture for 1954, 1959, and 1964. Intercensal year reduction factors were computed by linear interpolation.

NA = not available.

labor led to an increase in the amount of off-farm work performed by farm families. Apparently, the rate of technological improvements in agriculture outran the outward movement of farm families, because the data (Table 2-2) show a slower decline in the number engaged in farming than do parallel estimates (Table 2-1) of the volume of farm work performed. Thus, families who remained on the farm found it necessary to increase the proportion of labor time spent in nonagricultural employment.[1] For many marginal or "surplus" farm families, the shift from agriculture came in stages: part-time nonfarm work in rural areas, abandonment of farming as the primary source of income, and physical movement from the farm.

It should be recognized, however, that the counts in Table 2-2 are at best a rough measure of the volume of agricultural labor performed. For example, no consideration is given the changes through time in the age and sex composition of the farm labor force or the average proportion of a man-year spent in farm work by members of farm families. The last two columns in Table 2-2 were developed to correct for the latter defect. They convert the basic family labor counts to man-years by adjusting them for changes in average hours per week and average weeks per year worked by farm family labor (which includes the operator and numbers of his family). They do not, however, convert labor from heterogeneous sources–male, female, child, senior–to a common standard. Thus, they do not provide a completely adequate measure of family labor input. With this reservation in mind, one may note that the number of family workers declined from 3.339 million in 1950 to 1.351 million in 1969 (i.e., by 59.5%), but the decline was 71.4 percent in terms of the full-time equivalents–presumptive evidence of rising underemployment in agriculture. In addition, one may infer that an increasing proportion of southern farm work is done by hired workers, since labor requirements in 1968 were 39.8 percent of those in 1951, but the family labor input was only 29.6 percent as great.

The foregoing reduces to an observed trend and a derived proposition relative to agricultural displacement and regional manpower. Labor requirements in agriculture have declined drastically over the last two decades; that is, improvements in agricultural technology and productivity have led to correspondingly rapid reductions in labor utilization. This has made for large-scale displacement of labor away from agriculture. Between 1950 and 1969, the southern agricultural labor force declined by almost 2.7 million workers.

Population, Labor Force, and Nonagricultural Employment

The total population of the fourteen southern states increased from 43.399 million in 1950 to 62.798 million in 1970. The labor force expanded from 15.718 million to 22.797 million, an increase of 7.079 million workers. During the same period, nonagricultural employment grew, in approximate terms, from 9.810 million to 18.124 million, that is, by 8,315.2 jobs (Tables 2-3 and 2-4). The rate of employment growth was then more rapid than the rate of population and labor growth in the secondary and tertiary sectors. But, for the entire regional economy, the rate of employment growth lagged behind the rate of growth in the active labor force. The imbalance, of course, was occasioned by the reduction in agricultural employment. Between 1950 and 1968 the southern agricultural force declined by 2.6 million, thus expanding potential labor availability for employment in industry and services by 0.14 million workers annually and imposing a greater burden on those sectors than they could absorb.

The population and labor force counts in Tables 2-3 and 2-4 can be summarized to yield a simple arithmetic difference between potentially available labor and actual use of labor throughout the regional economy. True, the data–accumulated over all southern states and all industries–cover differences in labor skills, origin, and quality and reveal little about the level and changes in underemployment, sectoral or aggregate, or the marginal product of labor in various industries–or shortages of labor of certain types. But the counts do provide, in a rough-hewn and inelegant way, an estimate of surplus labor in the region–not where it is, or what kind it is, but simply that it exists. Furthermore, as shown below, they make it clear that displacement of agricultural labor was an important element in the development of the pool.

	Labor Pool (1950–1967)	*Millions*
$A=$	increment in regional labor force	4.712
$B=$	decline in farm labor force	2.600
$A + B=$	potential increase in nonagricultural employment	7.312
$C=$	actual increase in nonagricultural employment	6.574
$D=$	surplus labor	0.738

In the above tabulation, difference D is composed of individuals who increase sum $(A + B)$, or both.

TABLE 2-3. Population and Labor Force of the South (1950-1968; thousands)

	Population			Labor Force		
Year	Amount	Change from Previous Year	Cumulative Change from 1950	Amount	Change from Previous Year	Cumulative Change from 1950
1950	43,399			15,718		
1951	43,661	262	262	15,996	278	278
1952	44,129	468	730	16,167	171	449
1953	44,168	39	769	16,181	14	463
1954	44,464	296	1,065	16,289	108	571
1955	45,410	946	2,011	16,636	347	918
1956	46,323	913	2,924	16,970	334	1,252
1957	47,323	1,000	3,924	17,336	366	1,618
1958	48,144	821	4,745	17,637	301	1,919
1959	49,031	887	5,632	17,962	325	2,244
1960	50,166	1,135	6,767	18,438	476	2,720
1961	51,044	878	7,645	18,761	323	3,043
1962	51,908	864	8,509	19,079	318	3,361
1963	52,788	880	9,389	19,402	323	3,684
1964	53,593	805	10,194	19,698	296	3,980
1965	54,411	818	11,012	19,999	301	4,281
1966	54,873	462	11,474	20,169	170	4,451
1967	55,582	709	12,183	20,430	261	4,712
1968	56,275	693	12,876	20,685	255	4,967
1969*	59,534	3,259	16,135	21,741	1,056	6,023
1970	62,793	3,259	19,394	22,797	1,056	7,079

Source: Population data came from the U.S. Department of Commerce, Bureau of the Census, Current Population Surveys. All population figures are for July 1 of their respective years, the 1960 figure having been updated from April 1. Labor force data in 1950 came from the Statistical Abstract of the United States, 1950; in the sixties from the statistical summary in the Manpower Report of the President.

*Extrapolation.

It might be worthwhile to pause at this point to examine the extent to which the difference between labor available and labor required measures surplus labor. Looking at the counting process, we see, first, that members of the regional farm labor force in 1950 who migrated or

TABLE 2-4. Nonagricultural Employment in the South (1950-1967; thousands)

Year	Total Nonagricultural Employment	Change from Previous Year	Since 1950
1950	9,809.8		
1951	10,529.5	719.7	719.7
1952	10,892.3	362.8	1,082.5
1953	11,063.6	171.3	1,253.8
1954	10,894.3	-169.3	1,084.5
1955	11,343.6	449.3	1,533.8
1956	11,853.1	509.5	2,043.3
1957	12,096.8	243.7	2,287.0
1958	12,025.7	- 71.1	2,215.9
1959	12,450.1	424.4	2,640.3
1960	12,657.1	207.0	2,847.3
1961	12,716.3	59.2	2,906.5
1962	13,157.5	441.2	3,347.7
1963	13,595.1	437.6	3,785.3
1964	14,121.9	526.8	4,312.1
1965	14,934.8	812.9	5,125.0
1966	15,781.0	846.2	5,971.2
1967	16,384.2	603.2	6,574.4
1968	17,081.1	696.9	7,271.3
1969	17,817.9	736.8	8,008.1
1970	18,124.0	306.1	8,314.2
1971	18,386.3	262.3	8,576.5

Source: U.S. Department of Labor, Bureau of Labor Statistics; for 1950-1967, Employment and Earnings Statistics for States and Areas 1939-67 (August, 1968); for 1968-1971, Employment and Earnings Statistics for States and Areas 1939-71.

died or retired before 1967 reduced *A*, increased *B*, and thus have been netted out of *D*. Second, workers who entered the agricultural labor force after 1950 and later shifted to nonagricultural employment in the region would be counted under *A* and *C*, would not affect *B*, and hence would not alter *D*. Third, farmers who entered the labor force after 1950, then shifted to nonagricultural employment, and finally left the region do not affect *A*, *B*, *C*, or *D*. These individuals were not members of the labor force in either 1950 or 1967. *D* fails to capture this case and consequently understates the pressures generated by agricultural displacement. This is somewhat similar to the first case. *D* would have been greater if these individuals had not responded to the pressure of dwindling employment opportunities by leaving the region–their departure kept them from adding further to the pool of regional unemployment and underemployment.

The difference, *D*, is composed of individuals who increased the sum $A + B$ without increasing *C*, or decreased *C* without affecting $A + B$, or both. Those in $A + B$ who did not increase *C* would be basically of three types: post-1950 entrants to the nonagricultural labor force who were unemployed in 1967; post-1950 entrants to the labor force in agriculture who were displaced, remained in the labor force, but were unable to find employment in the nonagricultural sector in 1967; members of the 1950 agricultural labor force who left agriculture, remained in the labor force, but were not employed in 1967. Those who decreased *C* without affecting either *A* or *B* would be members of the nonagricultural labor force in both 1950 and 1967 who were employed in 1950 but not in 1967.

If the foregoing approach is correct in the main, then difference *D* is made up of surplus labor backed up in the region. This is true because it is net of retirements, deaths, and migration. Since metropolitan labor markets in the South are not particularly loose, the pile-up must be concentrated in the smaller urban centers and in rural nonfarm areas. As such, it poses a problem for future displaced agricultural labor in terms of its ability to find nonagricultural employment within the region.

Finally, no strong case should be made for the statistical accuracy or analytical elegance of *D*, which is shown as 0.738 million. Inevitably, there are discrepancies in the timing of the counts and imprecisions in labor force statistics. The variation might well be one or two hundred thousand. However, an error of this magnitude does not affect the essential conclusion that labor displacement from agriculture, given the limited labor absorptivity of the regional economy and the demand for certain types of skilled labor, is responsible for sizable unemployment and underemployment of low-skill labor in the region and contributed greatly to the pressure for outmigration.

For a variety of reasons–concentration on small farms, difficulty in

TABLE 2-5. White Family Worker Agricultural Employment in

	Basic Counts			
Year	Number	Index	Decline From Previous Year	Cumulative Decline
1950	2,741	100.0		
1951	2,629	95.9	112	112
1952	2,478	90.4	151	263
1953	2,368	86.4	110	373
1954	2,287	83.4	81	454
1955	2,203	80.4	84	538
1956	2,008	73.3	195	733
1957	1,932	70.5	76	809
1958	1,864	68.0	68	877
1959	1,831	66.8	33	910
1960	1,731	63.2	100	1,010
1961	1,695	61.8	36	1,046
1962	1,635	59.6	60	1,106
1963	1,613	58.8	22	1,128
1964	1,514	55.2	99	1,227
1965	1,389	50.7	125	1,352
1966	1,302	47.5	87	1,439
1967	1,271	46.4	31	1,470
1968	1,229	44.8	42	1,512
1969	1,192	43.5	37	1,549

Source: U.S. Department of Agriculture: Farm Employment
Farm Labor (1963-1969). Data for reduction to full-time
Agriculture, U.S. Department of Agriculture.

*Intercensal-year reduction factors were computed by linear

adapting to technological change, inability to convert to capital-intensive methods of production, poor vocational training, unavailability of credit, unfavorable land tenure arrangements, unequal treatment by government programs, lack of diversification–black farm families were disadvantaged in the struggle for survival in southern agriculture (discussed more fully in chapter 3). Consequently, it is not surprising to find that they were disproportionately displaced in this period of sharp decline in the farm population. Black family agricultural work-the South* (1950-1969; thousands)

Full-time Equivalents			
Number	Index	Decline From Previous Year	Cumulative Decline
1,961	100.0		
1,830	93.3	131	131
1,678	85.6	152	283
1,562	79.7	116	399
1,469	74.9	93	492
1,383	70.5	86	578
1,229	62.7	154	732
1,129	57.6	100	832
1,088	55.5	41	873
1,041	53.1	47	920
958	48.9	83	1,003
916	46.7	42	1,045
856	43.7	60	1,105
822	41.9	34	1,139
748	38.1	74	1,213
687	35.0	61	1,274
644	32.8	43	1,317
629	32.1	15	1,332
607	31.0	22	1,334
590	30.1	17	1,371

(August 1963), Number of Farms, 1910-1959 (June 1962), and
equivalents came from the 1954, 1959, and 1964 Census of

interpolation between census years.

ers dropped from 767,000 in 1950 to 349,000 in 1960 and 158,000 in 1969, with indices of 100, 46.9, and 20.6, respectively, in those years; the corresponding figures for whites were 2.741 million in 1950, 1.731 million in 1960, and 1.192 million in 1969, with indices of 100, 63.2, and 43.5. Thus, there were only one-fifth as many black families in agriculture in 1969 as in 1950, but more than two-fifths as many white families. Tables 2-5 and 2-6 present annual series showing the displacement of white and black labor between 1950 and 1969.

TABLE 2-6. Nonwhite Family Worker Agricultural Employment in the South* (1950-1969; thousands)

	Basic Counts				Full-Time Equivalents			
Year	No.	Index	Decline from Previous Year	Cumulative Decline	No.	Index	Decline from Previous Year	Cumulative Decline
1950	767	100.0			540	100.0		
1951	711	92.7	56	56	485	89.8		55
1952	646	84.2	65	121	427	79.1	58	113
1953	599	78.1	47	168	384	71.1	43	156
1954	561	73.1	38	206	348	64.4	36	192
1955	527	68.7	34	240	321	59.4	27	219
1956	467	60.9	60	300	275	50.9	46	265
1957	432	56.3	35	335	246	45.6	29	294
1958	397	51.8	35	370	221	40.9	25	319
1959	376	49.0	21	391	204	37.8	17	336
1960	360	46.9	16	407	187	34.6	17	353
1961	319	41.6	41	448	162	30.0	25	378
1962	298	38.9	21	469	147	27.2	15	393
1963	279	36.4	19	488	133	24.6	14	407
1964	264	34.4	15	503	130	24.1	3	410
1965	221	28.8	43	546	102	18.9	28	438
1966	197	25.7	24	570	92	17.0	10	448
1967	180	23.5	17	587	84	15.6	8	456
1968	171	22.3	9	596	79	14.6	5	461
1969	158	20.6	13	609	73	13.5	6	467

Source: Data are from the following publications of the U.S. Department of Agriculture: Farm Employment (Aug. 1963), Number of Farms, 1910-1959 (June 1962), and Farm Labor (1963-1969). Data for reduction to full-time equivalents came from the 1954, 1959, and 1964 Census of Agriculture, U.S. Department of Agriculture.

*Intercensal-year reduction factors were computed by linear interpolation between census years.

Inasmuch as the marginal product of displaced labor was near zero, such displacement can be taken as an index of surplus labor in southern agriculture. Much of this agricultural labor surplus becomes so for the entire regional economy to the extent that the demand for labor throughout the region did not expand sufficiently to absorb increments in the labor force associated with population growth, plus agricultural displacement and "immigrant" labor. Technically, unskilled labor becomes surplus in the region when its marginal product reaches zero in all sectors. Operationally, it becomes surplus at a level analogous to that defined for farm labor.

Black agricultural labor has been displaced at a rate faster than that of its white counterpart. A myriad of factors–among them smaller farm size, fewer financial resources, limited access to credit, and less adaptability to changing technology–must have induced a greater outflow of black labor.

Education

Southerners, black and white, urban and rural, have less education than their occupational counterparts elsewhere in the nation. Rural southerners of both races have been exposed to less education (actual years of schooling) than their urban counterparts. Bowman, in her study of southern underdevelopment, shows that in 1960, 92.8 percent of farm black males had less than a high school education, 82.2 percent had less than eight years of schooling, and 53.3 percent had less than five years. For white males the picture was better, albeit low by national averages; the respective percentages were 71.4, 46.4, and 19.0 (Bowman, 1965, p. 75; U.S. Department of Commerce, 1960).

The median years of education of employees in southern industries (two-digit SICs) that have had the highest growth rates between 1950 and 1960 are:

Industry	Years of Education
Electrical machinery manufacturing	12.38
Transportation equipment manufacturing	11.03
Metal industry manufacturing	10.78
Paper and allied products	10.48
Personal services	10.12
Tobacco products manufacturing	9.06
Mining	8.04

And the median years of education of employees in southern industries with large increases in the number employed are:

Industry	Years of Education
Professional and related services	17.21
Finance, insurance, and real estate	12.90
Government	12.46
Business and repair services	12.29
Wholesale and retail trade	11.84
Apparel products manufacturing	10.30
Food and kindred products	9.48
Construction	8.80

In both instances, the median years of schooling were taken for the typical SIC (U.S. Department of Commerce, 1960).

Clearly, the gap between the levels of education and vocational skills of the displaced agricultural labor and the manpower requirements of the growing regional industry was considerable. This is a dramatic case where the unleashing of technological change in agriculture caught southern institutions–and, in particular, education–at low levels of preparedness to facilitate a new arrangement of productive and human resources. The educational system of the rural South had failed to anticipate the oncoming socioeconomic changes and to prepare its people–black and white–for their massive relocation and the reallocation of its resources. And it had failed black males most of all.

On the whole, agricultural labor surplus has been a "noncompeting group." Its base of limited vocational and educational skills was lower than that needed by the industrial sector. Moreover, as a consequence of educational skill differences and regional racial attitudes, nonwhites were more disadvantaged in seeking employment outside agriculture than whites, leaving blacks disproportionately represented in the pool of "idle" labor.

Migration

In closing this sketch of the interaction between the displacement of agricultural manpower and surplus labor in the southern economy, let us look at migratory movements that at least in part were generated by the forces under consideration: (*a*) outmigration of semiskilled blacks who felt the pressure of the surplus labor pool created by displaced agricultural workers and (*b*) immigration of skilled labor in demand by the new growth industries. Yet net regional outmigration (for

TABLE 2-7. Annual Net Migration for the South* (1951-1969; thousands)

Year	South minus Florida	Entire South
1951	- 95	+ 67
1952	-388	-257
1953	-925	-822
1954	-784	-634
1955	-230	- 52
1956	-230	+ 9
1957	-144	+116
1958	-117	+ 81
1959	-106	+ 5
1960	+109	+206
1961, 1962	- 29	+311
1963	+ 56	+ 83
1964	- 14	+ 48
1965	+ 14	+108
1966	- 66	- 2
1967	+147	+251
1968	+ 66	+219

Source: U.S. Department of Commerce, Bureau of the Census, Current Population Reports, for the respective years. There was no Report published in 1961. Annual totals accumulated for the ten-year period 1950-1960 check very closely against those presented in Bowles and Tarver, 1965.

*South in this table is for the states of the Confederacy, plus Kentucky, Oklahoma, and West Virginia.

employment in the nonagricultural sector) did not expand sufficiently to drain off the agricultural surplus and the surplus increment in the labor force. The net migration data in Table 2-7 provide a useful summary,[2] but it is well to remember that net migration is but a part of the story. Indeed, net migration was merely the tip of the iceberg, with the great bulk of population movement not showing (Fein, 1965, pp. 122ff.). If we divide the South into subregions, we find the following:

1. In the southern coastal states, total migration was 7 times net migration for white males and 4 times the latter for black males.
2. In the eastern South Central states, total migration for white males was 8.5 times net migration, while for black males it was 2 times net migration.
3. In the western South Central states, the equations are 11 and 3.5 times respectively.[3]

In a special study of the educational qualifications of southern migrants, Fein found that immigrants, aggregated for both races, had higher educational levels than outmigrants (Table 2-8). This finding holds no surprise, for it has been thoroughly documented that black outmigrants usually have appreciably more education than those who remain in the region. It thus appears unlikely that displaced agricultural workers were a large portion of the black outmigrants from the South. If this were so, blacks who left agriculture, and then the region, were indeed the educational cream of the rural crop (for the migrants averaged far more years of schooling than rural southern black males in general).

Unfortunately, because there is little information on the levels of education of those actually displaced from agriculture, the above assertion cannot be rigorously defended. Even the fact that most of the migrants were living in urban areas when they left the South does not rule out the possibility that they could have entered the labor force in agriculture, then moved to urban areas before leaving. Nevertheless, the twin phenomena–high educational levels and urban departure–make it much more probable that the migrants were an upper level of black labor pushed from the region by the pressure of the pool of surplus labor, and that black displaced agricultural workers were a sizable component of the lower levels of the pool who remained in the South.

Black migration must have gained momentum because of the rising pressure of the pool of displaced labor. The dynamics of the pool operated in the direction of pushing a more than moderate share of the upper levels of black labor away from the region and into the industrialized and urban areas of the country. In the 1950s some 1.5 million black people migrated from the South; included were many of the region's most productive blacks.

TABLE 2-8. Composite of Educational Distribution for Southern Male Net Migrations*

(1955-1960)

Net Migrants	Years of Schooling (center of interval)						
	Five	Six	Eight	Ten	Twelve	Fourteen	Sixteen & Over
White	-6,200	-1,981	7,307	14,111	15,044	3,070	-7,109
Nonwhite	-6,575	-9,802	-6,620	-10,738	-8,248	-3,167	-3,312

Source: Fein, 1955, pp. 122ff.

*Aged 25 to 64.

The Immediate Future

The extent to which agricultural displacement has run its course is uncertain, although it is clear that the actual number leaving agriculture must go down. After all, more people *in toto* dropped out of southern agriculture in the 1950s and 1960s than were left in agriculture in 1970. But there is strong reason to suspect that the slow, steady trend toward mechanization will continue and that there will be further reductions in the farm labor force. More than that, the net reproduction rate of rural southerners is high enough to produce an excess of manpower over farm replacement needs, and several thousand rural youths each year must turn to the nonagricultural sectors in search of jobs. The region and the nation continue to have a stake in the adequacy of the South's rural schools.

This leads to a final summary statement in this examination of the interaction between agriculture and the regional labor force. It does not have the advantage of hindsight, or the force of statistical generalization, but it has a degree of inevitability, given the continuation of well-established trends.

Assuming additional labor-saving technological advances in agriculture and a high net reproduction rate for southern farm families, there will be a further, if diminished, flow of manpower from farm families into the nonagricultural sectors of the regional economy. Moreover, the existence of a pool of surplus labor in the region makes it likely that employment and migration patterns will not be significantly altered during the coming decade, although the outmigration of blacks, in absolute amount, will almost certainly decline.

Notes

1. The *Census of Agriculture* (1954, 1959, and 1964) shows this clearly.
2. The column "South minus Florida" is more relevant in this context because net migration to Florida was unique and of such great magnitude that it distorts the regional picture.
3. These are the census definitions. The data reflect the greater mobility, in and out, of the white population. Black movement, particularly in the cotton states, was generally out, so that net and gross migration were closer together, though even for blacks gross migration was twice as great in the region showing the smallest ratio (eastern South Central).

References

Bowles, Gladys K., and Tarver, James D. 1965. *Net Migration of the Population, 1950–1960, by Age, Sex, and Color*. U.S. Department of Agriculture Economic Research Service. Washington, D.C.: Government Printing Office.

Bowman, Mary Jean. 1965. "Human Inequalities and Southern Underdevelopment." *Southern Economic Journal* (July). Supplement, "Education and the Southern Economy."

Desai, M., and Muzumdar, D. 1970. "A Test of the Hypothesis of Disguised Unemployment." *Economica* (February).

Fein, Rashi. 1965. "Educational Patterns in Southern Migration." *Southern Economic Journal* (July).

Hayes, M. 1962. "A Century of Change in the U.S. Economy, 1860–1960." *Monthly Labor Review* (December).

Hiestand, Dale L. 1964. *Economic Growth and Employment Opportunities for Minorities*. New York: Columbia University Press.

Kaun, David. 1970. "Negro Migration and Unemployment." *Human Resources* (Spring).

Manpower Report of the President. 1968. Washington, D.C.: Government Printing Office.

Statistical Abstract of the United States, 1950. Washington, D.C.: Government Printing Office.

U.S. Department of Agriculture. 1962. *Number of Farms, 1910–1959*. Statistical Bulletin no. 316. Washington, D.C.: Government Printing Office (June).

———. 1963. *Farm Employment*. Statistical Bulletin no. 334. Washington, D.C.: Government Printing Office (August).

———. 1963–1969. *Farm Labor*. Generated by the USDA Crop Rotating Board. Washington, D.C.: Government Printing Office.

———. 1969. *Changes in Farm Production and Efficiency*. Statistical Bulletin no. 233. Washington, D.C.: Government Printing Office.

———. 1972. *Agricultural Statistics*. Washington, D.C.: Government Printing Office.

———. 1974. *Farm Labor*. Washington, D.C.: Government Printing Office (January 14).

———, Bureau of the Census. 1954, 1959, 1960, 1969. *Census of Agriculture*. Washington, D.C.: Government Printing Office.

U.S. Department of Commerce, Bureau of the Census. 1950–1970. *Current Population Survey*. Washington, D.C.: Government Printing Office.

———. 1951–1968. *Current Population Reports*. Washington, D.C.: Government Printing Office.

U.S. Department of Labor, Bureau of Labor Statistics. 1968. *Employment and Earnings Statistics for States and Areas, 1939–67*. Bulletin no. 1370-5. Washington, D.C.: Government Printing Office (August).

———. 1972. *Employment and Earnings Statistics for States and Areas, 1939–71*. Bulletin no. 1370-9. Washington, D.C.: Government Printing Office.

3

Agriculture

Virgil L. Christian, Jr.,
and Carl C. Erwin

A striking characteristic of the rural population of the South in the twentieth century has been its tendency to decrease compared to the total southern population. This decline has been particularly pronounced among the farm population. At the beginning of the century, 85 percent of the 22 million southerners were classified as rural. As late as 1920, nearly three-fourths of the total lived in rural areas, with 54 percent on farms and 20 percent on rural nonfarm locations (Table 3-1). By 1950, the southern population had reached 44 million, but only 53 percent lived in rural areas, with half of these on farms. Nonwhites accounted for 22 percent of the 1950 total, 55 percent of which were rural, and 65 percent of the rural residents actually lived on farms. Two decades later, there were more than 57 million people in the region, but only 21 million lived in rural areas, and fewer than 4 million resided on farms. The nonwhite population in 1970 had fallen to 18.6 percent of the total population, with only 6 percent of nonwhites living on farms. For the first time the percentage of whites on the farm was higher than that for nonwhites, but the percentages are very close, as they also are for the urban and rural nonfarm population.

Data on black farming inevitably mirror the foregoing population movements. The number of southern farms of all types operated by blacks reached a peak of 908,351 in 1920. Then the number began a slow and steady decline, falling to two-thirds of a million by 1940 and to a little over half a million in 1950. After 1950, the decline became more rapid, and there were only 184,000 black operators remaining in 1964–almost a third of the 1950 total. Also, the black share of southern farms went down steadily–from 23.4 percent in 1940 to 21.8 percent in 1950, 13.9 percent in 1964, and 7.4 percent in 1969.

These declines in black farms brought the percentage of nonwhites

TABLE 3-1. Population of the South by Place of Residence (Selected years; thousands)

Population Group	White	Nonwhite	White	Nonwhite
Urban	2,668	1,164	5,518	1,981
Rural*	12,136	6,363		
Nonfarm			4,546	1,502
Farm			10,967	4,958
Total**	14,804	7,527	21,031	8,441

Source: U.S. Department of Commerce, Bureau of the

* The farm and nonfarm breakdown was not made in the census

** May be off by one in the thousands place due to rounding.

living on southern farms in 1970 to less than that of whites. In fact, there are only four southern states–Mississippi, North and South Carolina, and Virginia–where the percentage of nonwhites on farms is greater, despite the blacks' historic concentration in southern agriculture. Not surprisingly, the greatest declines in the farm population for both races occurred in those states where the introduction of labor-saving equipment had the greatest impact–basically in the cotton states of Alabama, Arkansas, Georgia, Louisiana, Mississippi, and Texas.

Displacement of Black Farmers

Along with the decline in the southern farm population, there has been a pronounced decrease in the number of farms and a sharp rise in the number of acres per farm.[1] The decline in the number of farms reflects the combination of smaller farms into larger units, rather than the withdrawal of land from farming, and is a consequence of technological advances which have increased either the minimum size of an economically viable farm or the amount of land required for optimal

.nd by Race

White	Nonwhite	White	Nonwhite	White	Nonwhite
15,354	4,290	22,352	5,792	29,331	6,880
8,705	2,112	11,840	3,140	14,078	3,128
8,154	3,113	4,204	1,464	3,215	632
32,213	9,515	38,396	10,396	46,624	10,640

:ensus, Census of the Population, selected years.

before 1920.

combination with machinery and labor, or both. Indeed, the two phenomena–displacement of small farms and increase in average farm size–are opposite sides of the same coin but result from the same cause, that is, strong pressure of mechanization against small holdings. Accordingly, it is not surprising that black operators have found it more difficult than whites to survive in southern agriculture. They began the period of technological advance on much smaller farms–45 acres as opposed to more than 120 acres for whites in 1920–and have been at a serious disadvantage, for financial as well as institutional reasons, in trying to enlarge their farms. By 1964, farms operated by blacks had reached an average size of only 67 acres and had fallen from a third to a fourth of the average size of farms operated by whites. Two-thirds of all black farmers still operated holdings of less than 50 acres in 1964 (Table 3-2).[2] The data in Table 3-3 are not comparable with those in Table 3-2, because the 1969 percentages are for farms selling at least $2,500 of farm commodities and those in 1964 were for all commercial farms, which go down to $50 in sales. The 1969 breakdown leaves out nearly three-fourths (71%) of all farms operated by blacks.

The rapid increase in average farm size, following technological in-

TABLE 3-2. Percentage of Black and White Commercial Farm Operators by Size of Farm (fourteen southern states, 1964)

	Percentage Less than					
	10 Acres		50 Acres		100 Acres	
State	Black	White	Black	White	Black	White
Alabama	11.2	4.4	67.2	34.6	85.1	58.4
Arkansas	13.9	3.1	64.9	25.1	84.9	45.6
Florida	17.1	16.3	61.2	52.2	81.3	66.3
Georgia	9.8	5.2	49.7	26.4	73.3	48.0
Kentucky	35.5	10.7	70.4	32.7	85.3	57.5
Louisiana	10.9	6.9	74.9	45.4	91.2	65.2
Mississippi	4.1	2.9	67.6	27.9	85.8	51.9
North Carolina	16.3	7.9	71.8	42.3	89.9	68.4
Oklahoma	3.3	2.1	35.2	14.9	55.6	27.5
South Carolina	16.2	4.0	75.9	33.0	91.0	57.4
Tennessee	17.7	8.8	73.9	37.7	88.8	62.6
Texas	8.0	3.0	53.2	16.8	77.9	31.2
Virginia	18.6	6.7	60.5	31.8	81.5	53.5
West Virginia	9.8	2.6	52.2	26.4	77.2	52.2

Source: U.S. Department of Agriculture, *Census of Agriculture*, 1964.

novations that made agricultural production more capital intensive, has been used in turn to argue that small farmers were doomed by fundamental economic forces. That is, the presence of significant economies of size required that the minimum size of farm needed to produce at unit costs approximating those of the most efficient farms was large–larger, no doubt, than those operated by all but a very small fraction of black farmers in the South. It follows that most small farmers could not have been saved even by the most enlightened agricultural policy; those who have remained have done so only because of government subsidies or because of off-farm employment by family members.

Establishing that such economies have been present in southern agricultural production is a perilous task that raises as many questions as it purports to answer–the evidence is not all in yet. But there are three principal reasons for this:

TABLE 3-3. Percentage of Black and White Operators of Farms With At Least $2,500 in Sales (Fourteen southern states, 1969)

	10 Acres		50 Acres		100 Acres	
State	Black	White	Black	White	Black	White
Alabama	2.6%	3.1%	19.8%	16.0%	42.5%	33.7%
Arkansas	1.2	2.3	16.2	9.7	46.1	22.3
Florida	4.1	6.1	22.1	32.3	42.5	46.7
Georgia	2.8	4.5	16.0	14.8	37.4	29.6
Kentucky	13.1	5.7	30.1	13.9	52.1	34.3
Louisiana	1.3	1.6	34.0	11.0	63.2	26.9
Mississippi	2.3	1.1	19.9	6.1	45.6	18.4
North Carolina	9.1	5.9	55.0	29.4	80.4	55.1
Oklahoma	3.2	1.8	8.2	3.9	18.1	8.6
South Carolina	8.9	2.2	48.2	15.4	71.7	33.7
Tennessee	5.5	2.9	27.3	12.1	52.2	32.5
Texas	4.6	2.0	18.1	5.7	36.3	12.1
Virginia	7.8	3.8	32.4	12.2	58.1	28.6
West Virginia	10.0	2.6	10.0	6.0	40.0	14.9

Source: U.S. Department of Agriculture, Census of Agriculture, 1969.

1. Data from real farm operation reflect costs incurred from input combinations actually used, rather than costs which were generated by inputs optimally combined as required by economic theory.
2. Statistical measures require debatable specifications of agricultural production functions.
3. The construction of model synthetic farms, while potentially useful for estimating "within plant" economies that approximate the scale constructs of economic theory, yields little clue as to what has happened in southern agriculture because they begin at sizes larger than those available to the vast majority of southern farmers (Heady, 1953; Madden, 1967).

However, it is not necessary to maintain that this was the sole, or even the most important, cause of the disproportionate displacement of black farm operators in the South. For irrespective of the possible presence of economies of scale, there has clearly been a minimum farm size needed to sustain a southern farm family. The matter may be viewed in terms of indivisibilities, with the farm operator and his family making up a fixed quantum of labor input and with additional hired labor, land, and farm equipment considered as variable inputs added to the fixed family labor. Obviously, minimum amounts of land and equipment were needed to provide a bare subsistence to the family unit, and more were needed to make the farm a competitively viable economic entity.

Actually, the problem for the family farm may have been more a case of rapid technological changes, all of which increased the minimum size of a viable farm, rather than economies of size which are premised on fixed technology. The changes, particularly in cotton farming, operated in the direction of making the production process more capital intensive and led to higher capital/output ratios at all levels of output.

As Figure 3-1 shows, the expansion path of the farm would have swung closer and closer to the capital axis as technology improved. In the figure, *I I* and *II II* are isoquants in the old technology; *I' I'* and *II' II'* are isoquants in the new technology. If it is legitimate to plot "capital" on the same vertical axis, which implies that units of capital can be measured in the same way and priced the same way (parallel isocost lines for the two technologies), it is clear that the expansion path will lie closer to the capital axis for the "new," more capital-intensive technology. This is true because at any output level the ratio K/L is increased by virtue of the assumption of the capital-using nature of the technological change.

Optimal operation in the short run required that land and capital be applied to the available family labor on each farm in amounts sufficient to carry into the rational stage of production, that is, to reach levels of output such that average variable cost was rising. As technology improved, more and more capital and land were needed to be combined with the family labor before reaching rational combinations of the inputs, pushing the minimum size for an economically viable farm steadily upward. This conclusion is independent of economies of size. If such economies existed, they generated additional pressures for increasing the farm size beyond the minimum. But the economically feasible minimum size would have increased even if there had been constant or decreasing returns to scale, given that the operator's family unit on each farm was an indivisible minimum labor input.

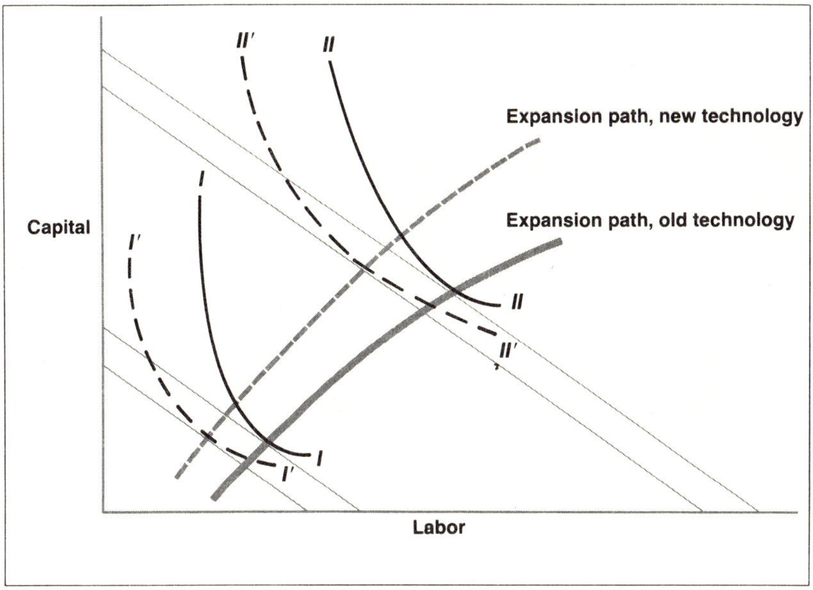

Fig. 3-1. Labor-capital combinations, old and new technology

Historically, one might arrive at a more realistic approximation of what has happened in southern agriculture by considering both labor embodied in the family unit and the amount of land available to it as fixed over a single growing season. Land tenure arrangements, even for nonowners, could hardly be modified rapidly enough to vary the amount of land usable by the family in a single year. Thus, the labor potential in the operator's family and the land under his control became fixed minima for these two factors, and the costs associated with them became fixed costs. The operator's short-run decision was simply one of determining optimal quantities of other inputs (including hired labor, perhaps!) to combine with them.

However, a critical point for efficient operation might already have been passed. Improvements in production methods since the last crop year could have meant that the quantities of labor and land involved in the old input structure were incompatible with minimum production costs attainable by the new methods. If labor had been the relatively short factor, more could have been hired; but this was not typi-

TABLE 3-4. Number of Farms by Farm Size, State, and Race (Fourteen southern states, 1949)

	Less than 50 Acres		Less than 100 Acres	
State	White	Nonwhite	White	Nonwhite
Alabama	71,396	40,025	40,087	10,250
Arkansas	54,609	33,160	35,179	5,230
Florida	26,123	4,880	8,358	1,510
Georgia	52,804	26,190	38,916	13,380
Kentucky	87,330	3,410	57,312	740
Louisiana	49,064	34,116	15,785	4,365
Mississippi	54,292	99,385	31,976	15,045
North Carolina	116,577	52,425	54,294	12,750
Oklahoma	25,850	3,485	20,403	2,055
South Carolina	36,967	46,145	18,762	9,425
Tennessee	97,103	17,275	53,928	3,950
Texas	71,574	19,870	49,833	7,760
Virginia	52,003	17,690	27,235	5,585
West Virginia	33,259	220	20,911	80

Source: U.S. Department of Agriculture, <u>Census of</u>

cally the case. For small farms, it was more likely that the amount of land was too small to accommodate optimal factor combinations. Hence, with zero marginal costs of labor use (up to the amount of family labor available), the sensible way to have produced in the immediate season was through labor-intensive methods. Family labor and land were fixed inputs, and short-run costs were independent of them. Thus, the decision to raise a crop depended entirely upon whether the crop yield would be sufficient to cover variable costs and contribute some surplus to the land and family labor already committed.

It is clearly impossible for the operator of the small farm to repeat this short-run solution year after year if more capital-intensive methods would have yielded lower unit costs. (This would be true even if the best technology exhibited constant or decreasing returns to scale.) Agricultural prices eventually must have reflected the lower costs of of Operator

Less than 220 Acres		220 Acres or More		
White	Nonwhite	White	Nonwhite	Total
28,193	5,731	14,520	1,159	211,361
34,483	2,245	17,034	446	182,386
8,085	810	6,874	203	56,843
35,975	7,775	20,643	2,354	198,037
53,121	420	15,818	86	218,237
10,486	1,772	8,046	388	124,022
26,985	7,332	14,684	1,587	251,286
34,702	5,305	11,558	862	288,473
41,920	2,365	45,264	826	142,168
14,103	4,355	8,493	945	139,195
42,982	1,800	14,194	292	231,524
83,469	4,765	93,107	1,038	331,416
28,790	3,380	15,383	757	150,823
19,441	40	7,461	6	81,418

Agriculture, 1949.

the more efficient methods, and the small farm was forced to sustain losses until some of its "fixed" resources (i.e., family labor) were driven out. The minimum-size farm that could have avoided this outcome would have been one in which there was sufficient acreage to permit the smallest indivisible units of technologically efficient capital to be combined with the family labor to produce at unit costs not appreciably greater than those of the most efficient farms (Tables 3-4 and 3-5). Thus, the implication for black farmers is straightforward: no matter where the minimum fell, it caught a higher percentage of blacks than whites below it, leading to disproportionate displacement of blacks. Incidentally, it was necessary that the operator have the capability of acquiring and using the new capital, even if he did operate a farm of more than minimum size. That black operators were displaced at a greater rate than whites, regardless of size, reflects their

TABLE 3-5. Percentage of Reduction in Farms by Farm Size, (1964 as percentage of 1949)

State	Less than 50 Acres White	Less than 50 Acres Nonwhite	Less than 100 Acres White	Less than 100 Acres Nonwhite
Alabama	0.6547%	0.6487%	0.5766%	0.6337%
Arkansas	0.6721	0.8318	0.5838	0.6718
Florida	0.2709	0.6463	0.3832	0.6251
Georgia	0.6415	0.7868	0.6021	0.8023
Kentucky	0.5130	0.4891	0.4373	0.5013
Louisiana	0.5379	0.7298	0.3752	0.5420
Mississippi	0.6349	0.7436	0.4665	0.5429
North Carolina	0.5725	0.5904	0.4334	0.5756
Oklahoma	0.5095	0.6909	0.4738	0.6953
South Carolina	0.6762	0.6775	0.5276	0.6859
Tennessee	0.5245	0.5441	0.4351	0.5989
Texas	0.5498	0.6890	0.4461	0.6298
Virginia	0.5825	0.6030	0.4563	0.5643
West Virginia	0.7281	0.7818	0.5775	0.7125

Source: Data generated from the 1949 and 1964 farm size because the counts can be calculated from the 1949 table 1964 Census of Agriculture rather than the census because size by race for farms selling less than $2,500 in farm operated by blacks, but only 49 percent of those operated that the relative displacement of blacks has been even support to the argument of the text than can be justified.

* Minus signs indicate a gain from 1949 to 1964.
** An increase from six to nine farms.

great disadvantage in this respect as well. But the two facts–(*a*) a very much greater percentage of black than white farmers operating farms of less than a hundred acres and (*b*) a much higher displacement of farms of less than a hundred acres than of larger farms–account numerically, albeit superficially, for much of the difference between white and nonwhite displacement.

It might be argued that the presence of significant economies of scale meant that the minimum-size farm needed to produce at unit

State, and Race of Operator

Less than 220 Acres		220 Acres or More*	
White	Nonwhite	White	Nonwhite
0.4220%	0.5812%	0.0738%	0.3719%
0.4397	0.5474	-0.1414	0.3700
0.3226	0.4938	0.0103	0.4187
0.4753	0.7172	0.1101	0.6602
0.2952	0.3357	0.1337	0.0349
0.1598	0.5090	-0.0657	0.4716
0.3054	0.4124	-0.0495	0.3453
0.2794	0.5338	-0.0578	0.3585
0.5029	0.6668	0.0928	0.3063
0.4190	0.6691	0.1462	0.6582
0.3004	0.4656	-0.1088	0.1986
0.4470	0.5952	0.0758	0.3863
0.3697	0.4917	0.1204	0.4240
0.4695	0.7000	0.1823	-0.5000**

ables in this group. The 1964 table is not included
nd these percentages. The calculations are based on the
he 1969 census does not provide a breakdown of farm
ommodities. The 1969 data exclude 71 percent of farms
y whites. Use of the 1969 data would therefore suggest
reater than it actually has been and would lend stronger

costs approximating those of the most efficient farms would have been large. If the state of technology had remained fixed for several years, farms that had not moved in the direction of optimal size would have operated at a cost disadvantage and finally at a loss, provided institutional factors did not divorce commodity prices from production costs.

But a key element in this argument is the notion of fixed technology: factors at all levels are combined optimally, given the state of technology. Hence, the scale question could not have been the central one in a situation dominated by rapid technological change, unless such change operated uniformly in favor of large farms. Changes in technology in southern agriculture have no doubt led to more capital-intensive methods, but these changes did not automatically lead to economies of size. A shift to more capital-intensive methods requires only that a farm be large enough to combine optimally with the smallest units of technologically efficient capital; the "economies of size" concept deals with unit costs for factor combinations at higher levels of output. Unfortunately, more land may have been needed than was or still is available to most black farmers, whichever was the case–either an increase in the minimum size of a viable farm or the creation of economies of size.

Clearly, it is possible for improvements in technology to increase the minimum size of an economically viable farm without leading to economies of size (Fig. 3-2). It *may* be true that unit costs drop drastically at low levels of output, indicating economies of scale up to output O_Q, that is, the output associated with the smallest-size viable farm. But what goes on before output O_Q is basically irrelevant, since such small farms cannot make it. We are arguing that increases in technology push O_Q to the right and that this may well be more important in black displacement than are possible economies of scale beyond O.

This point permits some modification of the argument advanced earlier. If the technological changes in southern agriculture all induced considerable economies of size, the position of the small farmer –and this includes a high proportion of black farmers–was fundamentally weak. But if the changes simply made agricultural production more capital intensive, many small farmers might have been saved by being provided (*a*) financial resources to acquire needed capital, (*b*) a necessary minimum amount of land, and (*c*) technical knowledge. It is one thing to say that small farmers were rapidly displaced because agricultural production became more capital intensive. It is quite another thing to say that the changes in production methods created economies of size that made the small farmer's position untenable, even if his holding was large enough to accommodate the smallest units of technologically efficient capital.

Mechanization in Cotton and Tobacco

The farm size problem has been more acute for blacks because of the effects of mechanization in the production of cotton and tobacco, the

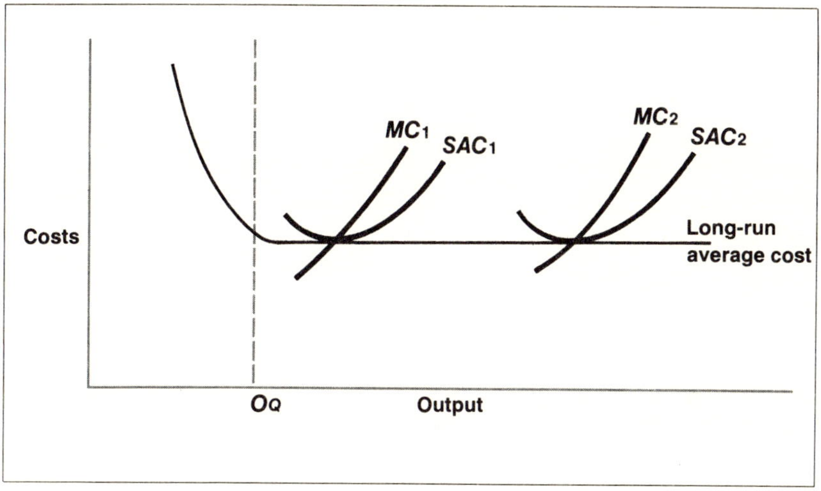

Fig. 3-2. Output associated with minimum size of economically viable farm

two most important farm enterprises for black operators in the South. Dependence of black farmers on these two crops at the time rapid mechanization began (1949) is indicated by the fact that they operated 41.8 percent of all southern cotton farms and 25.9 percent of tobacco farms, but only 3.5 percent of livestock and grain crops and 3 percent of dairy farms (U.S. Department of Agriculture, 1949, 1964). The data are for commercial farms, but they do leave a loophole. For example, if one counts all farmers who report any production of cotton, then one includes many for whom the crop is relatively unimportant. On the other hand, if only "commercial cotton farms" are counted, then one leaves out producers of cotton other than those who get more than 50 percent of their cash income from cotton, and this undoubtedly includes many large producers.

Data on the introduction of capital-intensive methods in the production of the basic crops in southern agriculture show wide divergencies. Mechanization in the production of cotton proceeded at a much faster rate than it did in tobacco. This is reflected in a series of index numbers developed by the Economic Research Service of USDA. From 1950 to 1969, production of cotton per man-hour increased nearly fivefold–a rise in the index of from 53 to 241 (Table

TABLE 3-6. Index Numbers of Cotton and Tobacco Production per Man-Hour (1957-1959 = 100)

Year	Cotton	Tobacco
1950	53	82
1955	81	94
1960	116	108
1965	209	118
1969	241	122

Source: U.S. Department of Agriculture, 1970, pp. 13-15.

3-6). But the increase for tobacco was much less–a rise in the index from 82 to only 122.

The failure of production methods in tobacco to improve as rapidly as those in cotton has been attributed in part to the differences in the administration of allotments assigned to farmers by the price support program of the United States Department of Agriculture. Owing to the possibility of combining allotments to make contiguous plots, acreages in cotton have become large enough to accommodate new capital-intensive methods. However, those in tobacco have been, and still are, too small to justify that introduction of machinery already developed. Sundquist commented on this question as follows: "Mechanization of tobacco has undoubtedly been slowed by the existence of farm programs which restricted the reconstitution of tobacco acreage into the size tracts of about thirty-five to forty acres required for efficient use of mechanical harvesters. The average tobacco allotment in the flue-cured tobacco area of the Carolinas, Virginia, Georgia, and Florida, for example, is only slightly more than three acres. In the coastal plain of North Carolina, where production is most concentrated and mechanized, production units (in contract to allotments) still average less than ten acres" (1971, p. 15).

Despite the lag in the adoption of capital-intensive methods of tobacco production, the introduction of the cotton picker alone reduced the labor needed to harvest cotton to about a fifth of that required two decades ago, assuming that cotton output was about the same then as now. (Actually it declined 10% between 1950 and 1964, from 12.8

million to 11.5 million bales. If that trend continues, the decline in labor use will be even greater than hypothesized here.)

The reduction was felt most by hired workers and tenant farmers, two categories of labor filled historically by blacks. Moreover, the introduction and widespread use of commercial insecticides, along with tractor tillage, virtually displaced the chopping operation, which was necessary to keep the weeds and insects from destroying the plants during the growing season. Thus, another hand task traditionally performed by blacks was almost eliminated.

The efficient use of capital-intensive methods (i.e., machine tools) in the production of both cotton and tobacco requires sizable contiguous acreages. Since cotton allotments under the federal price support and domestic allotment programs were transferable–while tobacco allotments went with the land–large-acreage plots could be developed more easily in cotton than in tobacco production. This tended to result in a greater proportionate increase in the number of acres of cotton than of tobacco per farm and, similarly, a greater reduction in the number of cotton than tobacco farms (Table 3-7). Consequently, the pressure on black operators, who were concentrated on small farms, has been greater, with some qualifications, in cotton farming than in tobacco farming.

During the past two decades white farmers have been able to expand the acres of cotton per farm in all the major cotton-producing states. But black farmers, with acreages in 1949 that compared fairly favorably with those of whites in all major growing states except Texas, had fallen far behind in 1964 (Table 3-7).

As a result, the participation of blacks in cotton production, as measured by the number of farms and by the number of acres under cultivation, declined sharply in the fifteen-year period from 1949 to 1964, especially in the large producing states of Arkansas, Georgia, Louisiana, Mississippi, and South Carolina (Tables 3-7 and 3-8). Moreover, the remarkable stability in the average acreages for blacks between 1949 (before mechanization) suggests that many black farmers are still struggling with labor-intensive methods on farms too small to use the best machinery (Fig. 3-3). However, this does not mean that optimal input proportions would not be more labor intensive for black farm operators. To the extent to which local labor markets pay lower wages to black labor in nonagricultural employment, the opportunity cost of black labor in agriculture is reduced. This alters the slope of the capital-labor isocost line for black farms, leading to a more labor-intensive expansion path.

TABLE 3-7. Average Acres of Cotton and Tobacco per Farm in
(1949 and 1964)

	Cotton					
	1949		1964		Ratio 1964 to 1949	
State	White	Nonwhite	White	Nonwhite	White	Nonwhite
Alabama	13.77	10.35	25.04	10.14	1.82	0.980
Arkansas	31.40	15.40	72.53	17.29	2.31	1.120
Georgia	14.66	13.24	32.58	14.43	2.22	1.090
Kentucky						
Louisiana	16.64	11.65	47.74	12.50	2.87	1.070
Mississippi	18.55	11.64	54.04	11.31	2.91	0.972
North Carolina	7.88	8.31	15.78	8.86	2.00	1.070
South Carolina	15.20	11.20	33.94	10.13	2.23	0.904
Tennessee	13.58	12.77	20.31	12.48	1.50	0.977
Texas	78.16	17.91	107.47	22.62	1.38	1.260
Virginia						

Source: U.S. Department of Agriculture, Census of Agriculture,

*The reader is warned to be wary of these figures. The 194
tobacco, and the 1964 data are for all commercial farms (at
of either commodity. The latter category includes all farms
practically all farms producing cotton and tobacco; but there
omission of farms selling very small amounts. It is unfortunatel
the "commercial farm" designation did not exist in 1949 and th
farms. Use of the 1969 Census of Agriculture only makes
farms selling at least $2,500 in farm commodities and thus mis
of those operated by blacks. Furthermore, exclusion of small

NA = not available.

Major Producing States by Race of Operator*

Tobacco					
1949		1964		Ratio 1964 to 1949	
White	Nonwhite	White	Nonwhite	White	Nonwhite
3.10	2.24	4.52	2.39	1.46	1.070
NA	NA	2.20	1.93		
4.09	3.91	4.99	3.74	1.22	0.957
3.68	2.74	5.32	2.29	1.45	0.836
NA	NA	1.20	1.88		
NA	NA	2.73	3.16		

.949, 1964.

.ata are for all farms that had sales of either cotton or
east $50 in sales of agricultural commodities) that had sales
with cash sales in excess of $50, which should capture
s a possible upward bias in the 1964 acreages due to the
mpossible to get comparable figures for the two years, as
creage breakdown in 1964 is available only for commercial
atters worse, as the racial breakdowns are restricted to
ore than half of all southern farms and more than 71 percent
'arms in 1969 would bias the ratios upward drastically.

TABLE 3-8. Commercial Cotton Farms in Nine Southern States (Selected Years)

State	White	Nonwhite No.	Nonwhite %
Alabama	51,138	24,107	32.0
Arkansas	42,625	30,807	42.0
Georgia	22,560	19,062	45.8
Louisiana	19,271	23,308	54.7
Mississippi	41,625	80,842	66.0
North Carolina	11,714	9,727	45.4
South Carolina	14,395	25,777	64.2
Tennessee	29,457	15,441	34.4
Texas	92,699	13,943	13.1

Source: U.S. Department of Agriculture, Census of

*The reader is warned that the data are potentially deceiving their income from cotton; 1964, for all commercial farms; 1969 counts are sharply reduced by that restriction and a distinction between "commercial cotton farms," which are income arising from cotton, and "commercial farms selling regardless of the proportion of the farm income generated whereas the following table is for "commercial tobacco "commercial farms raising <u>some</u> cotton or tobacco."

In Figure 3-3 the superscript *w* indicates "white," the *b* indicates "black." Each point on the capital axis, as K_1, generates two isocost lines, with the vertical intercept being greater for black labor–showing that a greater amount of black labor can be bought with the expenditure defined by the isocost line; that is, the slope of the capital, black labor isocost lines would be steeper than those of the capital, white labor isocost lines. The expansion path, if the farm uses black labor, would then be more labor intensive because the point of tangency on each isoquant with a capital, black labor isocost line would be to the left of that for a capital, white labor isocost line due to the concavity of the isoquant. This also implies that, of two identical farms producing the same output, a given increment in capital would displace more labor on the farm using black labor.

by Race of Operator and Percentage of Nonwhite*

White	Nonwhite No.	Nonwhite %	White	Nonwhite No.	Nonwhite %
12,742	9,369	42.4	2,552	395	13.4
9,735	4,650	32.3	3,785	577	13.2
3,800	3,155	45.4	731	106	12.7
6,147	4,919	44.5	2,497	428	14.6
13,634	21,939	61.7	4,510	1,048	18.9
1,625	1,483	47.7	286	18	5.9
3,423	5,062	59.7	605	96	13.7
9,961	6,111	38.0	1,752	303	14.7
32,142	1,206	3.6	15,804	211	1.3

Agriculture, 1949, 1964, 1969.

—1949 figures are for all farms with more than half of and 1969, for farms selling at least $2,500 in crops. The are not comparable with those in earlier years. There is commercial farms with more than 50 percent of the farm cotton," which are commercial farms with some cotton sales, by cotton. This table is for "commercial cotton farms," farms." Subsequent tables, on the other hand, are for

Since it has been impossible (because of the requirements of the domestic allotment program) for either white or black farmers to increase the average acres of tobacco per farm by as much as that of cotton, the black tobacco grower has not experienced such an increasing disadvantage in farm size in tobacco farming as in cotton farming (Table 3-9). Likewise, there has not been such a rapid decline in the number of tobacco farms for both races as there has been in cotton farms.[3] For example, the number of tobacco farms in the six major producing states, which produce virtually all tobacco grown in the South, fell from 180,641 in 1959 to 162,545 in 1964–90 percent surviving–while the number of cotton farms during the same period declined from 225,226 to 154,332–only 68 percent surviving (Table 3-10). The 1969 *Census of Agriculture* shows sharply reduced num-

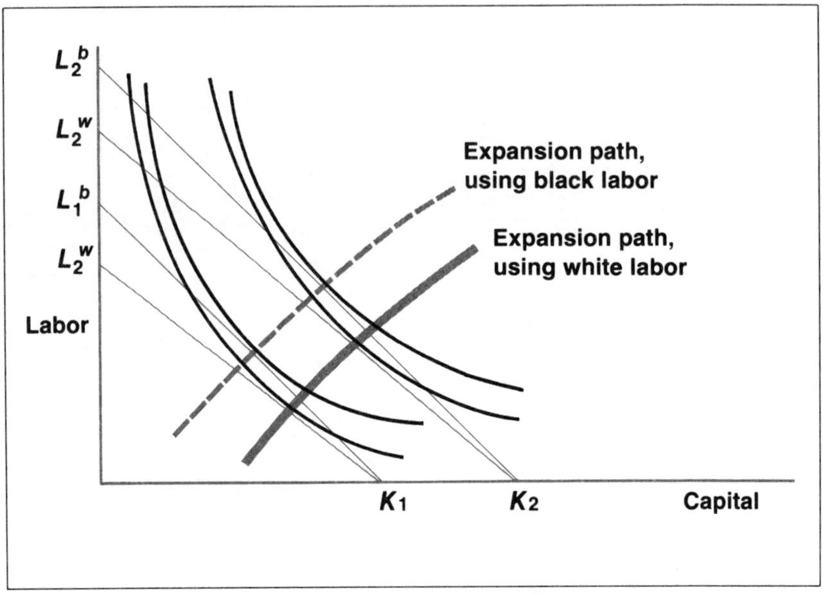

Fig. 3-3. Expansion paths, black versus white labor

TABLE 3-9. Commercial Tobacco Farms by Race of Operator (Selected years)

State	1949		
		Nonwhite	
	White	Number	%
Georgia	19,560	6,119	23.8
Kentucky	67,384	2,316	3.3
North Carolina	86,223	44,593	34.1
South Carolina	13,701	13,601	49.8
Tennessee	25,931	1,261	4.6
Virginia	19,169	10,530	35.5

Source: U.S. Department of Agriculture, Census of

* See footnote of Table 3-8 for comment regarding

bers in both categories, but the counts cannot be compared with earlier years, because they are restricted to farms with at least $2,500 in sales.

The relative pressure on black cotton farmers as opposed to black tobacco farmers attributable to the interaction of farm size and mechanization is difficult to measure. For one thing, there is the data problem (see Fig. 3-1). But this is not all. The crops are concentrated in different states, the land tenure arrangements and agreements are different,[4] the federal farm programs are not the same for cotton and tobacco, and the data cover operators only and not hired labor. Furthermore, there was little comparability in average acreages involving the two crops at the beginning of the period of rapid technological advance, since cotton farms were much larger, even then, than tobacco farms.

Although generalization is risky, the following seem warranted: First, black-operated commercial farms producing both cotton and tobacco show a later rate of survival than do white-operated farms–66.8 percent in 1959 compared to 69.6 percent in 1964 for cotton farms and 76.5 percent compared to 93.8 percent for tobacco farms during the same period. (Comparability of data requires that the survival rate for

nd Number and Percentage Nonwhite*

	1964			1969	
	Nonwhite			Nonwhite	
hite	Number	%	White	Number	%
5,509	824	13.0	3,329	330	9.0
2,418	1,051	2.4	20,554	223	1.1
8,385	17,596	26.7	34,952	5,318	13.2
6,976	5,060	42.0	5,342	1,550	22.5
7,265	698	3.9	4,899	150	3.0
1,641	5,122	30.6	7,052	1,193	14.5

griculture, 1949, 1964, 1969.

omparability of the data.

TABLE 3-10. Percentage of Acreage, Commercial Farms, Nonwhite Participation in Cotton and Tobacco Farming* (Selected years)

State	Cotton			Tobacco		
	1949	1964	1969**	1949	1964	1969**
Alabama	26.2%	23.0%	5.6%	***	***	***
Arkansas	26.2	10.2	4.1	***	***	***
Georgia	43.3	26.9	5.5	18.4%	7.3%	4.8%
Kentucky	***	***	***	NA	0.8	0.9%
Louisiana	45.9	17.3	5.5	***	***	***
Mississippi	54.9	25.2	4.9	***	***	***
North Carolina	46.7	33.9	7.8	33.1	21.4	9.7
South Carolina	56.9	30.6	6.8	42.5	23.8	12.3
Tennessee	33.0	27.4	5.8	NA	3.4	2.3
Texas	3.3	0.8	0.4	***	***	***
Virginia	***	***	***	NA	33.8	11.7

Source: U.S. Department of Agriculture, Census of Agriculture

NA = not available

*There is the inevitable comparability problem through time. The 1949 data are for all farms with cash sales of the commodity, the 1964 data are for commercial farms which require sales of $50 or more of farm commodities, and the 1969 data are for commercial farms with sales of at least $2,500.

**The 1969 data eliminate 71 percent of black farms and only 49 percent of white farms and bias the percentage sharply downward. They greatly overemphasize the decline in the black share from 1964 to 1969.

***Indicates that the state is unimportant in production of this commodity.

both commercial cotton and tobacco farms be based upon the five-year period from 1959 to 1964, as data on commercial tobacco farms by race were not collected in 1954. Commercial cotton and tobacco farms were used because they indicate that the major source of cash farm income is derived from these crops.)

Second, although black cotton farmers experienced more difficulty in surviving than did black farmers, the difference is not as great as expected. There is a strong suspicion that large numbers of southern black farm families continue to grow cotton as a submarginal enterprise simply because alternative uses for the family labor do not exist.[5]

Nevertheless, it is surprising that, in comparison to whites, black farmers have fared about as well in the capital-intensive cotton-producing enterprise as in the labor-intensive tobacco-producing enterprises (Tables 3-7 through 3-12). But the paradox fades when such considerations as acres per farm, cropsharing, and other similar factors are taken into account. United States Department of Agriculture data show that the blacks' share of the total tobacco output fell from 20.7 percent in 1949 to 14.3 percent in 1964, while that for cotton dropped from 19.2 to 11 percent during the same period.

Mechanization

Taken over all the southern states and if we consider all farming activities, the most far-reaching single change occurring in the last quarter-century was the introduction of the farm tractor. Before World War II most southern farmers, especially blacks, had used mules, partly because of their general adaptability for farm work and partly because their feed could be provided on the farm. The tractor had been used earlier, particularly on large farms, for spring plowing and in the preparation of the soil for planting field crops, but it was the wartime urgency to maintain productivity–together with the rise in farm commodity prices relative to price-controlled industrial goods–that made it advantageous for all farmers to mechanize their operations.

In 1950, the number of tractors reported on southern farms for the three major tenancy classes (full owners, part owners, and tenants) stood at 541,800 (Table 3-13). Only 5 percent of these, however, were operated by nonwhites. The number of tractors on farms continued to climb throughout the 1950s and early 1960s. By 1964, nearly half (47.2%) of all white farmers in the three major tenancy classifications operated tractors, compared with only a little more than a fifth (22.4%) of the nonwhite.

In this respect, black tenants did somewhat better than black full owners. In 1964, of all black tenants, 19.8 percent operated tractors as compared to 16.2 percent of the full owners. In 1969, for farms selling at least $2,500 in farm commodities, the situation was reversed, with

TABLE 3-11. Commercial Farms Producing Cotton by State ar

	1954			
		Nonwhite		
State	White	No.	%	White
Alabama	54,013	25,292	31.90%	20,57
Arkansas	36,701	24,388	39.90	14,48
Georgia	40,628	26,383	39.40	14,51
Louisiana	21,456	21,605	50.20	7,88
Mississippi	51,856	81,844	61.20	17,44
North Carolina	32,938	35,755	52.10	13,93
South Carolina	22,585	35,719	61.30	9,62
Tennessee	34,313	14,731	30.00	16,10
Texas	99,832	9,322	8.54	47,58
Total (average)	394,322	275,039	(41.10)	162,15

Source: U.S. Department of Agriculture, Census of

*These are commercial farms which reported the sale o received more than half their cash income from cotton. and cannot be used to show displacement since 1954.

75 percent of nonwhite full owners and 70.3 percent of nonwhite tenants having tractors; the corresponding figures for whites were 81.8 and 85.7 percent. However, it must be emphasized that the 1969 data exclude the smallest 49 percent of farms operated by whites and the smallest 71 percent of those operated by nonwhites.

The explanation for the relative disadvantage shown for farm owners among blacks appears to be that the owners were older and less able to compete in modern commercial-type farming activities. Their farms were small and capital was scarce. Hence, they were restricted primarily to those farm enterprises which required large amounts of hand labor. As a result, many owner-operators were pushed out of agriculture altogether.

y Race of Operator* (Selected years)

1964		1969			
Nonwhite			Nonwhite		1964 as %
o.	%	White	No.	%	of 1954
0,801	34.40%	10,187	1,005	9.0%	39.6%
4,869	25.20	10,557	1,158	9.9	31.7
5,501	27.50	7,836	992	11.2	29.9
5,867	42.70	5,321	875	14.1	31.9
3,125	57.00	11,442	2,127	15.7	30.3
2,575	47.40	4,755	1,273	21.1	38.6
0,457	52.10	4,548	1,158	20.3	34.5
6,484	28.70	9,595	751	7.3	46.1
1,494	3.04	41,159	362	0.9	45.0
1,173	(33.40)	105,400	9,701	(8.4)	(36.4)

griculture, 1954, 1964, 1969.

ome cotton, as opposed to "commercial cotton farms" which
969 data include only farms with sales of at least $2,500

Diversification and Tenure

One of the alternatives open to farmers faced with vast changes in the productive technology of their major cash enterprises is diversification. This is perhaps the most practical alternative for family-type farms where land and not labor is the scarce factor. Examination of data which differentiate types of farms by value of products sold shows that in 1964 most black farmers–82 percent–depended upon field-crop enterprises as their principal source of income (Table 3-14). As expected, cotton was the most important crop, accounting for 52.5 percent of the total with tobacco second, constituting 26.3 percent. Corresponding proportions for white farmers were 14.3 percent for

TABLE 3-12. Commercial Farms Producing Tobacco by State
(Selected years)

	1954			
		Nonwhite		
State**	White	No.	%	White
Georgia	21,393	5,147	19.40%	12,29
Kentucky	96,151	2,526	2.56	69,47
North Carolina	90,075	47,027	34.30	55,68
South Carolina	14,611	17,741	54.80	8,96
Tennessee	49,243	1,700	3.34	33,90
Total (average)	271,473	74,141	(21.50)	180,31

Source: U.S. Department of Agriculture, Census of

*These are commercial farms which reported the sale of
received more than half their cash income from tobacco.
$2,500 and cannot be used to show displacement since 1954

**Virginia is now a major grower but was not in 1954 an

cotton and 20 percent for tobacco. The black farmers' share of the other crop was quite low (Table 3.15).[6]

It is significant that, of all black farmers producing cotton, 97 percent had a volume of sales per farm of less than $10,000. For whites, the proportion was 60 percent. On the other hand, farming units organized primarily for the production of livestock enterprises accounted for only 5.3 percent of the total for black operators as compared to 37 percent for whites. The explanation for the lack of diversification on small farms in the South is that field crops are particularly adaptable to labor-intensive methods of production. On family-type farms, where the amount of land is fixed in the short run and the cost of capital is high, labor is the most plentiful and hence the lowest cost factor, d by Race of Operator*

964		1969			
Nonwhite			Nonwhite		1964 as %
No.	%	White	No.	%	of 1954
1,713	12.20%	8,539	624	6.8%	52.8%
1,359	1.92	49,295	475	1.0	71.8
20,398	26.80	41,996	5,931	12.4	55.5
6,961	43.70	6,316	1,810	22.3	49.2
953	2.73	20,728	270	1.3	68.4
31,384	(14.80)	126,874	9,110	(6.7)	(61.3)

griculture, 1954, 1964, 1969.

ome tobacco, as opposed to "commercial tobacco farms" which
he 1969 data include only farms with sales of at least

o data were collected there that year.

with a marginal cost near zero during any current growing season. Conversely, livestock enterprises are much more extensive types of operations, requiring more land and more capital per unit of labor than crops. Therefore, it is not surprising that a much smaller proportion of black than white farm operators engage in livestock production.

Another way of comparing the economic position of black farmers with white farmers in the South is to relate the scale of operations to the type of tenure. In 1964 more than two-fifths–44.8 percent–of all commercial farms operated by blacks were cultivated under some kind of tenant arrangement, and in 1969, 28.5 percent of Class 1–5 farms operated by blacks were in the tenant class. Comparable figures for whites were 14.8 and 14.4 percent in 1964 and 1969, respectively.

TABLE 3-13. Number and Proportion of Farms Using Tractors by Tenure Classification of Operator and by Race* (Selected years; thousands)

Tenure Classification	White 1949	White 1964	White 1969	Nonwhite 1949	Nonwhite 1964	Nonwhite 1969
			NUMBER OF OPERATORS			
Full owner	1,174.0	695.1	289.5	139.1	69.9	9.8
Part owner	265.0	263.0	175.0	51.4	30.9	7.5
All tenants	525.3	165.6	77.8	364.0	81.7	6.9
Total	1,964.3	1,124.7	542.3	554.5	182.5	24.2
			FARMS WITH TRACTORS			
Full owner	233.5	245.0	236.7	6.3	11.3	7.4
Part owner	135.4	192.1	161.2	5.4	13.3	6.5
All tenants	144.9	93.2	66.7	16.3	16.2	4.8
Total	513.8	530.3	464.6	28.0	40.8	18.7
			PERCENTAGE WITH TRACTORS			
Full owner	19.9%	35.2%	81.8%	4.54%	16.2%	75.7%
Part owner	51.1	73.0	92.1	10.50	43.0	86.4
All tenants	27.6	56.3	85.7	4.48	19.8	70.3
Total	26.2	47.2	85.7	5.05	22.4	77.5

Source: U.S. Department of Agriculture, Census of Agriculture, 1949, 1964, 1969.

*The 1969 data are restricted to farms with at least $2,500 in sales, which accounts for both the sharp reduction in the numbers and the sharp increase in the percentage with tractors. Racial breakdowns are not available for farms with sales less than $2,500. The 1969 data are not comparable with the earlier years.

While the trend in tenant-operated farms has been declining since 1920, the percentage for blacks in recent years has been nearly three times greater than that for whites.

It is important to note in this connection that, of the total number of commercial farms operated by blacks in 1964, only about 6 percent sold products valued at or above $10,000–the minimum amount, according to the United States Department of Agriculture, necessary to

TABLE 3-14. Number of Nonwhite-Operated Commercial Farms in the South by Principal Crop*

Principal Crop	1964 No.	1964 %	1969 No.	1969 %
All types	116,785	100.00	24,154	100.00
Cash grain	3,396	2.91	1,903	7.88
Tobacco	30,732	26.30	8,858	36.70
Cotton	58,159	49.80	3,195	13.20
Other field crops	3,593	3.08	1,735	7.18
Poultry	397	0.34	440	1.82
Dairy	1,129	0.97	947	3.92
Livestock	4,634	3.97	3,108	12.90
General	8,364	7.16	2,780	11.50
All others	6,381	5.46	1,188	4.92

Source: U.S. Department of Agriculture, *Census of Agriculture*, 1964, 1969.

*As is inevitably the case, the data are not comparable because of the 1969 restriction to farms selling at least $2,500. They do reflect, however, the continuing importance of cotton and tobacco and the greater relative disadvantage of the black cotton farmer.

maintain a $2,500 net income (Table 3-16). The corresponding figure for white operators was approximately 30 percent, or five times greater than for blacks. On the other hand, only 6 percent of all white operators and a mere 0.2 percent (227 in the entire South) of all black operators had gross sales of as much as $40,000 (the amount considered necessary to yield a $10,000 net income) in 1964; the percentages in 1969 were 11.1 for whites and 2 for blacks (Table 3-17).

Federal Agricultural Problems

In addition to the problems inherent in the black farmers' concentration on small acreages, involuntary programs of the United States De-

TABLE 3-15. Output of Major Southern Crops by Race of

Crop*	1949 White	1949 Nonwhite	1964 White	1964 Nonwhite
Cotton (bales)	10,392	2,477	10,278	1,271
Tobacco (pounds)	1,228,936	320,070	1,573,060	262,272
Grain corn (bushels)	392,744	68,907	324,707	30,936
Soybeans (bushels)	2,602	185	146,122	5,862
Wheat (bushels)	170,198	823	194,622	1,596
Rice (bushels)	42,284	369	127,292	688
Peanuts (pounds)	217,118	67,043	1,757,558	212,981

Source: U.S. Department of Agriculture, Census of

*Barley and sugar cane data were not collected in 1949 dropped in 1969. Census of Agriculture 1969 data are for of black farmers are in Class 6 (sales less than $2,500).

partment of Agriculture have operated to compound their difficulties.[7] Although justified on the grounds of "income parity," the programs continue to discriminate against the small farmer. The large, white landowners of South appear to have dominated the administration of these programs, perpetuating their control over farmers operating small acreages (especially the black operators) by means of a configuration of political and economic powers which extend from the Congress to the local administrative offices in the county seats. They control the Agricultural Stabilization and Conservation Service, which administers commodity price supports and establishes acreage quotas for the basic crops, of which cotton and tobacco are the two most important, especially for black farmers.

Operator (Selected years; thousands)

1969		Nonwhite % of total		
White	Nonwhite	1949	1964	1969
7,486	194	19.2	11.0	2.53
1,292,015	90,805	20.7	14.3	6.57
312,248	11,377	14.9	8.7	3.52
264,554	6,691	6.64	3.86	2.47
211,328	944	0.48	0.81	0.44
		0.86	0.54	
2,279,131	110,446	23.6	10.8	4.62

Agriculture, 1949, 1964, 1969.

:hough the output of each is now considerable. Rice was
:lasses 1-5 and are not comparable, since a high percentage

As recently as late 1968 no black farmer in the South had ever served as a regular member on a county Agricultural Stabilization and Conservation Service committee.[8] This is *the committee* which determines acreage allotments and conservation payments on individual farms. The record of black participation on the state and community levels is little better–blacks held only five of fifty-eight staff or community (grievance) committee positions in 1969.

Even in the Cooperative Extension Service, which was organized more than a half-century ago to help farmers improve productivity by providing technical assistance through the county agent's office, the record shows little black participation. The Cooperative Extension Service was totally segregated until 1964 and has done little since to help

TABLE 3-16. Value of Products Sold by Southern Commercial

Income Class	Full Owners No.	%	Part No.
$40,000 and over			
White	13,459	4.08	20,690
Nonwhite	36	0.12	143
$20,000 to $40,000			
White	20,779	6.29	28,086
Nonwhite	99	0.34	417
$10,000 to $20,000			
White	34,912	10.57	42,658
Nonwhite	446	1.51	1,696
$5,000 to $10,000			
White	56,490	17.11	47,962
Nonwhite	2,149	7.27	4,484
$2,500 to $5,000			
White	83,688	25.33	42,926
Nonwhite	6,447	21.82	6,470
$2,500 and under			
White	120,981	36.62	25,966
Nonwhite	20,364	68.94	7,963
Total Commercial			
White	330,309	100.00	208,288
Nonwhite	29,541	100.00	21,173

Source: U.S. Department of Agriculture, Census of
*The "percent" columns add to 100 vertically, by race.
(4.08) means that 4.08 percent of white full owners had
**Excludes some managers.

the poorest farmers improve their practices in either crop production or livestock management.

Perhaps the most ambitious, and most realistic, farm program ever attempted by the federal government to help small farmers is the Farmers Home Administration. It was set up in the 1930s to make loans to small farm families, to enable them to buy or expand their farms and improve their homes, to buy machinery to increase the pro-

Farms by Tenure of Operator and by Race* (1964)

Owners	All Tenants		Total	
%	No.	%	No.	%
9.93	6,392	5.01	40,541	6.09
0.68	48	0.07	227	0.19
13.48	11,284	8.84	60,149	9.03
1.97	262	0.40	778	0.67
20.48	23,277	18.24	100,847	15.14
8.01	3,768	5.70	5,910	5.06
23.03	31,789	24.91	136,169	20.44
21.18	14,862	22.49	21,497	18.41
20.61	29,712	23.28	156,307	23.46
30.56	21,565	32.64	34,482	29.53
12.47	25,181	19.73	172,131	25.84
37.60	25,564	38.69	53,891	46.15
100.00	127,635	100.00	666,144	100.00
100.00	66,069	100.00	116,785	100.00

Agriculture, 1964.
For example, the top percentage in the left-most column
sales of $40,000 or over.

ductivity of their farm enterprises, or to finance small businesses (especially farmers' cooperatives) in order to raise their incomes. Since the Farmers Home Administration directed its efforts largely toward farmers in the areas of greatest poverty, a large proportion of the loans made by the Economic Opportunity Act during the first four years of its existence were concentrated in the South. However, the Farmers Home Administration was required by law to help only those who

TABLE 3-17. Value of Products Sold by Southern Farms By

Income Class	Full Owners No.	%	Part No.
$40,000 and over			
White	24,798	8.57	28,143
Nonwhite	209	2.13	216
$20,000 to $40,000			
White	29,445	10.17	32,354
Nonwhite	345	3.52	490
$10,000 to $20,000			
White	42,357	14.63	38,643
Nonwhite	929	9.48	1,187
$5,000 to $10,000			
White	76,434	26.41	40,129
Nonwhite	2,746	28.02	2,328
$2,500 to $5,000			
White	116,431	40.22	35,733
Nonwhite	5,570	56.84	3,257
Total			
White	289,465	100.00	175,002
Nonwhite	9,799	100.00	7,478

Source: U.S. Department of Agriculture, Census of

* These totals are not comparable with those in the (those with less than $2,500 in sales).

could benefit most from the use of the loans. Hence, it helped the affluent more than the poor–the whites more than the blacks. During the period 1964 to 1967, black farmers, who constitute about a third of all farmers in the South, received only a fourth of all loans and only a seventh of the total funds.

Under the provisions of the law, the Farmers Home Administration undertook to maximize the use of its limited resources, even though most blacks were left out. For example, of the total recipients of the Economic Opportunity Act loans, 32 percent had a high school educa-

Tenure of Operator and by Race (1969)

Owners	All Tenants		Total	
%	No.	%	No.	%
16.08	7,145	9.18	60,086	11.08
2.89	59	0.86	484	2.00
18.49	11,071	14.23	72,870	13.44
6.55	238	3.46	1,073	4.44
22.08	16,720	21.49	97,720	18.02
15.87	1,084	15.76	3,200	13.25
22.93	20,662	26.56	137,225	25.31
31.13	2,329	33.87	7,403	30.65
20.42	22,195	28.53	174,359	32.15
43.55	3,167	46.05	11,994	49.66
100.00	77,793	100.00	542,260	100.00
100.00	6,877	100.00	24,154	100.00

Agriculture, 1969.

previous table because they do not include Class 6 farms

tion or more, a standard which could be met by only 3.2 percent of all black farm workers and less than 1 percent of the older black farm operators and farm managers. While this was not outright racial discrimination, favoring those with a high school education or more was equivalent to favoring whites.

But there was evidence of overt racial discrimination in the conduct of the Farmers Home Administration. In 1961 there was not a single black among some seven thousand members of the county committees which determine the eligibility of loan applicants. In 1969 there were only 385 black county committeemen in the South, the result perhaps of a 1965 directive which required at least one black committeeman in all counties where as many as 20 percent of the farmers were black. Although the Farmers Home Administration has improved its employment practices in recent years, blacks seem to have penetrated key positions on a token basis only. Hence, the conclusion that the administration of the programs of the Department of Agriculture has been discriminatory against small farmers in general and blacks in particular seems inescapable.

Income and Quality of Life Status

Wholly apart from the displacement of farm operators and farm family labor in the South, the technological revolution has had a profound effect upon the income and quality of life of the families remaining in agriculture. In this respect, one most interesting trend that shows wide racial divergences had to do with the number of automobiles operated by farmers in the South. In 1950 some 28 percent of all resident black farm operators and 60 percent of all whites had automobiles, but by 1969, for farms with at least $2,500 in sales, the percentages had grown to 64 for blacks and 71 for whites. However, it is important to remember that the 1969 data exclude the 71 percent poorest black and the 49 percent poorest white farmers, suggesting that the increase is not as great as the numbers indicate. For Class 1–5 farms, 67 percent of those operated by blacks have trucks, as do 82 percent of those operated by whites.

Another important measure of the socioeconomic well-being of the family is the number of people living in households. During the 1950s the average number of white persons per household on southern farms declined from 4.06 to 3.62 in 1960 and then to 3.15 by 1970, but in nonwhite households the average number increased from 4.06 in 1950 to 5.10 in 1960 before dropping to 4.43 in 1970.

Nor does the comparison for blacks improve appreciably when other characteristics of the household are examined. The percentage of children five to nine years of age living in households not headed by parents, although declining slightly since 1950, averaged roughly three times as high for nonwhites as for whites, and the proportion of occupied housing units considered in unsound condition, while also decreasing for both races, was 31 percent for nonwhite farm families as compared to only 7 percent for whites as recently as 1960. The percentage of housing units with both hot and cold piped water increased, and the increase among nonwhite families was more pronounced than among white families, owing largely to the fact that they started from a much lower base. But in the main, improvements in housing for nonwhite farm families have lagged behind those for white farm families during the entire period since World War II.

Racial differences in the income effects of recent technological changes have also been substantial in southern agriculture. The disparity in incomes between white and black farmers has always been significant, but not until recently have many white farmers (and these were made up chiefly of the larger landowners) enjoyed significantly larger incomes than black families. Income from sales of farm products was low for farmers of both races, and a sizable amount of the subsistence accruing to both groups came from produce raised on the farm. However, some indication of the position of blacks as compared with whites may be arrived at by taking the percentage of families receiving $3,000 in net income per year, a figure used by the Council of Economic Advisers as constituting the margin of the "poverty line."

The $3,000 annual income standard applied to the 1960 census data shows that 52 percent of white and 86 percent of black farm families fell below the poverty line. However, according to the 1970 *Census of Population*, the percentages had fallen to 18.8 for white and 50.9 for blacks.[9] Median income percentages for black vis-à-vis white farm families varied from lows of 43.8 in Mississippi and 49.5 in Louisiana to 60 in Kentucky and 58.3 in Texas. For urban families, the percentage which fell below the poverty line in 1970 was much less for both groups–9.2 for whites and 35.2 for nonwhites–but the difference in median incomes between whites and blacks was greater than that for farm families in all southern states except Mississippi and Texas (U.S. Department of Commerce, 1970; Cowhig and Beale, 1964, p. 42.).[10]

Hence, when almost any measure of the income/quality-of-life ratio is examined, sizable disparities between white and black families on southern farms become clearly evident. Not only are black farmers and their families at a marked disadvantage in comparison to white families, but also both institutional and technological forces beyond their control seem to keep pushing them back into a smaller corner of society. Worse than that, the prospects for improvement in the foreseeable future seem dim. Since the limiting factors for raising farm incomes are land and capital, significant changes in the labor/land and labor/capital ratios will take a long time, given the present institutional framework under which agricultural production is carried out in the South.

Notes

1. We wish to acknowledge the contribution of Adamantios Pepelasis to the development of this section.
2. The 1969 *Census of Agriculture* does not give a breakdown of farm size by race except for farms which sold at least $2,500 of farm commodities. This misses nearly three-fourths of the farms operated by blacks.
3. These are counts for commercial farms selling cotton or tobacco, as opposed to *commercial cotton* and *tobacco* farms. The footnote under Table 3-8 explains the difference.
4. USDA data show a heavy concentration of tenant farmers in states associated with cotton production. Tenancy agreements involving black operators are often pure "sharecropping," which requires the operator to provide only labor. Responsibility for acquiring needed capital would then fall to the white landowner, a situation favorable to the survival of many black cotton farmers.
5. In terms of the argument of the previous section, the family labor may be considered as a fixed input for a given growing season, with zero marginal cost involved in its use if there are not off-farm alternatives.
6. Data for 1969 are broken down by crop and by race only for farms with at least $2,500 in sales, which misses 71 percent of black farmers. The data cannot be used to update this section.
7. We are indebted to Ray Marshall for his help in the development of this section.
8. Much of the data for this section came from the U.S. Commission on Civil Rights (1965) as detailed in the references at the end of this chapter.
9. An increasing proportion of income from farm families is being generated by off-farm work. Hence, comparisons of farm family income, by race, by use of farm income alone are subject to qualifications.

10. More precisely, this statement read that the ratio of black median income to white median income was lower for urban than for farm families in all southern states except Mississippi and Texas.

References

Cowhig, James D., and Beal, Calvin L. 1964. "Socio-economic Differences between White and Nonwhite populations in the South." *Social Forces* (March).

Heady, Earl O. 1953. "Technical Scale Relationships and Farm Size Policy." *Southern Economic Journal* (January).

Madden, J. Patrick. 1967. *Economies of Size in Farming*. Washington, D.C.: Government Printing Office.

Sundquist, W. B. 1971. "Economies of Scale and Some Impact of Agricultural Policy on Farm Size." Paper prepared for *Human Resource Development in the Rural South*, edited by Ray Marshall. Austin: University of Texas at Austin, Center for the Study of Human Resources. Mimeographed.

U.S. Commission on Civil Rights. 1965. *Equal Opportunity in Farm Programs*. Washington, D.C.: Government Printing Office.

U.S. Department of Agriculture. 1949, 1954, 1959, 1964, 1969. *Census of Agriculture*. Washington, D.C.: Government Printing Office.

———. *Changes in Farm Production and Efficiency*. 1970. Statistical Bulletin no. 233. Washington, D.C.: Government Printing Office.

U.S. Department of Commerce, Bureau of the Census. 1900, 1920, 1950, 1960, 1970. *Census of Population*. Washington, D.C.: Government Printing Office.

4

State and Local Governments

David F. Ross

The employment of blacks in state and local governments in the South has undergone significant changes since the 1960s. No accurate count of numbers is available, but of much greater importance is the greater variety of job classifications in which blacks are now found. The old traditional "Negro jobs" still exist, but elsewhere blacks may now also be found in four quite different sets of circumstances: in what the Commission on Civil Rights has called "new traditional Negro jobs," in token numbers throughout the civil service, in all-black governmental units, and in fully integrated situations. Most of the change to date has been in the first of these categories.

If by "equal employment opportunity" we mean the full integration of public employment, then the surface of job discrimination has barely been scratched. "New traditional Negro jobs" and token integration have, however, accomplished certain things. They have helped to make government more responsive to the needs of black citizens, they have provided employment to substantial numbers of blacks, they have breached the first line of defense against equal employment opportunity, and they have provided experience which will be useful in identifying barriers and implementing programs conducive to the achievement of fuller integration.

"New traditional Negro jobs" refers to the fact that there are some positions, formerly closed to blacks, for which black skin is now becoming a prime requirement. Police forces which a short time ago were entirely white are now recruiting blacks for community relations work and as patrol officers for black and mixed neighborhoods. Agencies administering antipovery programs, such as public welfare and employment security, now employ significant numbers of blacks in white-collar, professional, and even supervisory positions.

"Token integration" is a term in common usage, the meaning of which is widely understood in a general way, but which had to be given a specific and quantitative meaning for the present purpose. It is recognized that it would be of considerable interest to know, when an agency is found to have a small number of blacks on its staff, whether this was the result of a policy of employing a few blacks to allay criticism or whether it was the first fruits of a policy of nondiscrimination.

For two reasons, however, no attempt has been made in this report to distinguish between such cases. One reason is that it would be impossible by survey methods to determine whether token integration was a policy or an accident. It simply cannot be taken for granted in the present climate of public opinion and legal jeopardy that candid answers would be given to questions pertaining to motivation. The other reason is that it is one of the conclusions of this study that a policy of nondiscrimination is ineffective as a means to the achievement of equal employment opportunities and that, for practical purposes, it is in fact equivalent to the policy of nonintegration or token integration.

Enough evidence now exists to make it clear that equality of employment opportunity can be achieved, but only through an aggressive policy which includes much more than merely removing the color ban. Additional features of an effective policy would include a program to recruit and equip blacks to meet existing requirements for civil service positions, a fundamental revision of civil service requirements to make them both job relevant and nonselective by race and economic class, and in some cases the redefining of jobs where, for example, work requiring a professional degree is combined in one job with work for which such a requirement does not exist. The failure of responsible officials in the present day to adopt such policy revisions, given the information that is now available, is in fact a discriminatory policy, regardless of conscious intent, and it is treated as such here.

Token integration is therefore defined as a situation in which an agency employs one black in a nontraditional job, or in which the number so employed, expressed as a proportion of total agency employment in such job categories, does not exceed half the proportion of blacks possessing appropriate educational qualifications in the state or other appropriate jurisdiction. The educational qualifications adopted as appropriate were completion of high school for skilled labor jobs and completion of four years of college for white-collar (i.e., clerical, professional, technical, and supervisory) positions. A variation was used in the case of supervisory employment, which was considered to be at a token level if the proportion of blacks in supervisory jobs did not exceed half the proportion of blacks in the agency's total work force.

The number of black-controlled governmental units is not statistically significant at this time. A few are discussed in this report, largely to establish the fact that qualified black applicants can be found for jobs at all levels of government employment when circumstances are favorable to their coming forward.

Fully integrated situations are similarly rare. Only in one small area (Tuskegee and surrounding Macon County, Alabama) were entire governments found which met this standard. It is significant, however, that almost every substantial government has an integrated agency. The lack of any identifiable pattern among such agencies suggests that their condition results from the personal convictions of their chief administrators, personnel directors, or other individuals in crucial positions.

There is yet no systematic and comprehensive available source of data for a study of black employment in state and local governments. Such governments were perhaps the only significant employers to be exempt from the employment provisions of the 1964 Civil Rights Act and hence from the reporting requirements, although they were included through amendments by the Equal Employment Opportunity Act of 1972. The Census Bureau collects detailed periodic information on employment in state and local governments but omits race and color from its categories. Some agencies receiving federal financial assistance are subject to a nondiscrimination requirement and since 1972 have had to report employment by race and other categories to the Civil Service Commission. The coverage is far from complete, however, even among federally aided agencies (it omits, for example, police forces, highway departments, and agricultural extension personnel). In any case, the Commission has received neither money nor manpower for the analysis and publication of the results.

It is indeed one of the major findings of this report that the federal government has been seriously remiss in not providing for the most obvious and rudimentary data needs in this important area. The fault is shared by Congress and the executive branch and by Republicans and Democrats. All have joined in a consensus decision to make state and local governments (with some exceptions) islands of exemption from federal concern for the rights of black citizens. As a result, it has been necessary for the purposes of this report to rely on a varied assortment of (*a*) one-shot surveys, (*b*) surveys conducted on noncomparable bases, (*c*) unevaluated data presented in hearings and court actions or in the press, and (*d*) such other miscellaneous sources of information as could be gathered. The report is accordingly spotty in its coverage and more impressionistic than statistical in its methodology.

If, therefore, the findings depended upon marginal classifications, their value would be doubtful. In fact, however, this has proved to be largely an area of strong blacks and whites, not delicate shadings. Great numbers of agencies still exist in which no blacks are employed except in "traditional Negro jobs." The differences are immense. The patterns among agencies with token integration and agencies providing "new traditional Negro jobs" are sharp and clear. The findings, whatever their statistical significance, provide important indicators both of data needs and of directions for the formulation of public policy.

State Governments

Comprehensive reports on employment in state government by race, agency, and job level have been published by state agencies in Kentucky, North Carolina, Tennessee, and Texas. Virginia's Department of Personnel has not published such a report but has made available the necessary data in the form of IBM printouts. A study conducted by the Commission on Civil Rights provides similar information for state employees in the SMSAs containing the capitals of Georgia and Louisiana (as well as the cities of Houston and Memphis).

Additional data were made available for this report by the Civil Service Commission in the form of unprocessed questionnaires by certain federally aided state agencies in all thirteen states which, for purposes of this study, are defined as "the South." Finally, some data for the state of Alabama are available in the records of the U.S. District Court in Montgomery and in a report of hearings conducted in Montgomery by the Commission on Civil Rights.

North Carolina is one of the states where government has made an effort to purge itself of job discrimination. In January 1963, Governor Terry Sanford created the North Carolina Good Neighbor Council, with the purpose of (among others) encouraging the employment of qualified persons without regard to race. At the same time, he said that there would be no discrimination in state jobs, and he directed agency heads to implement this policy. In 1967 the state legislature gave statutory recognition to the Good Neighbor Council, which had previously existed only by executive order, and Governor Moore continued his predecessor's policy of providing support and leadership to the movement for nondiscrimination. The climate has thus been relatively favorable, and it would be expected that North Carolina would serve as an example of what could be achieved under optimal conditions. If so, the outlook for other states is not too bright.

About 25 percent of North Carolina's residents (but only about 17% of state employees) are black.[1] Among the whites in state employment, 68 percent are skilled labor or white-collar workers, compared to 30 percent of blacks (86% for whites and 58% for blacks in 1970 for the categories in note 2). Blacks are 5.2 percent of all skilled workers employed by the state, which is slightly better than the token integration:[2] 9.9 percent of North Carolina's high school graduates are black.[3] The overall picture, however, is not particularly significant: 74 of the 196 black skilled workers, for example, are employed in the state's ten predominantly black educational and medical facilities.

Most skilled labor in state government, in North Carolina and elsewhere, is employed in the highway department. In 1968, for example, North Carolina employed 2,201 skilled workers in its highway department and only 1,568 in all 105 other agencies and institutions. Highway departments are traditionally important sources of patronage, which may explain in part why, although heavily subsidized by the federal government, they are exempt from federal regulation of their hiring policies. North Carolina's highway department employs seven blacks as skilled labor, for a token integration rate of 0.3 percent. There are twelve integrated agencies which employ black skilled labor at more than a token rate, none of which are of significant size: five institutions of higher education, three health facilities, and the Board of Juvenile Corrections.

Much more important in state government is white-collar employment. More than half of North Carolina's total employment is in this category, and 8.8 percent of the category are black. Since the state's college graduates are 12 percent black, this appears to be substantially better than token integration.[4] Again, however, when we examine the picture on an agency-by-agency basis, quite a different impression is gained. The predominantly black institutions employ over half of the black white-collar workers, and seventy-nine agencies, accounting for 68.5 percent of all state white-collar employment, employ either no blacks or only token numbers of blacks in such jobs. Of the seventeen agencies remaining, only three are of significant size: the University of North Carolina, the Agricultural Extension Service, and the Board of Juvenile Corrections.

None of these three represents a response to the governor's initiative or the work of the Good Neighbor Council. The university has led rather than followed official policy; the other two have also long been important employers of blacks, and the jobs involved are mainly examples of "new traditional Negro jobs." The extension service employs a large number of black women as home demonstration agents to visit black homes, and the Board of Juvenile Corrections serves a clientele (youths in trouble with the law) among whom the poor, and hence the black, are disproportionately represented. Moreover, of the seventeen "integrated" agencies, only one is integrated at the level of supervisory employees: Pembroke State College, with a total employment of only 203.

Where the influence of pressure from the governor's office can perhaps be seen is in the forty agencies practicing token integration, which include most of the larger state agencies, and in some small agencies closely connected to the governor's office (and lacking independent power bases). An example of the latter case would be the personnel department, all of whose employees are at the white-collar level. As recently as 1966, this department employed no blacks; by 1968, its work force was 7.4 percent black, or fully integrated by our standard. Its total employment, however, was only 54, so that the impact of its integration on job opportunities was negligible.

In Kentucky, 7.2 percent of the population and 5.3 percent of state employees are black, as in North Carolina; however, the black employees are found mainly at the level of unskilled labor.[5] Only 398 (30%) of total black employees were found to be employed as skilled labor (89) or at the clerical (128), professional (167), or supervisory (14) levels. Of the forty-nine state agencies for which data are reported, thirty-nine had either no integration at the skilled-labor level or only token integration. These included highways, parks, agriculture, corrections, public safety, and conservation, along with thirty-three others which are either very small or have negligible skilled-labor requirements.

Of the remaining ten, only two are significant employers of skilled labor, the Department of Mental Health and the Tuberculosis Commission. Both operate hospitals. This differs from the picture in North Carolina only in that it omits educational institutions from the integrated category, and this difference is not significant because the Kentucky data do not cover educational institutions.

Fifteen Kentucky agencies were found to employ blacks beyond the token level (which is only 1.85%) in white-collar jobs. Only six of these were of significant size: economic security, education, mental health, child welfare, finance, and a basket category ("other commissions"), which includes the Human Rights Commission. Of all blacks in white-collar jobs in the state, 62 percent are in the first three of these, with an additional 15 percent in the other three. All but the finance department involve significant numbers of old or new "traditional Negro jobs." The Department of Finance stands, with North Carolina's Department of Personnel, as an apparent special case.

Data available for Tennessee are not so complete or recent as those previously discussed, but comparing the statewide survey of 1962 with the Memphis data of 1967 clearly establishes three things:

1. There has been a significant increase in black employment beyond the unskilled-labor level.
2. This has come about not so much by the spread of equality in employment opportunity through the state government as by the relative expansion of those agencies which already employed blacks to a significant extent.
3. These agencies are once more primarily those which deal with the poor: public health (which in Tennessee includes mental health), welfare, corrections, and employment security.

It is not necessary to delve beneath the surface to discover that in Louisiana very little opportunity exists for blacks in state employment. The state is 31 percent black in population, but only 3.5 percent of state employees in the Baton Rouge area are black, and less than a quarter of these are above the unskilled level. Of the sixty-seven agencies reporting, fifty-seven employ no blacks above the unskilled level. Both the highway department, which elsewhere displayed token integration, and the health facilities, which elsewhere were among the most integrated, are included in this group. Token integration is found in Louisiana in such agencies as employment security and welfare, which elsewhere were found to have passed that mark. Apart from the five-person Office of Economic Opportunity, only the Louisiana State Library in Baton Rouge is fully integrated at the white-collar level, evidently another special case.

The state of Georgia, represented by the Atlanta SMSA, presents an intermediate kind of situation. Its total employment of blacks (5.7% of state employment, where blacks are 25% of the population) is closer to the Louisiana pattern than to that of Kentucky, North Carolina, or Tennessee. Their distribution, however, more closely approximates that found in the mid-South and border areas.

Of twenty-nine agencies in Georgia, only eleven (all with total employment under a hundred) have no integration of either white-collar or skilled employees. Token integration, however, is more commonly of the classical variety–one black face in the office. This was found in nine agencies at the white-collar level, including highway departments and public safety. Another four were integrated to less than the 5 percent level–in a state where 10 percent of the college graduates are black–and the USDA just barely exceeds the 5 percent mark. "New traditional Negro jobs" account for the proportionately full integration of two departments, labor (employment security) and family and children's service (welfare). Like most states, Georgia also has its one exceptional agency, the Department of State, with 10 percent of its 163 white-collar employees black.[6]

The Virginia data permit, in addition to the analyses by agencies, an analysis by occupational titles. There are 1,956 occupational titles in the Virginia civil service, and 1,539 of these are held exclusively by whites. One black each is found in an additional 140 occupations, while another 48 appear to be "traditional Negro jobs" by the evidence that they are held by more blacks than whites. This leaves 229, or 11.7 percent of all occupational titles, which appear to be open to employees of all colors.

About 40 percent of all black employees in Virginia are in "traditional Negro jobs"–these are principally custodial or kitchen workers and the lower echelons of hospital employees. About 30 percent of all white employees are in jobs which are either all white or have only one black in the classification. In only four areas are there occupations dominated by whites which employ as many as a hundred blacks: the clerk-typist field, mental hospitals, highway departments, and higher education.

Among clerk-typists in Virginia, over half of the blacks are employed in predominantly black institutions, and there are indications that a significant number of the others are employed to perform secretarial work for black professionals and executives. The blacks employed in mental health and higher education are largely accounted for by the three predominantly black mental hospitals and two predominantly black colleges operated by the state. The case of highway work, however, is something else.

Virginia's highway department employs 258 blacks as skilled labor, 5.7 percent of its total skilled work force. Since 9 percent of the state's high school graudates are black, this rates as better than token integration; it is also far in excess of the rate found in any other state covered in this survey.[7] These are not only skilled jobs; they are also strictly nontraditional for blacks, including such occupations as heavy machine operation and repair and surveying. Moreover, they are performed primarily out-of-doors in rural areas where the work crews are highly visible to a motoring public, which is still predominantly white. It is particularly significant when employment barriers are broken down in highway departments, because this is a field that has not only economic but also political importance due to its patronage potential. It is also the one area of state employment where a significant breakthrough could be made for the upgrading of black manual laborers. Granted that 5.7 percent is only a beginning in a state whose population is 21 percent black and granted that the Virginia highway department employs only trivial numbers of blacks as white-collar workers and supervisors, it remains true that something very special and significant has taken place here.

The same phenomenon is found in other agencies in the state. In all, thirty-four agencies in addition to the predominantly black institutions employ black skilled labor at better than token rate, their average being 9 percent, while token integration is found in only nine. The remaining thirty-seven agencies–which, while having skilled work forces, employ no blacks in that category–account for only 6.6 percent of the state government's total skilled jobs.

Whatever may have brought about this favorable development for black skilled labor in Virginia, it has not affected white-collar workers. Over 60 percent of black white-collar workers are employed in the state's nine predominantly black institutions. Of the 151 state agencies, 79 employ no blacks at this level, another 13 employ one each, and 21 others employ them at a rate of less than 3.6 percent, which is half the proportion of the state's college graduates who are black.

Of those whose white-collar work forces are integrated beyond the token level, most are in the fields where new and old "traditional Negro jobs" are found: health, education, welfare, and employment security. The apparent exception is the Department of Alcoholic Beverage Control. This agency employs some 1,640 people in white-collar jobs, 129 of whom are black, an integration ratio of 7.9 percent. The exception is more apparent than real, however. First, these are mainly blacks employed in retail stores located in black neighborhoods, and, second, the data are consistent with a charge by the Virginia Council on Human Relations that the department systematically withholds promotions from blacks.

Available data for the state of Texas add another dimension to our analysis, for they include a classification by race and salary level. It is obvious that there are wide variations in the level of remuneration connected with different white-collar jobs and that hiring a black stenographer at $6,000 a year is a different kind of breakthrough from hiring a black administrator at $20,000. Much can be inferred in a general way about salaries from the data for other states. Only for Texas, however, can a really clear and specific picture be derived.

Of 132 state agencies, 14 were identified as being fully integrated and significant, and these were subjected to a detailed analysis by salary level. "Fully integrated" means integrated at more than the token rate among either skilled or white-collar employees. "Significant" means that the agency is "fully integrated" among *both* skilled and white-collar employees, or that it is "fully integrated" among skilled employees and has more than a hundred such, or that it is "fully integrated" among white-collar employees and has more than two hundred.

In all, these agencies employ 36,547 people classified as "Anglo" or "Negro" by the state of Texas. They include seven colleges and universities, the education and the mental health departments, the tuberculosis hospital, the employment commission, and the Texas Youth Council. The only two unexpected members of the group are the forest and the agricultural services. Except for two predominantly black educational institutions, these fourteen represent the greatest opportunities and successes of Texas blacks attempting to move up into nontraditional jobs in state government. The salary data clearly demonstrate that, even under the most favorable circumstances, equality of opportunity is still a long way from achievement.

Of 5,121 blacks employed in the fourteen agencies, only 6 (0.1%) earn more than $15,107; yet 2,037 of the 31,426 "Anglos" (6.5%) are above this level. At $12,000 and above, we find 12 percent of the "Anglos," compared to 0.3 percent of the blacks. Earning as much as $6,407 are 43.2 percent of the "Anglos" but only 8.3 percent of the blacks. These fourteen agencies employ 1,326 blacks in white-collar jobs, yet they pay only 426 blacks as much as $6.407. Obviously, the integration either is limited largely to the lower echelons of white-collar jobs or does not involve equal pay for equal work.

Looking beyond these fourteen agencies, at the statewide level we find an absolute majority of all black employees at salary levels down to and including $8,075 working in the two predominantly black institutions and 45 percent of all those at $6,407 and above. Even in segregated institutions, however, the opportunity to earn a good salary is far from equal. Texas colleges and universities employ a total of 30,875 people, of whom 927 (3%) earn more than $20,000. The two black colleges employ 984 people, only 6 of whom (0.6%) are paid at that rate.

Only fragmentary data are available for the state of Alabama, but Alabama has special significance as the only state which has been taken to court by the federal government because of job discrimination. Federal "Standards for a Merit System of Personnel Administration," which apply to certain state agencies receiving federal funds, include the requirement that discrimination because of race be specifically prohibited and that appeal procedures be provided. The requirement is weak, and most states have found it possible to go through the expected motions without making traumatic substantive changes in their personnel policies.

The state of Alabama, however, chose to make a stand on principle and refused to state that discrimination was contrary to its public policy. Finally, in June 1968, when Alabama had been defying the regulation while continuing to receive federal aid for five and a half years, the Justice Department brought suit to force compliance. Exhibits presented as evidence in the case showed that in six affected agencies, having 3,071 full-time employees, there were 87 blacks, all but 25 of whom held custodial jobs.[8] The 25 included one (out of 194) in the occupation classified as "Employment Interviewer I and II"; 13 (out of 649) classified as "Case Worker, Grade I"; 2 (out of 1,052) classified as "Clerk-Typist and Clerk-Stenographer, Grades I and II"; and 9 others whose occupations were not identified.

In the same year that the suit was brought, hearings were held by the U.S. Commission on Civil Rights for sixteen black-belt counties (to be discussed later) in Alabama. In four state agencies having offices in the sixteen counties, the Commission found blacks in non-custodial employment only in the Alabama Cooperative Extension Service, which was formed by the 1965 merger of formerly separate black and white extension services.

The federally aided agencies required to report their employment practices to the Civil Service Commission provide not only the most recent data available but also the only data for some of the states in this region and the only data on a uniform basis for all the states. The reporting agencies cannot be taken as representative of the state governments to which they pertain, for they are specifically and exclusively those which are subject to a federal requirement of nondiscrimination. They are of particular interest, however, for the light they shed on the effectiveness of that requirement in bringing about equality of employment opportunity.

One conclusion that emerges clearly is that employment opportunities for blacks in the affected agencies are increasing rapidly. The 25 black noncustodial employees in Alabama in 1968 had grown to 202 by 1970. For the thirteen southern states in the study, between 1969 and 1970 the number of black white-collar workers increased from 4,147 to 5,843. By 1970 every state except Alabama had at least one category of agency integrated beyond the token level, and even in 1969 every state except Alabama and South Carolina met this test. Kentucky and Virginia, by 1970, were beyond token integration in all categories of agency, with Florida, Georgia, Oklahoma, Tennessee, and Texas in all but one.

The categories of agency referred to are health, welfare, employment security, aid to the handicapped, and a small miscellaneous category including civil defense, surplus property disposal, and personnel administration. The federal law applies equally to all categories, but its enforcement has been left largely to the corresponding federal agencies and has varied in intensity, depending upon the interest of the respective agencies.

At one end of the spectrum, the Labor Department, which is concerned with the programs that have been classified here as employment security, has pressed hard for the employment of blacks at all levels in the administration of those programs. At the other end, there is no indication that the Office of Civil Defense has been aware of a nondiscrimination requirement. The fact that pressure from the federal government does have an effect seems clearly to be shown from a comparison of the employment security and miscellaneous categories. The former was integrated beyond the token level in eight of the thirteen states in 1969, and in ten in 1970; the same could be said of no states for the miscellaneous category in 1969, and of only two in 1970.

In 1969, two states still had no black white-collar employees, while six others had only one each in the latter category. By 1970 these extreme forms of discrimination had been reduced in frequency to one and three states, respectively. But this remained the only category in any state with fewer than ten blacks in white-collar jobs.

At the same time, it seems clear that the effect of federal pressure is limited and that other kinds of pressure must also be taken into account. Employment security was the most integrated field in only four states in 1969 and five in 1970. It ranked second in four states in 1970, third in three, and fifth in South Carolina. Welfare was more highly integrated in seven states and on the average for all states. The various programs for the rehabilitation of the handicapped were in general the third most integrated, although ranking first in two states and second in two others in 1970, while programs in the health field generally ranked fourth but were second in three states and third in four. Evidently, something is needed to account for the generally greater degree of integration in welfare than in employment security, despite the greater federal pressure in the latter field, and for the state-to-state variations from the general pattern.

It is submitted as a hypothesis that (*a*) client pressure is generally strongest in the welfare field and is evidently somewhat more effective than federal pressure and that (*b*) individual variations are accounted for largely by differences among state agency administrators, some of whom will resist pressure to the utmost while others gladly yield to it. The fact that various welfare rights organizations have sprung up in recent years–without any equivalent manifestation among the sick, the handicapped, or even the unemployed–lends support to the first assumption; while, without the second, it seems impossible to account for such data as that a larger proportion of white-collar workers in vocational rehabilitation are black in Mississippi than in any other southern state.

Other Governments

Governmental units below the state level include school districts; cities, towns, and villages; counties; and occasionally other special districts. For present purposes, both the nature of the problem and the availability of data dictate that those be considered in two categories: school districts and "all other."

The problem of blacks with regard to employment in school districts is in some ways opposite to that which they face elsewhere in government. Public school teaching has long been a profession open to blacks in the South and has been one of the major avenues of upward mobility. Black colleges in the South have been geared to this market, and black aspirations have been built on this foundation. It was not, of course, equal employment opportunity that created this situation; it was the maintenance of separate school systems for blacks and whites. To a significant extent, desegregation has resulted in termination of employment or demotion of black teachers; to a greater extent, it has resulted in the closing off of entry to the public education field for black college graduates.

There are two reasonably systematic data sources on public school employment by race in the South. One is a report of the U.S. Commission on Civil Rights, which presents data as of 1965 on number of teachers by race and by racial composition of school enrollment (1967). The other is a report of a survey by a task force of the National Education Association, in which 668 cases of black teachers, whom the association was able to identify as having lost their jobs during 1965 directly or indirectly because of school desegregation, are discussed (1965). Reports of court actions and legislative hearings provide additional information useful in updating these more comprehensive reports.

It will be recalled that before 1954 the provision of "separate but equal" public education for blacks was a legally acceptable means of meeting the requirement of the 14th Amendment to the Constitution that the states provide the equal protection of their laws to all citizens. It is true that for many years no serious attempt was made to make black school systems equal to white systems, except in the sense that each provided some kind of education. After World War II, however, and until the Brown decision of 1954, the trend of court decisions conveyed to many southern policy makers the message that the best defense against desegregation was to upgrade the quality of the black schools to the point where a court could not find clear evidence that they were in fact unequal.

By 1965, however, it was obvious that, whatever per pupil expenditures or any other "objective" measure might have shown, southern school officials had never considered the education that was provided to black students as being good enough for white students. In many districts, desegregation revealed the overcapitalization of the school system and permitted an increase in efficiency by closing some facilities. In virtually every such case, the buildings taken out of service were among those that had housed black schools.

Much more generally, the consolidation of black and white schools permitted the more efficient use of personnel and consequent release of teachers and administrators. The persons so dispensed with were in almost all cases black. In many cases, quite apart from any considerations of efficiency, black teachers, principals, coaches, and so forth were released or demoted as simply not qualified, although they had been employed and retained for varying numbers of years to work in the "separate but equal" black schools. In some of these cases, no doubt, officials simply felt that no black teacher was qualified to teach a white student and that no black principal was qualified to supervise a white teacher. The National Education Association has collected accounts of instances, however, in which superintendents appeared to show true compassion for and regret at the plight of displaced black personnel and urged them to return to school so that they could become qualified to work in the integrated system.

For some years, there has been a movement to standardize teacher certification requirements nationally, a movement conceived and promoted without any thought of lending itself to racist purposes. The National Teacher Examination has been resisted by commissioners and boards of education, jealous of their prerogatives or interested in preserving peculiar local requirements. Suddenly, in 1961, there began a great upsurge in the popularity of the examination among southern school administrators.

The state of Florida was the first to institute the National Teacher Examination requirement in 1961. Teachers in that state, whether newly employed or already in the system, were required to pass the examination with a score of 500 (or higher by county option). Those who failed to do so could remain in the school system, at the discretion of the county superintendent, only under so-called Rank V certificates, at a salary limited to $2,800 per year and with no tenure. As is being discovered of many supposedly objective tests, the examination is highly selective on a racial basis. With suitable academic caution, the National Education Association task force on teacher displacement concluded: "It is highly probable that scores in the National Teacher Examination are affected by the social class and geographical section from which the candidate comes. . . . It is therefore probable that the application of the [examination] cut-off scores to teacher certification, appointment, and promotion procedures will bear most heavily upon the Negro teaching population" (1965).

A few years later, in ruling on an exam score requirement of 1,000 in the Columbus, Mississippi, school district, federal district Judge Orma R. Smith was more specific: "Under this standard, 90 percent of the white graduates from Mississippi institutions of higher learning are eligible to teach in the Columbus school district, and 89 percent of the black graduates from Mississippi institutions are disqualified." In forbidding use of the exam scores, the judge cited a March 1971 Supreme Court decision that employers cannot screen out blacks by the use of tests which do not measure their qualifications and that "good intent or absence of discriminatory intent does not redeem employment procedures or testing mechanisms that operate as 'built-in headwinds' for minority groups and are unrelated to measuring job capability."

The matter of the National Teacher Examination score has been discussed at some length because it is representative of a significant method of job discrimination throughout the public service. It has probably passed its zenith in the schools, where the employment situation for blacks is currently undergoing rapid change. The 1954 Brown decision was concerned exclusively with student desegregation and left a legal vacuum within which school districts had considerable freedom to phase out their black employees in the process of eliminating their black schools. Under more recent decisions, however, and under mounting administrative pressure from HEW, more and more southern communities have accepted the inevitable and are in the process of discovering that white students can learn under the direction of black teachers. The trend still appears to be downward among black principals (and possibly coaches) and will probably remain so for some years to come.

The principal source of information on municipal governments is the report of the Commission on Civil Rights (1967). The four southern SMSAs (Atlanta, Baton Rouge, Houston, and Memphis) include 115 governmental units below the state level, with 47,572 employees, 14,045 of whom are black. Because of uniformity in the collection of data, they lend themselves to comparisons not only among municipalities but also between municipal and state governments. Some heterogeneous data have also been located for other communities.

Perhaps the most significant comparison to be made is between state and central city governments in the same SMSA. In each of the four cases, the central city is by far the larger employer of blacks, while the state is far ahead in opening nontraditional jobs to blacks. The city of Atlanta employs 1,716 blacks, but only 32 are in white-collar jobs while in the same area the state of Georgia, with only 342 blacks on its payroll, has 205 in white-collar jobs. Baton Rouge employs 307 blacks, only 5 in white-collar jobs; the state has 197 blacks, 23 in white-collar jobs. Of the 159 black employees of the state of Texas in the Houston area, 76 are in white-collar jobs, compared to 91 of 1,479 black city employees.

In Memphis, 582 of the 4,226 blacks employed by the city are white-collar workers–an impressive number but not an impressive proportion in comparison to the 131 of 411 black state employees in the Memphis area. It is true that white-collar jobs constitute a much greater proportion of total state jobs than of total city jobs in each of the four SMSAs, but even after allowing for this, the state emerges as a relatively bigger employer of white-collar blacks in all cases and substantially so in all but Memphis.

While cause and effect cannot be proved, these observations are consistent with causal factors which are known to differentiate the situations in which city and state governments must operate. One factor of probable significance in explaining the greater proportion of total jobs for blacks in city government is that so much of the city's business involves waste disposal, a traditional field for black employment. A second factor, reinforcing the first, is that city governments are much more sensitive to pressures emanating from the urban poor, among whom blacks are heavily represented, while state governments are correspondingly more subject to outside pressure, particularly from the federal government.

Federal pressure, where it has been exerted, has been largely to get blacks into nontraditional jobs. Conversely, pressure from the urban poor is more effectively met by hiring black janitors at City Hall than by adding a black professional (probably from the middle class or even from out of town) to the white-collar staff.

An apparent exception tends to prove the case that has been made. Police work is nontraditional employment for blacks, yet in the four SMSAs studied, 8.2 percent of city police jobs are held by blacks, compared to only 2.7 percent of state police jobs. This conflicts with our findings by type of job but not by source of pressure as causal factors. State police departments receive financial assistance from the federal government, but the legislation does not require them to be nondiscriminatory in their hiring policies. City police departments, on the other hand, are under considerable pressure from black neighborhoods to provide black patrol officers, not so much because of the jobs but because of the kind of police protection desired.

Among city fire departments, in many respects similar to police departments in their personnel procedures and requirements, no corresponding degree of integration is found. One reason is that firefighters often work a twenty-four–hour shift and must sleep at the fire station, and it is taken for granted (probably correctly) that whites in this occupation would strenuously object to sharing their domestic facilities with blacks. It is also relevant, however, that individual firefighters are not identified with particular neighborhoods, as police officers are.

Among municipalities other than central cities and other governmental units in the four SMSAs, and among scattered communities elsewhere for which data could be obtained, much less of analytical interest was found. Black employment is almost everywhere limited to old or new traditional jobs. Where a county or special district operates medical facilities (Atlanta) or a bus system (Dade County, Florida), we find significant numbers of blacks employed in addition to those found everywhere in street cleaning, garbage collection, and the like. Small towns and rural counties generally have too few employees (other than elected officials) of any color to permit statistical comparisons. The most significant development there is the result of changing voting patterns.

Stretching through the midsections of the Deep South states is the so-called black belt, a series of counties in which blacks make up a majority, or very close to a majority, of the population. Until the late 1960s, these counties were controlled politically by whites, but legislation on voting rights and voter registration drives are bringing about rapid changes, and increasing numbers of governmental units are now black controlled.

Not unexpectedly, though regrettably in terms of integrationist sentiment, the result has been in almost every case a change from all-white to all-black government. The one notable exception is Tuskegee–Macon County, Alabama, where full integration has been achieved in both the city and county governments. Tuskegee is dominated by two large institutions–Tuskegee Institute and a Veterans Administration hospital–both of which employ unusually large proportions of highly educated people, black and white, from cosmopolitan backgrounds. It would be fatuous to attempt generalizations from such a situation.

The Weaponry of the Struggle

The struggle for equal employment opportunities for blacks is largely a technological race, as are most prolonged engagements between opposing forces. Weapons have been devised against known barriers to equality, and when they have proved effective, new types of barriers have been devised. At each stage, the weaponry has become more sophisticated, more difficult for nonprofessionals to comprehend, and more expensive. In the days when doors bore signs reading "White" and "Colored," it required little argument to prove that discrimination existed and little expertise to perceive that its elimination required removal of the signs. Removal of the signs, however, did little to alter the fundamental inequality that existed. Like the abolition of slavery, it removed a constant reminder to blacks of their oppressed condition but left their economic, social, and political status virtually unchanged.

A historical review of exclusionary devices and how they have been combatted is beyond the scope of the present study. It is important to keep in mind, however, as we survey the arsenals on both sides, that these are the results of a developmental process which is still going on.

One of the most effective barriers to the employment of blacks that has been developed is called "waiting for qualified applicants." The policy is adopted, and it is then announced that, if at any time the best qualified applicant for any position is black, that applicant will be hired. Under examination, the appointing official usually expresses the classic liberal position that any policy other than total colorblindness would be discriminatory and that discrimination in favor of blacks is just as bigoted and degrading as discrimination against them. Such a position is philosophically sound and intellectually defensible. It also results in virtually no hiring of blacks for nontraditional jobs.

In the first place, blacks long ago learned that the most significant messages they receive from whites are not expressed in words. If they hear that a certain agency is an equal opportunity employer and they see that in that agency all of the people sitting at desks are white, they believe what they see and not what they hear. This, of course, is effective only to the extent that potential black applicants are not militants, "troublemakers," and so forth, who will perceive a racial barrier but apply for a job anyway. Even in such a case, however, the defense is still effective because only rarely will a black applicant be the best qualified applicant.

There are fewer blacks than whites in most jurisdictions, and generations of oppression have kept them from developing knowledge, skills, and interests appropriate to nontraditional black occupations in the same degree that these have been developed among whites. Finally, even in those exceptional cases where the best qualified applicant is black, there is a high probability that the qualifying examination will not correctly assess his qualifications. This brings us to the second barrier.

The merit system of civil service has long been pushed by reformers and resisted by politicians as a means of selecting among applicants for public employment. It was first introduced into the federal service in 1883 under President Arthur, who succeeded to the presidency when Garfield was assassinated by a disappointed office seeker. In a similar manner, the death of a Michigan governor while weakened with flu and harassed by office seekers at the outset of his term provided the impetus for civil service reform in that state.

Where such martyrdoms have not been available at crucial times, the advance has been slow, and as always in such cases, reformers have turned to the federal government to exert pressure on the states to adopt a merit system. The pressure has come in the form of a requirement that agencies administering certain federally aided programs must use a merit system in selecting their employees. Even today, half of the state governments in the Union exclude a majority of their employees from the merit system.

Most merit systems, and all merit systems meeting federal standards, are explicitly nondiscriminatory. Until recently, however, most applicants were from the white middle class. Now that significant numbers of blacks are applying for public employment, it is becoming evident that civil service examinations intended to test qualifications for employment have unconsciously been loaded with white middle-class questions. This discovery has led in some quarters to a re-examination of civil service tests and in others to a new assessment of their utility. There are few things which could be more conducive to the comfort of a southern public agency administrator–wanting to avoid litigation, to retain federal funding, and to keep the agency white–than an objective examination prepared by northeastern liberal experts in Princeton, New Jersey, to test qualifications for employment which systematically select out blacks. The sudden popularity of the National Teacher Examination as a case in point has already been discussed, and we need not belabor the point.

The Civil Service League, a private reform group founded during the Garfield presidency to promote the merit system, has recently adopted the position that unconscious bias is so deep seated and pervasive that the only practical solution is to abolish most written tests and replace them with performance tests. It can safely be predicted that the response to this initiative by governmental units will be no more alacritous than was the response to the league's ninety years of pressing for increased reliance on written tests.

The third barrier of major importance today is that which we have referred to as token integration. This may come about, as we have seen, in many ways. In a study of policy, however, its greatest significance is found when it comes about as the response of an agency head or personnel officer to irresistible demands that some blacks be hired in the office. Token integration, in such a situation, buttresses the policy of waiting for qualified applicants and makes this barrier virtually impregnable.

Recruitment and training are the weapons appropriate to an attack on the policy of waiting for qualified applicants. The policy succeeds only because in the absence of an organized response few blacks apply, and most of them are not too well qualified. Training is also the most immediately effective response to the use of inadvertently biased "objective" tests. To the extent that such tests measure relevant job qualifications, training in the skills required on the job will be effective. In other cases, training in the taking of irrelevant tests can be effective.

Either way, an energetic and effective program of recruitment and training of black job applicants will eventually produce one of two results: if it does not get some blacks employed, it will generate evidence, for judicial or administrative evaluation, that discrimination is being practiced.

When the agency falls back on token integration–which is the familiar tactic of giving up some territory in order to gain a stronger line of defense–recruitment and training remain necessary but are no longer sufficient. This stage has been reached in the kind of situation exemplified by North Carolina, where the governor pressed for equal employment opportunities in state government and in 1963 established the Good Neighbor Council (discussed earlier), whose function, among others, is to locate and recruit blacks who could qualify for nontraditional jobs and assist them in locating suitable vacancies and making application. The agency has not been lavishly budgeted, but it has had able and dedicated leadership. In part as a result of its efforts, blacks are now found throughout the agencies of state government–but almost everywhere in token numbers. If the governor had taken the most effective advocate of job integration and put him or her in charge of a major operating agency (e.g., the highway department) instead of in the Good Neighbor Council, the total impact on black employment in state government would probably have been many times greater.

Where agency directors are not committed to equal employment opportunity and use token integration as a defense, there appear to be only two really effective means of achieving further progress. And under present circumstances, both are capable of being used only on certain types of targets. One is constituency pressure. Where an identifiable bloc of blacks is served by a particular agency (i.e., where it operates by neighborhoods, as with state liquor stores, or concentrates its efforts on the urban poor, as with welfare agencies), its clients can often exert extremely effective pressure for blacks to be hired.

The other device is legal action, where job discrimination is prohibited by law. In most instances, this means federal legal action and can be used only with those federally aided agencies for which such a prohibition has been enacted by Congress. It is generally regarded as a last resort, but the recent case in Montgomery, Alabama, shows that it can be effective. The court in that case directed the state to employ certain specific blacks and to employ unspecified blacks in certain agencies and positions in preference to whites until prescribed proportions had been reached. In effect, it imposed a quota system.

Such a solution is distasteful to many proponents of equal employment opportunity, but it remains the one device capable of meeting tokenism on its own terms and destroying it. Unfortunately, Congress to date has limited its applicability to only a few state agencies.

Recommendations

Implicit or expressed in the above findings are various recommendations for means of achieving greater equality for blacks in state and local government employment. These are brought together and summarized in three parts–recommendations (*a*) to Congress, (*b*) to various agencies within the federal executive branch, and (*c*) to others, which includes men and women of good will, whether black or white and whether in or out of state or local government.

Congress, no doubt for urgent political reasons, has granted to state and local governments a large measure of immunity from federal law requiring nondiscrimination in employment. This has been accomplished by exempting these governments from the employment provisions of the 1964 Civil Rights Act and by failing to incorporate a nondiscrimination provision into all legislation providing federal aid to programs administered by subordinate governments. This special treatment should be ended. Congress has also assigned to an office of the Civil Service Commission the responsibility to oversee the operation of those nondiscrimination provisions which it has enacted, but Congress has left the office inadequately funded to do the job. This deficiency should be corrected.

Given the nature and extent of the problem, the Census Bureau can no longer effectively defend its policy of omitting race from the data collected and published in its *Census of Governments*. Surveys of several SMSAs, sponsored and published by the Civil Rights Commission and frequently cited in this report, provide a model of what the Census Bureau should do nationally and at regular intervals. In the absence of effective supervision by the Civil Service Commission, enforcement of federal nondiscrimination requirements is left to the agencies administering the respective aided programs at the federal level. Some of these (e.g., labor) take this responsibility seriously, while others (e.g., civil defense) do not. The practice should be made uniform.

Some attention should also be directed to the means of enforcement. Agencies have required reporting and have used threats and moral suasion, but in no case has an agency employed the only real muscle it has under the law, the power to cut off funds. The reasoning has been that it would be the citizens (who would benefit from the program) rather than the offending state agency that would suffer from a cut-off of federal funds. It is clear in many cases, however, that what state and local officials really want is no longer to preserve segregation but merely to end it on terms that will not hurt them at the polls. If an actual cutting off of funds would make it possible for state officials to end job discrimination while at the same time make this look good to their own constituency, at the cost of having a federal agency look bad, this could be a small price to pay for a significant breakthrough.

As we have seen, the federal government over the years has pressured the states into adopting many of their present merit system procedures for civil service. Now that it is clear that these procedures involve a good deal of inadvertent bias, the federal government is obliged to take the lead in exploring new procedures and promoting their adoption. This would be the responsibility primarily of the Civil Service Commission. Simultaneously, much needs to be done in the recruitment and training of blacks for nontraditional jobs. Some federal agencies, particularly the Labor Department and HEW, are already involved in this work, but not with specific reference to government employment.

Recruitment and training are also primary ways that persons outside the federal government can promote the cause of equal employment opportunity. Colleges and universities, high schools and adult education programs, voluntary organizations, and individuals in government employment–all can make significant contributions in this important area. In addition, the main work of organizing community action groups must fall on individuals and organizations outside government. Experience has shown that federally funded and promoted community action groups can function successfully only to the point at which they begin to be effective against local politicians.

Perhaps the persons best able to effect positive changes in the situation are state and local government officials. Many of these do not want changes to occur, of course, but others do. For the latter, the greatest value of this study and others like it can be in providing suggestions as to what sort of action is effective and what is not. In almost every case, where a southern official has appointed a black to a position of high rank for the first time, that position is a "new traditional Negro job" outside the regular hierarchy of administration, for example, minority representative, community relations officer, and so forth. Such people can coordinate, expedite, lobby, negotiate, flatter, cajole, and persuade; but they cannot hire. Their efforts uniformly produce token integration and no more.

If a governor, mayor, or the head of an executive agency would find one qualified black and place that person in a position where he or she administers the recruitment program, interviews applicants, processes applications, and makes recommendations for appointment, promotion, tenure, and the like, not only would the complexion of that agency undergo a rapid change, but also the attitudes of whites toward their black co-workers would be profoundly improved.

Finally, for everyone involved in this struggle, it is necessary to make the conversion that the courts have already made, from our traditional thinking in terms of the removal of barriers to the uncongenial process of thinking in terms of targets or quotas. The Alabama case of Brown previously discussed is of great significance in this connection. Alabama was hailed into court because it refused to remove a barrier: specifically, it refused to state officially that its hiring practices were nondiscriminatory, as the law requires it to do for covered federally aided programs. In its ruling, the court did not bother to require that such a statement be adopted and published. Instead, it simply said to the state–in effect–"you will hire so-and-so many blacks in such-and-such positions."

Job discrimination is like an old dog who has been trained to stay within a fenced yard. When the fence is removed, he still patrols the perimeter of the yard, refusing to go beyond and growling menacingly at anyone who ventures to cross the imaginary line. Even posting a sign that says "Do *not* beware of the dog" makes little difference. What we must do is to get a new dog and train it in new ways. When that has been done, the liberal ideal of "best qualified applicant regardless of color" can be realized and the hated quota system done away with. Until then, liberal color blindness may well prove to be the last of the effective barriers to equal employment opportunity.

Editors' Note

The Labor Department issued additional information after the original study was completed. Excerpts from its letter with suggested updated material are as follows:

> There have been major developments and initiatives taken by federal agencies (including the U.S. Civil Service Commission) in the field of equal employment opportunity affecting state and local governments since the original data for "Employment of Blacks in the South" were compiled. The following notes are intended to update the reader's knowledge of actions and significant accomplishments by the federal government since that time.
>
> 1. An interagency agreement was jointly signed and issued by the Equal Employment Opportunity Commission, U.S. Civil Service Commission, Department of Justice, and the Office of Federal Contract Compliance dealing with equal employment opportunity and the setting of quotas. This agreement was designed to ensure a consistent federal position on matters of compliance under Title VII of the Civil Rights Act of 1964 and maintains that "there is no conflict between a true merit selection system and equal employment opportunity laws."

2. Because it was felt that passive nondiscrimination is not enough to ensure full equality of opportunity and to ensure that merit principles be properly applied at all levels of government, the U.S. Civil Service Commission called for the use of positive, affirmative action. In conjunction with this effort, the USCSC Bureau of Intergovernmental Personnel Programs developed an informative and widely distributed pamphlet, "A Guide for Affirmative Action," for use by state and local governments. Also, by providing technical assistance to state and local jurisdictions to develop affirmative action plans, over 95 percent of all state merit system and affected grant-aided agencies now have affirmative action plans. All thirteen southern states (except the state of Alabama which, under a court order, believes it is precluded from compliance in this area) have developed statewide affirmative action plans.

3. To ensure continuity and progress in the administration of the federal merit system standards, the U.S. Civil Service Commission has allocated funds and issued directives through its Bureau of Intergovernmental Personnel Programs for USCSC regional staff to conduct qualitative evaluations of all state merit system and affected grant-aided agencies. Almost 90 percent of the comprehensive on-site evaluations of state merit system agencies in the thirteen southern states were completed in the latter part of fiscal year 1973, with a heavy emphasis on equal employment opportunity. Problems have been identified and negotiations and technical assistance have been conducted to bring about improvement.

4. In cooperation with the U.S. Department of Labor's Emergency Employment Program during fiscal year 1973, the U.S. Civil Service Commission utilized over $1 million to increase its technical assistance efforts to state and local governments. Approximately 30 percent of these funds were used to provide technical assistance in the thirteen southern states. Many of the personnel system changes effected were geared to facilitate the hiring of the disadvantaged in programs under the Emergency Employment Act of 1971.

5. Under the Intergovernmental Personnel Act of 1970, during fiscal year 1972, over $300,000 were awarded in grants to state and local governments for projects specifically related to EEO activities. Approximately 20 percent of these funds were awarded to the states of Florida and North Carolina for activities in the

area of EEO. Through the comprehensive approach of the IPA, efforts are continuously being made to help build the kind of open, merit-based systems that will provide full equality of opportunity for all qualified persons.

Notes

1. These percentages had become 22 for residents and 20 for state employees by 1970 (U.S. Bureau of the Census, 1973, North Carolina, table 17, p. 54, and table 173, pp. 695–703).
2. Fourteen percent of the following categories were black in 1970: professional and technical; managers; sales workers; clerical workers; craftsmen; operatives; transport operatives (ibid., table 173, pp. 698–700).
3. Ten and three-tenths percent in 1970 (ibid., table 51, p. 209).
4. The 8.8 percent had risen to 12.5 percent in 1970, with 9 percent of the state's college graduates black. The decline from 12 to 9 percent is not surprising, given that black out-migration from that region is positively selected for education (ibid., table 173, pp. 695–700, and table 51, p. 209).
5. These percentages had become 7.4 and 5.7, respectively, by 1970 (ibid., Kentucky, table 16, p. 43, and table 173, pp. 714–719).
6. 1970 Census data show the black share of total state employment to be very close to the black share of the state's population–slightly over 20 percent. These are statewide data, however, and not directly comparable with the Atlanta SMSA percentages in the text (ibid., Georgia, table 173, pp. 850–855, and table 17, p. 55).
7. Blacks were less than 8 percent of high school graduates in 1970, but the percentage of blacks in the population had fallen from 21 to 18.5 (ibid., Virginia, table 51, p. 216, and table 17, p. 46).
8. *Brown* vs. *State of Alabama* (1954).

References

National Education Association. 1965. *Teacher Displacement in Seventeen States*. Washington, D.C.: National Education Association (December).

U.S. Commission on Civil Rights. 1967. *Racial Isolation in the Public*

Schools. Washington, D.C.: Government Printing Office (February).

U.S. Department of Commerce, Bureau of the Census. 1973. *Census of Population: 1970*. Washington, D.C.: Government Printing Office.

5

Federal Employment in the Sixties

R. Lynn Rittenoure

During the 1960s, approximately 40 percent of total employment in the United States was in the nonprofit-making sector, a significant component of which was in the federal civilian service. By the end of the decade, in civilian capacities alone, the federal government employed well over 4 percent of the nonagricultural work force in the South. Although the 4 percent figure represents a significant slice of the employment pie, the qualitative aspects of federal service employment are equally as important as the quantitative ones. Federal jobs are more secure and stable than many found in the private sector, and many are policy-making positions which influence employment policy in other sectors. Also, the leverage which disadvantaged groups can exert on the federal sector for equal treatment in employment opportunities is probably greater than in any other area.

By virtue of the quantitative and qualitative importance of Federal employment in the South, a study of federal service employment practices with regard to the black minority in the 1960s is necessary to an understanding of the total minority employment picture of the region in the recent past. The study may also contribute to an improvement of minority employment opportunities in the late 1970s and early 1980s by projecting pathways which public policy must follow to ensure equality of employment opportunity.

At the end of the 1960s, there were well over 700,000 federal employees in the South, an increase of over 100,000 from the early part of that decade. Of the total in 1969, barely more than 90,000 were black, about 15,000 more than in 1963 (the date of the first complete census of federal employment). Although black employment increased more rapidly than total federal employment, blacks in 1969 were still represented to a much smaller extent than was their ratio to total population.

If in 1969 blacks had been employed in the federal service in the South to the extent of their representation in the population, they would have held an *additional* 42,645 jobs, all in white-collar occupations. This condition contrasts drastically with the situation elsewhere in the United States, where if blacks had been employed in the federal service proportionate to their representation in the work force, they would have held approximately 45,000 *fewer* jobs in 1969.

The black "job deficit" in the South is a glaring indication that there have been limitations on the opportunities afforded blacks for employment in the federal sector in the South. As a result, this chapter has a fourfold objective:

1. To describe the pattern of black employment in the federal government in thirteen southern states and fifteen southern metropolitan areas[1] and to compare the pattern with that in nonsouthern states and with nonsouthern SMSAs
2. To report some results of regression and correlation analysis designed to provide an account of the determinants of black employment patterns
3. To examine the various programs designed to change the structure of black employment
4. To offer some suggestions which will facilitate improvement of black employment opportunities in the federal service

Profile of Federal Employment of Blacks

The objective of this section is to describe black employment in the federal service in the South with respect to location by pay system, by state, by SMSA, and by agency. The black penetration rate, which is simply the proportion of black employees of the total federal work force in any given framework, is the primary device for identifying black employment location. As will be seen, blacks are found primarily in blue-collar occupations and in the lowest-paying categories of all pay systems.

An effort is also made to identify the relative position of blacks within pay systems in states and SMSAs. The device used for this purpose is the index of occupational position. The ratio of blacks' indices of occupational position to those for "all others" in the federal work force indicates the approximate earnings ratio of the two groups. It has been found that blacks have gained improved relative earnings positions outside white-collar occupations. However, in all pay systems, blacks have apparently become "locked into" given occupational categories, and their progress as a group (in terms of grades and earnings) has not been sufficient to even begin to approach the grade and earnings structure of the remainder of the federal work force. Each of the federal government's statutory pay systems is under consideration: the general schedule (predominantly white collar), the wage board (predominantly blue collar), and the postal field service.

The last part of this section describes the black employment situation in several selected agencies, each of which has at least one significantly large bureau with low black penetration rates.

Black Employment Totals in the South

Table 5-1 lists total and black employment for the federal service in southern states. It also lists the black penetration rate by state and an "adjusted penetration rate," which is simply the federal service penetration divided by the proportion of the total population that is black. It should be noted that the data are totals and do not reflect differences between pay systems. It is significant to note that, with the exception of Oklahoma, Tennessee, and Virginia, black employment falls far below proportional representation.

Nearly 29 percent of all federal service jobs were located in the thirteen southern states in 1969, an increase from 27 percent in 1963. A like proportion, 29 percent, of total general schedule positions were in the South in 1969, whereas only 18 percent of the total number of black employees in this pay system were in the South. Although the 18 percent figure seems quite small, it represents a significant improvement over 13 percent in 1963. Of the total wage board and postal field service jobs, the South had 36 and 21 percent, respectively, of total employment in these systems. The wage board portion is somewhat large because of the many defense installations which require large numbers of blue-collar workers in service capacities. The large number of wage board positions in the South is a fortunate circumstance for the black worker, since of the total number of blacks employed in this category in the United States at the end of the decade, 41 percent were from the South. The comparatively small proportion of total postal field service employment located in the South is due to the relatively nonurban characteristic of the South, compared to the rest of the nation.

Almost 25 percent (nearly 91,000) of the total number of blacks in

TABLE 5-1. Black Penetration of Federal Jobs in Thirteen Southern States (1969)

Region & State	Total Federal Jobs (1)	Total Blacks (2)	% of Blacks in Federal Jobs (3)	% of Blacks in Total Population (4)	Adjusted Penetration Rate (3)÷(4)
Total					
United States	2,569,646	389,443	15.2%	11.2%	1.357%
Non-South*	1,852,910	298,730	16.1	8.1	1.988
South	716,736	90,713	12.7	19.1	0.665
Alabama	53,340	5,182	9.7	26.4	0.364
Arkansas	16,146	1,549	9.6	18.6	0.516
Florida	67,503	5,661	8.4	15.5	0.542
Georgia	74,072	13,159	17.8	26.0	0.685
Kentucky	34,518	3,388	9.8	7.5	1.307
Louisiana	26,253	5,361	20.4	29.9	0.682
Mississippi	19,353	2,198	11.4	36.8	0.310
North Carolina	35,174	5,250	14.9	22.4	0.665
Oklahoma	54,055	3,450	6.4	7.0	0.914
South Carolina	28,451	4,633	16.3	30.5	0.534
Tennessee	40,609	5,779	14.2	16.1	0.882
Texas	143,058	13,076	9.1	12.7	0.717
Virginia	133,682	27,189	20.3	18.6	1.091

Source: Calculated from U.S. Department of Commerce, Bureau of the Census, 1970; and U.S. Civil Service Commission, 1970*c*.

*Includes the District of Columbia.

federal civilian jobs were employed in the South. Of this number, nearly half were employed in the wage board system and a quarter each in the other two. Well over half of total black employment in each of the pay systems in the South in 1969 was concentrated in Georgia, Texas, and Virginia. More than a fourth of the total black federal service employment in the South was concentrated in the fif-

TABLE 5-2. Percentage of Total Federal and Black Employees in Various Pay Systems by Region (1963 and 1969)

Regional Aggregations	General Schedule Total	General Schedule Black	Wage Board Total	Wage Board Black	Postal Field Service Total	Postal Field Service Black
Non-South						
1963*	0.454%	0.339%	0.234%	0.276%	0.312%	0.386%
1969	0.440	0.298	0.207	0.204	0.353	0.465
South						
1963	0.466	0.196	0.314	0.602	0.199	0.191
1969	0.513	0.266	0.283	0.486	0.204	0.248

Source: U.S. Civil Service Commission, 1964 and 1970c.

*Computed without the totals for the District of Columbia.

teen SMSAs upon which this study focuses. The lion's share of employment in the SMSAs was found in Atlanta, Houston, New Orleans, Norfolk-Portsmouth, and San Antonio.

Employment by Pay System in Closer Perspective

Table 5-2 demonstrates that the pattern of federal civilian employment differed somewhat between the two regions in question. Whereas in the non-South general schedule employment remained a relatively constant proportion of total federal employment between 1963 and 1969, in the South it became increasingly significant. The proportion of total black federal service employment concentrated in this system increased in the South, but not so rapidly as total employment in general schedule–type jobs. Whereas more than half of the total federal work force in the South were found in white-collar occupations, barely more than a quarter of the blacks were similarly situated. Thus, well over half of all federal service employment opportunities existed in an area in which blacks have traditionally been denied acceptance.

The picture was almost reversed in wage board employment in the South. Nearly half of the South's black federal employees were found in blue-collar occupations, whereas only slightly more than a quarter of all employees occupied wage board positions. This situation contrasted drastically with that in the non-South, where the proportion of both total and black employees in wage board jobs was 20 percent. However, the historical trend demonstrates that in the South there has been a structural shift of black employment from the wage board to the general schedule system.

There has also occurred in the South a structural shift of black employment from wage board to postal field service. Although most in the latter system are of a blue-collar variety, many of the positions are more secure and stable than wage board jobs, and the shift indicates job improvement. However, the prospect of increasing mechanization in the new U.S. Postal Service may nullify the gains by displacement of a large body of black employees.

Table 5-3 lists black penetration rates by pay systems and categories within pay systems for the South and elsewhere in 1963 and 1969. Black penetration in general schedule and postal field service jobs increased in both regions in all categories. There have been significant changes in wage board penetration, but they are due primarily to a change in categories for data collection (see footnotes to Table 5-3) and significant change in the method of determining compensation of wage board employees: the Coordinated Federal Wage System was put into operation in 1967 and changed the method of wage determination for wage board jobs from an agency-by-agency basis to common pay scales for all agencies within specified geographical areas (Donoian, 1969, p. 30). In any case, it is obvious that black penetration in the general schedule occupations is far less than in either of the other two in both regions.

Although the South lagged far behind the non-South in black penetration in the general schedule and postal field service jobs, black penetration was much greater in the South than elsewhere. The profile of black employment by pay systems indicates that in the federal service, as in the private sector, the cornucopia of black employment opportunities was in blue-collar employment.

Occupational Concentrations

Regardless of pay system, black employment in the federal service, as suggested by the penetration rates, was concentrated in the lowest

TABLE 5-3. Black Penetration Rates, by Pay System, for the South and Non-South (1963 and 1969)

Pay System	1963 South	1963 Non-South	1969 South	1969 Non-South
Total general schedule	4.9%	9.3%	6.9%	9.8%
GS-1 to GS-4	10.3	18.3	14.7	19.2
GS-5 to GS-8	4.0	8.0	7.0	10.9
GS-9 to GS-11	1.3	3.2	3.2	4.6
GS-12 to GS-18	0.4	1.2	1.3	2.2
Total wage board*	22.3	14.7	22.8	14.3
$5,499 or less	50.6	30.3	50.5	24.5
$5,500 to $6,999	19.3	18.0	33.3	24.9
$7,000 to $7,999	2.6	6.6	12.8	14.3
$8,000 and over	0.1	0.9	5.1	7.9
Total postal field service	12.0	15.4	16.1	19.1
PFS-1 to PGS-5**	12.5	16.8	17.8	20.3
PFS-6 to PFS-8	4.4	8.3	9.7	13.5
PFS-9 to PFS-11	0.3	1.7	1.6	4.6
PFS-12 to PFS-21***	0.1	0.8	1.3	4.2

Source: Calculated from the U.S. Civil Service Commission, 1964 and 1970c.

*The categories for the wage board minority census in 1963 were $4,499 or less; $4,500 to $6,499; $6,500 to $7,999; and $8,000 and over.

**This category was PFS-1 to PFS-4 in 1963.

***This category was PFS-12 to PFS-20 in 1963.

grade or earnings category. For example, in 1967 more than 50 percent of total wage board employment in the $5,499 or less category in the South was black. Table 5-4 lists the proportion of total and black employment in the lowest paying category in each of three major pay systems. It also contains an index of black concentration relative to total employment concentrations in the lowest paying category; the index is simply a ratio of black to total employment concentrations.

TABLE 5-4. Proportion of Total Federal and Total Black (1963, 1967, and 1969)

Year and Region	General Schedule GS-1 to GS-4 Total	Black	Ratio of Concentration
1963			
Non-South***	0.337%	0.661%	1.961%
South	0.327	0.687	2.101
1967			
Non-South	0.286	0.559	1.955
South	0.311	0.619	1.990
1969			
Non-South	0.239	0.476	1.992
South	0.255	0.547	2.145

Source: Calculated from U.S. Civil Service Commission,

*The earnings category for 1963 is $4,499 or less.

**The grade for 1969 data is PFS-1 to PFS-5.

***Non-South data do not include the District of Columbia.

A value greater than one indicates that blacks are concentrated in the lowest paying category to a greater extent than the total work force in each pay system.

Although the proportion of black employees concentrated in GS-1 to GS-4 positions declined between 1963 and 1969 in general schedule occupations in both regions, it did not decline as rapidly as the concentration of the total work force in that system. Thus, the ratio of concentration actually increased in both regions over the decade. A similar comparison is difficult to make for wage board occupations be-

Employees in the Lowest Paying Category of Each Pay System

Wage Board			Postal Field Service		
$5,499 or less*		Ratio of Concen- tration	PFS-1 to PFS-4**		Ratio of Concen- tration
Total	Black		Total	Black	
0.108%	0.221%	2.046%	0.861%	0.937%	1.088%
0.203	0.460	2.266	0.851	0.953	1.120
0.118	0.352	2.983	0.874	0.939	1.074
0.323	0.613	1.898	0.810	0.921	1.137
0.038	0.098	2.579	0.857	0.911	1.063
0.152	0.335	2.204	0.826	0.912	1.104

1964 and 1968b and 1970c.

cause of the fluctuating data base (see footnotes to Table 5-4). However, in this system in both regions, the concentration of blacks in the lowest earnings category is more than double that of the total wage board work force. In postal field service, the ratio of concentration declined in both regions between 1963 and 1969, despite the fact that the data for 1969 reflect employment in PFS-1 to PFS-5 rather than the PFS-1 to PFS-4 category used in 1963. The ratio of concentration in this pay system in both regions at the end of the decade was only slightly greater than one.

TABLE 5-5. Summary of Index of Occupational Position Ratios for Pay Systems by Regional Aggregations of States (1963 and 1969)

	Black Index Divided by All Other					
	General Schedule		Wage Board		Postal Field Service	
Regional Aggregation	1963	1969	1963	1969	1963	1969
United States	0.734%	0.724%	0.838%	0.871%	0.964%	0.971%
Total						
Non-South	0.729	0.719	0.855	0.869	0.966	0.973
Non-South*	0.748	0.742	0.879	0.890	0.966	0.973
South	0.741	0.727	0.821	0.818	0.969	0.963

Source: Calculated from U.S. Civil Service Commission, 1964 and 1970c, and U.S. Civil Service Commission, Bureau of Manpower Information Systems, 1964 and 1970.

*Does not include the District of Columbia.

Index of Occupational Position

A far better measure of occupational distribution than the ratio of concentration, from both a descriptive and an analytical standpoint, is an index of occupational position of blacks and an "all other" employee group in the federal service. The index of occupational position is calculated for a group (blacks and "all other") by multiplying the average income of all employees for each of the congeries of grades or earnings brackets (a category) used to tabulate minority employment data (see Table 5-3) by the proportion of a group in each category and summing over all categories. In the general schedule system, for example, the categories are GS-1 to GS-4; GS-5 to GS-8; GS-9 to GS-11; and GS-12 to GS-18.

Since salary structures vary between states and SMSAs because of different structures of employment, the index in dollar terms is not

TABLE 5-6. Summary of Index of Occupational Position Ratios for Pay Systems by Regional Aggregations of SMSAs (1963 and 1969)

	Black Index Divided by All Other					
	General Schedule		Wage Board		Postal Field Service	
Regional Aggregation	1963	1969	1963	1969	1963	1969
United States	0.713%	0.684%	0.843%	0.822%	0.961%	0.964%
Total						
Non-South	0.693	0.682	0.799	0.816	0.959	0.967
Non-South*	0.716	0.708	0.834	0.868	0.963	0.969
South	0.705	0.697	0.860	0.839	0.947	0.943

Source: Calculated from U.S. Civil Service Commission, 1964 and 1970*c*, and U.S. Civil Service Commission, Bureau of Manpower Information Systems, 1964 and 1970.

*Does not include the District of Columbia.

useful for comparisons. The ratio of black earnings to "all other" earnings is therefore used to make comparisons and to analyze variations among states, SMSAs, and regions. Tables 5-5 and 5-6 summarize the index of occupational position ratios for aggregations of states and SMSAs[2] for 1963 and 1969 by pay systems.

The most discernible feature of the tables is the increase of the index of occupational position ratio from about 0.700 in the general schedule pay system to well over 0.800 in the wage board system and above 0.960 in the postal field service system. The vast difference between the pay systems explains the logic of analyzing each pay system separately, as is done in the following section of this chapter.

Perhaps the second most notable feature of the data is that the relative earnings position of blacks deteriorated in the decade in general schedule occupations outside the South and in all pay systems in the

South in both state and SMSA aggregations. In all cases the deterioration is less and the improvement is superior outside the South when the District of Columbia is not included in the totals. (In 1969 blacks in Washington, D.C., earned approximately 66 percent of whites' earnings in both general schedule and wage board occupations.) In all cases when the District of Columbia is not included in the totals, the relative earnings of blacks in the South, both in states and in SMSAs, were lower than elsewhere.

Another important observation taken from the data is the significant difference between the state and the SMSA ratios. For the most part, outside the major SMSAs, where penetration is low, the extent of black upgrading is relatively greater. Thus, the penetration advantage that blacks find in major SMSAs is offset by their inability to penetrate the higher grades and earnings brackets. Still another interesting feature of the data is that, in wage board jobs in the non-South, the relative earnings position of blacks improved in both SMSAs and states but deteriorated in the South. The southern index-of-occupational-position ratios in wage board jobs were far below those of the non-South when Washington, D.C., is included at the end of the decade. The index ratios in postal field service jobs have been subject to little fluctuation over the decade, remaining at a relatively high value. However, in the southern SMSAs, the index ratios are markedly below those for the total South.

At least a brief note should be made at this point concerning the relative ranks of individual states and SMSAs in the South. Throughout the decade, Kentucky has consistently maintained a higher than average index ratio in general service jobs (0.787 in 1969), whereas Florida and Tennessee have consistently had the lowest (0.678 and 0.679, respectively, in 1969). The Tennessee rank depends substantially upon Memphis, which had an index ratio of 0.660 in the general schedule system in 1969; the Florida rank depends to a large extent upon Miami, which had a 0.676 ratio in 1969. However, in 1969, Houston was far behind with an index ratio of 0.598, placing it last among all SMSAs, a position of honor held by that city throughout the decade.

Oklahoma and Texas have ranked quite well in the wage board system, although their index ratios are somewhat higher than in other states because of the larger number of native Americans and chicanos in their populations. Both groups are included in the "all other" category for purposes of computing the index ratio. The single state with a consistently superior index ratio in this pay system is Virginia, the position of which is improved significantly by a large amount of employment and a relatively good index of occupational position performance in Norfolk-Portsmouth. The lowest index ratio is found in Tennessee (0.562 in 1969). The Tennessee ratio is heavily influenced by very low ratios in Memphis and Nashville, although other SMSAs, including Atlanta, Birmingham, and Fort Worth, certainly rank alongside the Tennessee cities.

No single state has consistently ranked high in index ratios for the postal field service pay system, although Georgia–with the significant help of Atlanta–has ranked very low. Whereas most of the index ratios for this pay system are well over 0.900, Atlanta had 0.868 in 1969, a value which declined steadily from a high of 0.963 in 1963.

It is obvious that for the most part southern states and SMSAs rank as regional aggregations and individual entities far below those outside the South. Average earnings of blacks in the federal service are far below those of "all other." There is, however, a host of variables–which take on significantly different values in the two regions under consideration–that influence the pattern of index ratios and penetration rates. But before we look at the pattern of determinants of black employment, we should see a profile of black employment, by agency, in the South.

Black Employment in the South by Agency

Twenty governmental agencies hire 96 percent of the total employment in the South. Table 5-7 shows that an agency's mission is an important determinant of black participation in its work force. Large portions of total employment will be black if the agency offers large quantities of blue-collar work (such as the General Services Administration, the Veterans Administration, the Navy, the Army, and the office of the Secretary of the Department of Defense) or has a quantitatively significant black clientele (such as the Office of Economic Opportunity, the Equal Employment Opportunity Commission, the Department of Housing and Urban Development [HUD], the Department of Health, Education, and Welfare [HEW], or the Department of Labor).

An exception to the above rule, both nationally and in the South, is the Air Force. In both regions, the Air Force has well over half its total employment in the wage board system of payments, but the black penetration rate in the nation is 7.3 percent, while in the South it is

TABLE 5-7. Employment of Blacks in the South* by Twenty

Agency	Total Employment		
	Total	Black	%
Air Force	117,699	10,031	8.5
Army	144,805	18,554	12.8
Civil Service Commission	675	70	10.4
Commerce Dept.	5,846	1,100	18.8
Defense Dept.	18,208	3,140	17.2
Equal Employment Opportunity Commission	157	75	47.8
General Services Administration	7,418	2,927	39.5
HEW	18,705	2,224	11.9
HUD	3,286	201	6.1
Interior Dept.	8,184	524	6.4
Justice Dept.	7,563	190	2.5
Labor Dept.	1,491	133	8.9
NASA	17,829	391	2.2
Navy	99,144	16,915	17.1
Office of Economic Opportunity	295	79	26.8
Postal Service	145,864	23,557	16.2
Transportation	18,846	744	3.9
Treasury Dept.	17,671	1,029	9.8
USDA	24,753	1,220	4.9
Veterans Administration	40,244	11,011	27.4

Source: Calculated from U.S. Civil Service Commission,

*The South refers to the 13 states used elsewhere in this

Agencies of the Federal Government (1969)

General Schedule			Wage Board		
Total	Black	%	Total	Black	%
61,862	2,151	3.5	55,538	7,860	14.2
90,513	5,531	6.1	54,157	13,017	24.0
672	68	10.1	3	2	66.7
5,145	908	17.6	577	188	32.6
15,571	1,411	9.1	2,623	1,729	65.9
157	75	47.8			
3,516	701	19.9	3,901	2,226	57.1
16,432	1,815	11.0	977	394	40.3
3,284	201	6.1	2		
6,748	269	4.0	1,626	255	15.7
6,814	165	2.4	413	16	3.9
1,489	132	8.9	2	1	50.0
16,737	260	1.6	963	131	13.6
42,995	2,694	6.3	55,714	14,191	25.5
295	79	26.8			
16,831	380	2.3	2,015	364	18.1
17,535	986	5.6	135	43	31.9
23,147	992	4.3	1,173	212	18.1
31,103	6,276	20.2	8,475	4,494	53.0

1970*c*.

ook.

8.5 percent. However, part of the reason for the low penetration rate of blacks is the location of major Air Force bases in areas of heavily concentrated chicano rather than black employment. Other exceptions are HEW, HUD, and the Labor Department. Penetration rates in the South for these agencies are far below those on the national level. The wide divergence between the southern and the national penetration rates for these three agencies is accounted for by the fact that data for the District of Columbia are added to the national figures.

Other agencies also have significantly lower penetration rates in the South than at the national level (e.g., the Treasury Department and the Civil Service Commission) without benefit of the fact that most of their employment is found in the District of Columbia. Yet the Departments of Agriculture, Interior, Justice, and Transportation, as well as NASA, have low penetration rates in both regions. A partial reason for this is simply that there are proportionately fewer black lawyers, foresters, and engineers available in comparison to the number available in many other occupational categories.

Conclusion

By whatever index used, the pattern of black employment in the two regions under consideration is somewhat different. In the South, blacks–with respect to their proportion in the population–are severely underrepresented in white-collar occupation. The representation of blacks, as reflected in the penetration rate, is increasing, but the relative earnings position of blacks is low and did not improve throughout the 1960s.

All the data used in this chapter indicate that equal employment opportunity is not a demonstrable reality within the federal service. The multitude of programs and policies designed by the federal government to ensure the equality of employment opportunity within its ranks has not produced demonstrable improvement, except in the area of overall penetration rates, in the black employment pattern. Penetration rates in themselves are not a satisfactory measurement of equal employment opportunity.

There is, of course, a large and complex constellation of factors influencing the structure of black employment in the federal service. A thorough understanding of all the variables and their influence on employment patterns must be developed before a rational equal employment program is devised. It is the purpose of the following section to account for the patterns of employment by evaluating the determinants of the pattern. An equal employment program, it is hoped, can then be designed that will permit significant improvement in the employment prospects of blacks.

Conclusion to the Analysis

The major hypothesis–that the pattern of determinants of black employment in the federal service is substantially different in the two regions under consideration–was thoroughly substantiated by regression analysis, though space limitations prevent the presentation of these results in detail. In southern cities, for positions in the general schedule pay system, relatively distinct hiring queues, delineated by race, exist. In the South, there has been a much stronger emphasis upon black penetration (relative to upgrading) than in the non-South. Federal employers in the non-South are apparently conducting a relatively more thorough search for qualified black employees and are thus able to hire more highly qualified blacks.

Finally, housing segregation in the South presents a major obstacle to black federal employment in major southern cities, a situation not found in the non-South. Although there are definite problems with respect to black employment in federal service jobs outside the South, the problems in the South are different in nature or are more pervasive. Programs and policies must be designed to pierce or circumvent the barriers in both regions. However, some special efforts must be made in the South to create equal employment opportunity for all people in such jobs.

Equal Employment Opportunity Programs and Policies

If employment opportunities for blacks in federal jobs, especially in the South, are to improve, significant alterations in the format of the U.S. government's in-house equal employment opportunity programs are required. The current format is discussed in the four sections below.

Administrative Structure, Evaluation, and Control

The responsibility for equal employment opportunity program design and implementation currently rests with the Civil Service Commission,[3] as it has since 1965 (Krislov, 1967; Garfinkel and Cahn, 1969, pp. 357–372). Overall responsibility rests within the office of the executive director; but within the Commission itself, activities with equal employment implications are contained in many bureaus, offices, and boards, such as the following:

1. The Bureau of Policies and Standards, which oversees the establishment of suitability standards for federal employment
2. The Bureau of Training, which is responsible for assuring equality of employment opportunities in federal training programs
3. The Bureau of Manpower Information Systems, which collects and disseminates minority employment data
4. The Board of Appeals and Review, which hears appeals from agency decisions on discrimination complaints
5. The Bureau of Personnel Management Evaluation, which is responsible for reviewing and evaluating agency equal employment efforts and monitoring agency self-evaluations of such programs (a crucial role in equal employment implementation)

Individual agencies and their assorted installations are required to conduct "self-evaluations" of their entire personnel function as it relates to equal employment opportunity. Problems are to be reported to the Commission's inspection teams, along with plans for their correction. If the Commission finds in its periodic review of agency self-evaluations that the efforts are not in line with expectations, it "requires improvement or corrective action to bring them into conformity" (U.S. Civil Service Commission, 1970*b*, chap. 713, subchap. 1, install. 135).

The efficacy of agency self-evaluations and Commission review is subject to some question, despite the rhetoric. If an agency does not take corrective action in the case of discriminatory practice on its own initiative, corrective action will not likely occur. The report is an in-house document, and unless the agency voluntarily takes corrective action, neither the Commission nor any other institution is likely to bring effective pressure to force change.

Although any one of the ten regional directors of the Civil Service Commission has the authority to seize the personnel functions of any federal government installation if the policies of the Commission are not carried out, such an action has never occurred and will most likely never occur. The Civil Service Commission is a relatively small agency and is completely unequipped to do anything more than make an example of a few installations, which it is fearful of doing because of the possibility of setting a dangerous precedent which it could not pursue if required. Thus, the Commission "requests" rather than "requires" corrective action in any case of nonconformity with regulations. The real responsibility for equal employment evaluation and control is to be found at the agency level of operation.

Affirmative Action Plans

Although the Civil Service Commission is responsible for government-wide equal employment principles and coordination, individual department or agency heads are responsible for the development and implementation of "plans of action" designed to promote the affirmative action directives of two recent presidential administrations. Presidents Johnson and Nixon both ordered the necessity of eliminating discrimination not only in hiring and upgrading but also, as Nixon put it, "through positive action, making it possible for our citizens to compete on a truly equal basis for employment and to qualify for advancement with the federal service" (Office of the White House Secretary, 1969). There are great differences of opinion, however, on what constitutes "positive" action. Confusion as to precisely what this means led Roger Wilkins, formerly of the Community Relations Service in the Justice Department, to argue that "without a clear interpretation by the [Commission] of the meaning of nondiscrimination in government employment, clearly defined standards of performance, and an understanding that penalties will be imposed for failure to comply, agencies' plans of action and their self-evaluations have proved ineffective in achieving full realization of equal employment opportunity" (1969, p. 5).

Although the present study is not yet ready to pass judgment on their effectiveness, it can be argued that agency plans have thus far been much less than imaginative. They have evolved for the most part because of fear created by misunderstanding and confusion, merely an expression of desire to adopt for the individual agency or department programs which have been designed by the Commission. There are few interagency or interdepartmental differences in plans of action. The effectiveness of such plans is reduced if they are all the same and if agencies do not know what is required and cannot feel free to be imaginative and inventive in discovering ways and means of reducing inequities and promoting equality of opportunity in hiring and upgrading.

An interesting example of the problem outlined above can be found in a program initiated by the Federal Aviation Administration. It has instituted an inventive program to increase minority participation in the air traffic controller ranks. The administration in its southwest region (Arkansas, Louisiana, New Mexico, Oklahoma, and Texas) is offering summer employment to minority group college students who simply *pass* the air traffic controller examination.[4] The individuals do not have to rank in the top echelons or pass medical and security qualification standards for summer employment.

Upon graduation from college, students are requested to take a "junior federal assistant" examination, and the names of those who pass are put on a register. The administration then requests individuals from this register who have air traffic control experience. The likelihood of being able to hire its summer employees is relatively high, and the administration can then upgrade minority group employees through the ranks to positions for which they could not qualify if they attempted entry from the external labor market. According to Morris Brooks, chief of the staffing branch in the Bureau of Recruiting and Examining of the southwest regional office, the only civil service requirement for conducting this type of program is that the experience obtained by summer employees can be also obtained outside the Federal Aviation Administration.

It is significant to note, however, that the same innovative and obviously "positive action" program used in the southwest region has been "nixed" by the regional director of the Civil Service Commission in the southeast region (Alabama, Florida, Georgia, Mississippi, North and South Carolina, and Tennessee). The inconsistency of the Commission in interpreting acceptable positive action programs has contributed to a lack of innovative agency efforts. In at least one instance the Commission has condoned "negative" action. The Internal Revenue Service has recently decided–with the blessing of the Civil Service Commission–that the position of "estate tax examiner" requires a law degree. The Commission accepted the Internal Revenue Service's request for increasing the qualification standards despite widespread acknowledgment that a law degree is quite unnecessary.[5]

Nevertheless, even though the Commission has been derelict in its duty to become partners with agencies in discovering acceptable positive action programs, it has been somewhat active in developing new programs of its own, although the efficacy of the programs is subject at times to serious question. Only a brief description of the most wide-ranging programs will be included here.

The worker-trainee program is perhaps the most widely known of the several programs to promote the entry of "disadvantaged" individuals into federal service. (The term "disadvantaged" is used here to indicate that the program is designed for all citizens, not just minority groups.) The essence of the worker-trainee program is to administer nonwritten performance examinations designed to test five key job elements–reliability and dependability, dexterity and safety, ability to handle weights and loads, ability to follow direction, and likelihood of succeeding in job assignments for which the examining plan is appropriate (U.S. Civil Service Commission, 1968, p. 1). Traditional testing techniques have been abandoned to allow for entry into the federal service by certain disadvantaged individuals. The jobs for which worker-trainee eligibles are hired are low-level GS-1 positions. Worker-trainee eligibles are appointed on a career-conditional basis and, with satisfactory service, may become full-fledged employees. In order to improve their occupational state, however, they must perform adequately on any number of traditional examinations.

Worker-trainee announcements have been issued in sixty-three cities, eighteen of which are in the South. More than 35,000 placements have been made from the worker-trainee register, including 9,529 in fiscal year 1969; 17,127 in fiscal year 1970; and 9,000 in fiscal year 1971.[6] Obviously, the appointments contribute nothing to improving the occupational position in the federal service, since all appointments are at a low earnings level.

Two additional civil service programs, however, are designed to improve the blacks' relative occupational position: the Upward Mobility for Lower Level Employees and the Outstanding Scholar programs. The former has been designed to provide an "opportunity for all persons, with full recognition of their dignity as individuals, to seek and to achieve their highest potential and productivity in employment situations" (Office of the White House Secretary, 1969). The program contains eight areas of action (U.S. Civil Service Commission, 1970c):

1. Job redesign and redevelopment
2. Adjustment in career systems to permit easier entry by lower-level employees onto higher-level career ladders
3. Redesign of qualification standards
4. Provision of enough information on job opportunities to lower-level employees to permit sound planning on career development

5. Provision of career counseling and guidance
6. Provision of education and training
7. Assurance of proper placement of individuals for full use of skills, abilities, and interests
8. Thorough communication of the nature of the program

Although the program incorporates a grand concept, there is little chance that anyone will ever know how well it works. As of 1970, there were no plans on the part of the Bureau of Training, which provides leadership to all civil service departments and agencies for program implementation, to collect data by race on program participation.[7] Therefore, without effective monitoring, the success of the Upward Mobility program rests entirely on the initiative of the individual departments and agencies.

The Outstanding Scholar program provides that individuals ranking in the top 10 percent of their graduating class or completing college with a 3.5 grade-point average ($A = 4$) can establish GS-5 eligibility without the Federal Service Entrance Examination, which is the major exam used to establish registers for career management position in the federal service. The importance of this program can be seen by comparing the federal exam performance by race. Although the Civil Service Commission does not collect data on any examination by ethnic group, some record of the federal service exam results can be obtained by comparing those from predominantly black and white colleges. For example, in 1967 a survey of 191 colleges and universities showed that 71.7 percent of those taking the federal service exam passed it; but only 29.6 percent of the students from predominantly black colleges passed the exam (Reeves, 1970, p. 45).

Thus, it is safe to conclude that a much larger proportion of black individuals graduating in the top 10 percent of their class fail the federal service exam than the same elite group from predominantly white colleges and universities. Given the argument upon which the Outstanding Scholar Program is based–that persons graduating in the top percentage of their college class are qualified for management positions in government service–an inefficient allocation of resources has been generated in the past by exclusive reliance on the federal service examination.

Although few general schedule appointments have been made from the Outstanding Scholar Program register, there is obviously the possibility of a highly selective regional impact of the program. Because most black colleges are found in southern states, the increase of blacks in the federal service due to the program should be greatest in the South. There is, of course, the possibility that graduates from predominantly black colleges could be engaged in positions outside the region, but a large-scale raiding of the South should not be expected. At the time of this writing, no evaluation of the program was completed, and there was some question whether it ever would, which left still another hiatus in the area of meaningful review of equal employment opportunity programs.

The Civil Service Commission has also engaged in directing a few other "affirmative action plans." In 1973, in conjunction with the Educational Testing Service, the Commission was conducting a test for possible cultural biases in suitability examinations. Although a few preliminary reports were issued, no final reports or changes had occurred when this chapter was written (Educational Testing Service, 1969, 1970). The Commission, however, is duty-bound to eliminate all examinations that screen out blacks without realistically measuring their qualifications for work, according to the Supreme Court's *Griggs* vs. *Duke Power Company* decision in March 1971 and U.S. District Court's *Douglas* vs. *Hampton* in February 1972.

Aside from developing a culturally unbiased test which reflects prospective job capabilities, the Supreme and District Court orders can be complied with by not placing exclusive reliance on the federal service entrance exam, a test which has been used on an exclusive basis to fill openings in well over three hundred occupational categories in the federal service. Such a change was then under consideration by the Commission.[8]

The Commission also directed agencies to participate in community affairs which affect the employability of minority group members. Agency heads or their designated representatives act individually or as members of a federal executive association, executive board, or business association. The activities of the agency officials must have a direct relationship to employability but may include working with schools to improve curricula or working to improve transportation facilities, housing accommodations, and so forth. To the extent that this program is working, it is probably the best example of an affirmative approach to improving minority employment opportunities in the federal service. President Johnson, for example, recognized in March 1966 that the regulations requiring agency participation in community affairs affecting employability "go beyond the limited objective of eliminating discrimination. If we are going to have equal employment opportunity in the federal government, we must attack the problem on many fronts" (U.S. Civil Service Commission, 1966, p. 3).[9]

The Civil Service Commission's community effort program, like all others, is marked by a lack of effective alliance with and evaluation and control of agency efforts. A thorough understanding of "positive action" and effective alliances for problem-solving purposes has not yet emerged within the federal community–all efforts to date are best described as desultory.

Complaint Procedure

The nondiscrimination aspect of the federal government's equal employment opportunity program could not possibly be effective without a complaint procedure through which employees or prospective employees can make their feelings known concerning individual acts of alleged discrimination. As of July 1, 1969, a new administrative procedure for processing complaints was introduced by the Civil Service Commission. The new procedure stressed "independent" investigations and hearings as opposed to the previous interdepartmental procedure.

The newest portion of the complaint procedure provided that an agent, not associated with the agency in which the formal complaint arises, conduct an investigation. Independence and impartiality were sought by designating a person who was not directly or indirectly operating under the jurisdiction of the head of the agency in which the complaint arose. The guidelines for providing investigators were as follows (U.S. Civil Service Commission, 1969*b*, p. 3):

1. For complaints arising in the *departmental service*, the "head of that part of the agency in which the cause of the complaint arose" shall normally be considered to be the director of that bureau or its equivalent (i.e., one of the primary organizations into which the departmental headquarters of the agency is divided) involved in the complaint.
2. For complaints arising in the *field service*, the "head of that part of the agency in which the cause of the complaint arose" shall normally be considered to be the director of the field installation involved in the complaint.

The investigation of the complaint will be followed by a hearing, if the complainant so requests, before an "independent" appeals examiner who will make an analysis of the case and recommend a decision, based upon a judgment of the merits of the complaint, to the agency head in whose department the complaint originally arose. The agency head, however, still has the final decision in the matter. The agency head may accept, reject, or modify the decision recommended by the appeals examiner. Nevertheless, if the complainant is dissatisfied with the disposition of the case, the agency head's decision may be appealed to the Commission's Board of Appeals and Review.

The formal complaint procedure is viewed as the second line of defense for those who feel themselves discriminated against. The first step is a grievance procedure which makes use of equal employment opportunity counselors whose job is to "establish an open and sympathetic channel through which employees may raise questions, discuss grievances, get answers, and on an informal basis get resolutions of problems connected with equal employment opportunity" (U.S. Civil Service Commission, 1969*a*, p. 1). The equal employment counselors, however, have a very important role in that it is their duty to advise the aggrieved employees of their rights and duties, such as the existence of formal procedure, time limits for appeals, and so on.

Unfortunately, as is the case with many of the Commission programs, data concerning the number, type, and disposition of complaint cases are not collected on a regional basis. For the purposes of this study, then, an analysis of the complaint procedure can be undertaken only deductively. In accordance with provisions of the Equal Employment Opportunity Act of 1972, the aggrieved individual, if dissatisfied with the final action taken in his or her case by an agency or by the Commission's Board of Appeals and Review, may file civil actions in Federal District Court.

Minority Statistics

The Civil Service Commission conducts a biennial minority census in the federal service on a head-count basis. However, agencies and installations can maintain minority employment data on a continuing basis, if it is maintained on automated data processing equipment that ensures individual privacy and separation from personnel records (U.S. Civil Service Commission, 1970*b*, chap. 713, subchap. 3, install. 133). The system is at all times under full control of the agency's equal employment director, thus to minimize the possibility of misuse. The great advantage of using data processing equipment is the possibility of maintaining current data and of conducting detailed analyses of the data.

The Commission's suggestions for agency self-evaluation of equal employment opportunity programs emphasize that maintenance of raw data should simply be a prelude to a detailed investigation of problems relating to the employment of minority groups. The Commission suggests that the data be used to determine relative turnover rates, types of jobs filled by minority groups, whether there have been patterns of nonselection, the effects of positive action, and so forth. Although most agencies now maintain minority statistics on data processing equipment, virtually no detailed analysis of the data was being conducted at the time of this writing.

Although not all the data collection programs in all agencies were investigated, the most thorough program appears to be that of the Navy, for it has collected statistics by state and by SMSA for a variety of occupational categories. The SMSAs in the South for which the Navy has data are Charleston, Jacksonville, Louisville, Memphis, New Orleans, Newport News, and Norfolk-Portsmouth. The state and SMSA data are collected by occupational series group and grade and are summarized in various ways. Data are available on the number of apprentices, Federal Service Entrance Examination annual appointments, blue-collar supervisors, production-facilitating occupations, and inspectors. In this way, the Navy can isolate minority participation in those areas that are crucial for both present and future employment of blacks. For example, the apprenticeship program in the Navy is the largest in the federal government because of the quantity of blue-collar craftworkers in its employ. The statistics program designed by the Navy is almost necessary to adequately anticipate and promote the employability of blacks. Other agencies would do well to follow the Navy's lead.

Although agencies are authorized to use their minority employment data for a wide variety of reasons, they may not under any circumstances establish a quota for the employment of persons on the basis of race, color, sex, religion, or national origin. It should be noted that the "no quota" regulation is somewhat of a change from an earlier regulation which specifies that the purpose of the minority data program is to ensure "equality of opportunity, not to give preference in opportunity to any one group. Unless this point is made, agency managers may issue statements and take actions (such as *setting numeri-*

cal quotas and goals) which are contrary to public policy and which lay the program open to charges of preferential treatment" (U.S. Civil Service Commission, 1967, p. 4-6-4, emphasis added). Minority employment data may and should be used by agencies to spotlight areas of scanty minority representation and the formation of goals to reach specific objectives.

Conclusion

An attempt has been made in this section to recount the variety of programs used to promote black employment opportunities in the federal service. Many of the programs are general in nature, although some are designed specifically to increase the number of blacks on the federal payroll and to improve the promotion opportunities of those already employed. Unfortunately, scant documentation of the effects of the programs is available. In some cases the programs do not lend themselves to quantification; however, there appears to be a lack of emphasis upon and promotion of schemes to quantify program results. Although the existence of a diabolical plot is not being suggested, it appears as if there is no great interest on the part of program directors to allow thorough analysis of what is happening in the equal employment opportunity office.

The responsibility for an adequate data program–as well as adequate evaluation and control, affirmative action, and complaint procedures–is one which is shared by the Civil Service Commission and individual agencies. Often one will blame failures or simply disappointments on another. A successful partnership between civil service and individual agencies is necessary for equal employment to become a reality in the federal service. A large number of improvements can be made in this area, many of which will be discussed in the next section. However, not one of the policy recommendations will serve its intended purpose in a vacuum of noncooperation.

Recommendations for Renovating the Federal Government's Equal Employment Effort

The major emphasis of this report is that the pattern of black employment in the federal service and the structure of determinants of that pattern are very different in the South compared with the non-South. The applications of a given set of policies and programs in two such different contexts have not been and cannot be equally successful. There is a strong indication, for example, that penetration as opposed to upgrading has been the relatively more important measure of equal employment performance in the South (compared to the non-South). Although there are a host of reasons for the difference, programs must be designed which take cognizance of and seek to correct the divergent patterns. The primary objective of this section is to scrutinize the regional impact of the current set of equal employment policies and programs and to design appropriate policy alternatives to improve black employment opportunities in the federal service in the South. The policy alternatives can be placed in two categories: (*a*) those which suggest changes in the organization and direction of the equal employment opportunity program at the national level and (*b*) those which are designed to take into account and correct macroregional differences.

Administrative Structure, Evaluation, and Control

Since 1965, the responsibility for in-house equal employment efforts has been housed in the Civil Service Commission. The raison d'être for such an arrangement is that the personnel arm of the federal service should also hold ultimate responsibility in the entire equal employment area, including program development and operations along with evaluation and control. There has never been, to my knowledge, a serious suggestion that the Commission be subjected to independent evaluation of its role as guardian of the "merit system." However, in light of the sensitive nature of equal employment system, it has often been argued that the Commission should not have the responsibility of evaluating the federal government's equal employment efforts. The success of the program rests most heavily on acceptance by and active participation of individual agencies and their various installations. Although the success of the "merit system" also rests upon agency acceptance, there is little resistance to the merit system, whereas there is definitely some resistance to equal employment oportunity in all its ramifications. The pertinent question is, then, whether the Civil Service Commission has the commitment to ensure agency compliance with directives of equal employment opportunity legislation.

A large number of arguments have been marshaled in favor of federal service equal employment evaluations and control being administered by a separate independent agency. One of the most outspoken critics of the present arrangement is Clifford Alexander, past chairman of the Equal Employment Opportunity Commission. Alexander argues that the Civil Service Commission's own record with respect to the employment of blacks has been poor and that, as a result, the Commission could not be expected to be an effective watchdog of the equal employment program (*Washington Post*, April 13, 1969).[10]

In 1969 in the South, the Civil Service Commission employed sixty-eight blacks, a tenth of its total employment, forty of whom were employed in GS-1 to GS-4 positions. The penetration rate for blacks in the South was 6.5 percent in GS-5 and above. Not a single black employee was hired by the Commission in Tennessee, and only one black each in Arkansas, Kentucky, Mississippi, and North Carolina. It seems reasonable that the Commission's black employment record in the South may indeed hamper its enforcement efforts. (Although I am not in sympathy with the argument, many agency officials have stated off the record that they will begin sincere efforts in the area of minority employment when the Civil Service Commission demonstrates a definite commitment by increasing its own minority representation.)

There are others, both in and out of the federal service, who argue that, regardless of its record on black employment, the Civil Service Commission has a poor image in the field. It is accused of being tradition bound, institutionally defensive, and an isolated agency. If the accusations have any merit, the Commission is hardly the appropriate repository for responsibility in such a sensitive and vital area as equal employment opportunity. It is virtually impossible, however, to determine the extent of disaffection toward the Commission; it is similarly impossible to determine the effects of any disaffection on the equal employment opportunity program. There may be enough circumstantial evidence, however, to suggest that the current path is not necessarily the road to true equal opportunity.

The Civil Service Commission's evaluation of agency equal employment opportunity programs remains a clandestine operation. For example, the Commission, through its regional offices, periodically conducts "community progress reviews" that are designed to interpret and promote equal employment opportunities in a system of federal installations. The equal employment programs were evaluated in terms of the climate of the community in question, where "climate" refers to housing, educational, and attitudinal patterns. In order to review the results of the community reviews, I was required to sign a "memorandum of understanding," which was obtained only after extensive negotiations. The contents of the reviews cannot be disclosed, even though it appears that *some* of the information contained in the reviews would be useful in mobilizing public opinion to support expanded black employment opportunities.

The policy of the Civil Service Commission is somewhat restrictive when viewed in light of the policies of the Equal Employment Opportunity Commission, which has conducted open hearings ("forums"), for example, on employment in the textile industry of North and South Carolina, on white-collar employment in New York City, and on total black employment in Houston. Furthermore, whenever charges are filed through the Justice Department, the facts in all cases become public knowledge.

It has been emphasized that "*some* of the information" contained in the reviews could be usefully publicized. Unfortunately, most of the information contained in the reviews is simply useless or not thoroughly used and analyzed. There is no reason to believe that the Civil Service Commission's reviews of equal employment opportunity programs by installation–reviews which are *not* available to the public–are any better. In all cases, the reviews are conducted by persons who make use only of available data. It is beyond question that the available data are not adequate to effectively evaluate equal employment opportunity programs. No effort has been made, for example, to use index-of-occupational-position ratios or to require installations to develop relative turnover and promotion rates for blacks versus whites. The reports required of the private sector by the Equal Employment Opportunity Commission are a great deal more extensive than those required of the federal sector.

It has been mentioned that the Civil Service Commission has the authority to usurp the personnel functions of any installation where it is found that the agency is not performing its duties satisfactorily. Although the data which are analyzed in any individual case may not be adequate to fully evaluate the equal employment performance, it is perhaps significant to note once again that the Civil Service Commission has never seized the personnel functions of any installation.

The story is told about a speech made by Robert F. Kennedy in Birmingham in which he urged the business community of that city to open its doors to black employment. The speech was greeted with sarcastic remarks concerning the poor record of federal government with respect to black employment. The then Attorney General, it is said, investigated the complaints of the business community and found them to be justified (Krislov, 1967, p. 37). This story, apocryphal or not, points up an important fact: there has traditionally been a significant difference between how the federal government deals with discrimination in the private sector and how it deals with in-house discrimination. The difference is just as obvious to federal personnel administrators as it is to the Birmingham business community.

One final argument remains which may have some bearing upon the image of the Civil Service Commission as it seeks to carry out its equal employment opportunity duties: a vast difference exists between the formal requirements of the Civil Service Commission and the requirements it actually places on federal agencies. In a document designed to "transmit instructions and guidelines for reviewing, evaluating, and reporting agency equal employment opportunity programs," the Commission requests that agencies and installations ask if selection criteria are valid and if they are applied equally to all persons (U.S. Civil Service Commission, 1967*b*, p. 4-6-9). It also asks the installations to determine if there are any variations in the use and nonuse of selection panels and, if so, whether there are valid reasons for the variation. At the time of the distribution of the above document, the Civil Service Commission had not gone beyond investigating the feasibility of testing the validity of the criteria for employment selection. The large divergence between the rhetoric of action and the requirements of action surely contributed to the opinion that the Commission is not seriously concerned with equal employment opportunity.

The Ad Hoc Congressional Committee on Discrimination in Federal Employment and Federal Contractor Employment, whose chairman at this writing is Representative William F. Ryan of New York, has stated: "The Civil Service Commission has failed to even adequately, let alone aggressively, conduct the equal employment opportunity program. Its institutional orientation toward neutrality, its institutional disinterest in combating discrimination, its inadequate staffing, and its numerous other program missions all militate against its being the suitable body within the federal government to conduct a nationwide, intensive program of this nature" (1970, p. H8772).

The ad hoc committee recommended that the responsibility for the in-house program be lodged in the Equal Employment Opportunity Commission or a totally new agency. Many other individuals have suggested the same (U.S. Senate, 1969; U.S. House of Representatives, 1970). There is generally less enthusiasm for the establishment of a totally new agency than for transferring responsibility to the Equal Employment Opportunity Commission. Representative Ryan, for example, has argued that "there reaches a point where the disadvantages of the multiplicity of bureaucracies outweigh the benefits of new agencies."[11] However, all congressional attempts to effect the transfer have failed. There also appears to be no immediate prospect of success for any legislation on the matter, despite overwhelming evidence in favor of a change.

What is urgently needed at the present time is for the evaluation of in-house equal employment opportunity programs to be placed in the hands of inspection teams independent of civil service control. The inspection teams should be designated by the President and given the authority to review not only equal employment opportunity programs but also the entire personnel functions of a multitude of agencies and their installations.

The inspection teams should work in those states, SMSAs, and agencies which have relatively poor black employment patterns. The results of the current report suggest that evaluations should begin immediately in the South, particularly in Arkansas, Florida, and Tennessee, and in Houston, Memphis, and Miami. Specific bureaus within agencies–such as the Social Security Administration, the Federal Aviation Administration, the Internal Revenue Service, the Soil Conservation Service, and the entire defense establishment–are good starting points.

Open hearings should be held or, at the very least, reports should be published and made public. Such a procedure would bring public pressure on federal administrators or managers whose actions have for too long been sheltered from public scrutiny. The essence of a responsive bureaucratic structure is public review of actions taken. For example, given the importance of federal employment and the relatively poor pattern of black employment in the federal service in Houston, it would have been beneficial for hearings on federal employment to have been held in conjunction with the Equal Employment Opportunity Commission hearings held in that city on June 2 through 4, 1970. In fact the Commission could have been given authority to include federal administrators among its witnesses. Such a program would doubtless have promoted the effectiveness of the hearings held for the private sector.

Given the lack of demonstrable progress in the area of equal employment opportunity, especially in the South, the federal administrator's argument that public exposure would produce reactions which would have a negative impact on black employment opportunities no longer has a defensible basis.

Affirmative Action Plans

No amount of independent evaluation, however, can make equal employment opportunity a reality if guidelines to action are not clearly and succinctly stated. One of the major problems proscribing the success of programs and policies to promote the improvement of black employment opportunities is the lack of concrete program objectives. "Affirmative action" can be meaningful only when objective goals for black employment are established.

Within the current administrative framework, the responsibility for establishing numerical objectives rests both with the Civil Service Commission and with the individual agency or installation. It has been noted previously that the Commission only recently dropped its prohibition on setting goals and had not reached the stage where it required agencies to develop objective numerical goals for black employment when this report was written. Although it is impossible to determine the precise date when the Commission ceased its objection to goals, it apparently did so after the application of the "Philadelphia Plan" to federal contractors in that city by the Office of Federal Contract Compliance. The federal government, in the area of hiring blacks, requires less of itself than it does of private contractors with whom it does business. Many agencies and individual installations have developed goals in the absence of civil service direction, but the lack of enthusiasm in the civil service reflects to many a lack of enthusiasm for the entire equal employment opportunity program.

Federal employers should aim at increasing black penetration at all grade and salary levels, at least in all installations of notable size, to reflect the proportions of blacks in the local population. If, in 1969, blacks had been represented in federal service employment to an extent which reflected their proportional representation in the southern population, more than forty thousand additional blacks would have been employed. Table 5-8 indicates the black "job deficit" in federal service white-collar positions in the South in 1967 and 1969.

If a constant rate of decrease in the deficit is maintained, it will be possible to achieve black employment parity by the year 2030, but that parity will be only in the general schedule pay system. The black job deficit actually increased between 1967 and 1969 in the GS-9 to GS-11 and GS-12 to GS-18 categories. Employment in the two categories expanded in the South by nearly ten thousand each. A strong positive approach to the establishment of goals must be taken by the Civil Service Commission .

TABLE 5-8. Black "Job Deficit" in the General Schedule Pay System
(1967 and 1969)*

Year	Total	GS-1 to GS-4	GS-5 to GS-8	GS-9 to GS-11	GS-12 to GS-18
1967	44,107	6,771	12,591	13,546	11,199
1969	42,645	3,496	12,368	13,779	13,002

Source: Calculated from U.S. Civil Service Commission, 1968b and 1970c.

*Data for 1963 were not used because they were collected on June 30, whereas the other data were collected on November 30 of the respective year.

The establishment of explicit goals, however, is merely a starting point to effective affirmative action. Affirmative action in this context actually has two connotations:

1. Design and implementation of programs to eliminate existing barriers to equal employment opportunity which have been woven into the administrative structure
2. Design and implementation of programs to provide special treatment for the disadvantaged

The former type of program includes the redesign of tests and test administration to eliminate cultural biases and adjustments in the hiring process. The latter type of program is primarily the responsibility of individual agencies or groups of agencies. This type of program, as Chairman Hampton explains, involves the "*moving out* by agency heads and their managers to make equal opportunity a reality" (U.S. Senate, 1969, p. 132; emphasis added).

Examinations

One affirmative action issue, discussed previously, is that regarding pre-employment and promotional examinations. It is the overwhelming opinion of outside observers that many federal service entrance examinations are culturally biased; the validity of the examinations is low for all test takers but is particularly low for ethnic minorities. Invalid employment tests are no longer lawful, and the Civil Service Commission is making many changes to comply with the law. Even completely valid, culturally unbiased examinations will not solve the problems posed by the existence of given test administration procedures. That is, the content of a highly structured, competitive examination is apparently not the only condition which has caused differential performances of blacks and whites on entrance examinations. One civil service official stated unofficially that blacks are intimidated by standard test-taking procedures. If more than one black were taking a given examination, or if black examiners were present to advise the blacks to (for example) proceed to another question if they are having difficulty, performances of the black test takers would improve significantly.[12]

Other factors may also influence the relative performances of blacks and whites on examinations. It has been learned that prospective black clerical employees perform far better, compared to whites, on the state of Louisiana's clerical examination than they do on the federal examination.[13] Two realistic explanations for such a phenomenon are (*a*) the equipment used for the state examination more closely approximates the type upon which the black candidate has achieved facility or (*b*) there is a personal element involved which works to the disadvantage of the black on the federal examination.

In either case, two important considerations are brought to the surface by the above example. Any examination, especially a performance examination, should be administered to different groups based upon a consideration of the conditions under which they gained their skill. Approximation of the conditions for test-taking purposes would not be outlandishly difficult in many instances. Second, the Civil Service Commission should make an effort to determine the reasons for geographical differences between relative (i.e., black/white) performances on given examinations. Although the differences may often be due to differences in skill ratios, an investigation may demonstrate that presence of certain examiners militates against the success of black candidates. Both of the above considerations should be within the purview of the independent inspection teams.

One final aspect of the examination evaluation procedure should be adjusted. A low scorer on any examination is treated unfairly, whether black or white. The Equal Employment Opportunity Roving Task

Force of the U.S. Postal Service explains the situation and proposes an alternative: "Civil Service regulations prohibit an individual who passes a pre-postal entry examination with a low score from improving his standing by taking a subsequent examination until one year elapses from the date of his notice of rating on the previous examination. The individual who fails the examination may apply for re-examination as long as the examination is open and until he achieves a passing score. . . . Action should be taken to change the civil service regulation in order that the low scorer may be accorded the same opportunity as the unsuccessful competitor to improve his status" (U.S. Post Office Department, 1968, p. 8). There seems to be no reason not to follow the task force's advice and remove all obstructions to low-scorer re-examinations.

The Hiring Process

Another area in which changes are vitally needed is the hiring process itself. Perhaps the most vilified portion of the process is the procedure which allows the appointing officer to choose an employee from the top three individuals on the eligible list. This provision is an ancient one. Herbert Kaufman explains:

> The Attorney General, in 1871, ruled that a provision of the Act of 1871 requiring appointment of the person who scored highest on the examination for the position for which he was applying was unconstitutional. It conflicted, he said, with the Constitutional provision that appointments be made by the President, the courts, and the heads of departments because it made the examining agency the appointing power. In order to comply with the Constitution, the Attorney General concluded, a range of latitude for choice and judgment must be left the appointing officer. Civil Service rules of 1883 met this standard by allowing the appointing officer to select one of the top four on any eligible register; this was changed to "the rule of three" in 1888, which is still in effect today. (1965, p. 38)

The existence of the "three-person-eligible" provision, regardless of the direct constitutional issues involved, permits discrimination by appointing officers if they are so inclined. It is equally true, however, that it permits preferential treatment to minority groups if the appointing officer is so inclined. If there are a hundred individuals on the eligible list, and the probability of a black's making a given score is equal to that for anyone else, the probability of a black's being among the three persons eligible is 3 to 100. In the absence of any avoidance of or preference for blacks, the chances of being chosen from the three persons are 1 to 3. The probability of being selected is a joint or multiplicative probability equal to 1 to 100 (3/100 × 1/3). If discrimination exists, the probability of being selected is less than 1 to 100. If there is a preference for blacks, the probability of a black's being selected is greater than 1 to 100. An important policy issue involved is whether black employment opportunities can be increased by a change in the hiring rule.

The argument could be made that the greater the flexibility in the system, the greater the possibility for improving job opportunities for blacks. In such a case, the appropriate policy alternative is an expansion of the number of individuals on any register eligible for selection. It is true that an expansion of the number of eligibles may de-emphasize some of the problems caused by culturally biased examinations by, in some cases, raising the probability of a black's being selected.

The other side of the argument is that as long as any discrimination exists or as long as discriminatory practices exist to a greater degree than preferences for blacks, the three-person-eligible rule permits a reduction in the probability of a black's being selected. The three-person-eligible rule is a portion of the Washington Urban League's case against the federal government charging discrimination in employment practices (see Civil Action No. 2603-69, Paragraph 93 [2], filed September 12, 1969, in the United States District Court of the District of Columbia). The usual recommendation is that an appointing officer be required to hire the number-one eligible. As pointed out earlier, if everything else is equal, the probability of selecting a black out of 100 prospective employees is 1 to 100 under the three-person-eligible rule. The probability is less than that if discrimination exists. The probability of hiring the same black is 1 to 100 under a "one-person-eligible" rule.

It is true that a one-person-eligible rule would reduce discrimination in the actual appointment process. Not all discrimination in the actual employment process would be eliminated, however, since the employing agency can often promote from within to fill the open position and open a new position to be filled which does not list a black as the first eligible. It is also true that, since the likelihood of discrimination in the appointment process is greater in the South, the three-person-eligible rule has a differential regional impact with respect to black employment opportunities in the federal service. However, that is no assurance that a one-person-eligible rule would actually expand the number of job opportunities for blacks.

A third alternative, which combines the best features of the other alternatives, is to expand the eligible list and require that, whenever a black (or a member of any other minority group) who is listed as the number-one eligible is refused appointment, the action must be justified in writing to the equal employment opportunity officer of the agency in question. Furthermore, the action should be justified to the independent inspection team when the action is taken in any agency which has been pinpointed as exhibiting a "pattern of discrimination" in employment. Although the eligible list was not expanded, the Post Office Department in 1968 introduced a plan in which justification in writing is required whenever a black first eligible is refused appointment (see U.S. Civil Service Commission, 1968, p. 3). Like many such programs, however, there has been no attempt to evaluate anything but the complaints of administrators.

The Civil Service Commission can also play an important role by permitting individual agencies to make special requests from existing registers. The Federal Aviation Administration's program in the southwest region (Dallas) to request individuals from the Junior Federal Assistance Examination register with previous air controller experience is the perfect example of an innovative program designed to increase minority employment which the Civil Service Commission should encourage.

In the southwest region, the Social Security Administration requested that the Civil Service Commission permit employing agencies "to request persons with special background in the Negro community using the same rationale for this that we apply to persons who have competence in a language spoken by a minority group such as Spanish or one of the Indian languages. If no persons with such experience were available from registers, special examinations could be held to locate a sufficient number who would be able to qualify."[14] The Social Security Administration argues that "there is real substance to the proposition that special background in the Negro community is a marketable skill in a public service organization, such as the Social Security Administration, delivering benefits in an area with high Negro population. *Communication is more than a facility in language*."[15]

The Civil Service Commission has not yet permitted the Social Security Administration to conduct its proposed program, arguing that current procedures are adequate to improve minority participation in the federal service work force. The Social Security Administration cannot, of course, blame its poor performance on the Civil Service Commission. Nevertheless, its effort at an innovative procedure should not be squelched.

The Civil Service Commission should also look beyond the worker-trainee and Outstanding Scholar programs to others which could be developed to allow entry into the federal service without an examination. For example, members of the upper 10 percent of a graduating class from any accredited institution should be eligible for employment in the federal service without examination. The expanded program should include junior colleges, business schools, and vocational schools. Of course, the entry-level requirements would be adjusted for the type and length of educational experience.

One final aspect of the hiring process which is due review by the Civil Service Commission is the current emphasis on prior earnings as a determinant of entry-level appointments in the federal service. Roger Wilkins argues: "Federal recruiters also place a great emphasis on the previous earnings of job candidates–rather than on their previous work experience and levels of responsibility. The result is that black candidates who have a history of low earnings get jobs which are less responsible and which pay salaries that are lower than jobs received by their white counterparts" (1969, p. 1). It is difficult if not impossible to determine the extent to which the prior-earnings approach is used for entry-level appointments. If, however, the procedure is used equally throughout the federal service, the black applicant is at a colossal disadvantage in the South, where the ratio of earnings for blacks compared to whites is far lower than in the rest of the country. The possibility that black applicants may have been discriminated against, in terms of pay and position, in their previous employment must also be considered.

In all cases, although the Civil Service Commission has a vital role to play in the federal government's equal employment opportunity program, much of the responsibility rests with individual agencies and their approach to affirmative action.

Barriers to Affirmative Action

It has been demonstrated that nonsouthern employers have been more successful than their counterparts in the South in locating qualified black personnel and in upgrading existing black employees. In the South, in major SMSAs, the problem is most acute because of a multitude of labor market problems compounded by residential housing patterns which tend to limit black participation. Federal employers have been less than enthusiastic about black participation, demonstrated by the apparent existence of relatively distinct hiring queues. Although some of the responsibility for the above phenomena rests with the Civil Service Commission, the primary responsibility for action and change rests with the individual agencies.

It has been relatively easy in the South to emphasize penetration as opposed to upgrading as an indicator of successful implementation of equal employment opportunity. The problem of inadequate dispersion of black employees throughout the employment structure is particularly acute in the South and has not improved throughout the decade of the 1960s. It should not be expected that recruitment programs aimed at increasing black penetration in high-level entry positions and on definite ladders–even if the programs have a bias toward improving such penetration in the South–can solve the problem of inadequate dispersion. A great portion of the burden must be placed on in-house training and upgrading.

This study is not designed to analyze the vast internal labor market of the federal service. The subject needs study, however, and provides a rich opportunity for future research. Nevertheless, a few observations and hypotheses can be advanced at this stage. Given the proposition that in-house training and upgrading must share an equal burden with recruitment techniques in promoting the dispersion of black employment throughout the federal service, they have failed, especially in the South. There are several reasons for the severity of the problem in the South.

Although a drive may have been launched to upgrade black personnel to positions which reflect their ability and experience, there is, due to past discrimination, simply a much smaller proportion of blacks on career ladders which have maximum grades above GS-7. The problem of past discrimination exists not only in white-collar employment. In blue-collar employment and in the postal service, there has has been strong resistance to blacks' employment in supervisory, managerial, or any other positions of authority. The network of black and white employment creates, in effect, *separate seniority rosters*. Furthermore, the pattern of past discrimination colors and compounds any problem of current discrimination, especially in the South, since advancement is based to a large degree upon supervisory evaluations.

Again, although this report does not bear directly on the operation of the internal labor market in the federal service, there is ample reason to suggest that the Civil Service Commission's Upward Mobility program is correctly conceived. However, there is no way to ensure that agencies are actively conducting the program. The Commission's Bureau of Training, the entity in charge of the program, should collect and analyze data on black/white training opportunities. The data would then be available for intensive evaluation by independent evaluators. Agencies should establish goals for the proportion of training slots filled by minorities, and supervisory ratings of all employees should be evaluated by the equal employment opportunity office to pinpoint possible sources of discriminatory employment practices. In the Dallas region, HEW has instituted for that area a program which requires individual bureaus of HEW to submit monthly reports on promotions and new appointments by grade level for sex and ethnic categories. The program is designed to create individual accountability for patterns of appointment and upgrading. Unfortunately, attendance by agency managers or their representatives at monthly meetings to evaluate the reports has been spotty.[16]

Another method to improve the dispersion of black employees is to improve recruitment of quality black personnel, a procedure in which southern federal employers have engaged somewhat less enthusiastically than their nonsouthern counterparts. Nevertheless, the opportunity to recruit blacks is much greater in the South with the advent of the Outstanding Scholar program. There is an abundance of predominantly black colleges in the South from which blacks can be recruited. However, there are basically three restrictions (discussed below) which proscribe effective recruitment.

Recruiters are often white, which places a constraint on their credibility, and often they do not have concrete offers of employment to extend to interested individuals. (I have been unable to obtain a satisfactory sample of opinions concerning attitudes toward white recruiters on predominantly black college campuses. However, a feeling of significant resentment against white recruiters was conveyed on the Texas Southern University campus in Houston.) Many of the black college campuses are in out-of-the-way places, and it is simply much easier to find qualified white candidates. It is true that extended effort and attention must be devoted to seeking black job candidates. The task would be much simpler if agencies had realistic educational requirements for available positions. For example, the Internal Revenue Service requires that an appraiser be an engineer, a revenue agent, an accountant, an estate tax examiner, and an attorney. Realistic standards on the demand side of the market influence the supply picture; the two are not independent. The three restrictions to effective recruitment could be easily solved by joint agency efforts to send racially mixed recruiting teams with full slates of job opportunities. It would be difficult for independent inspection teams to judge the quality of recruiting efforts; however, they could easily bring pressure to change unreasonable educational requirements.

The regression results indicate that residential housing segregation poses relatively more severe problems in the South. Agencies have been urged by executive order to become concerned about all aspects of the community which may affect the employability of the disadvantaged, such as housing, transportation, and education. Although concern may be present, action, except by the U.S. Postal Service, is notoriously absent in the South. There has been no coordinated effort by groups of agencies, through federal executive boards or executive associations, to work at outreach efforts. Although individual agencies have made spotty efforts at outreach, no efforts have been successful.

Outreach can be successful if agencies work together to improve community relations and to expand communication of employment opportunities. Agencies should work together to identify skills which are used by all and recruit trainable members from the minority community for classes sponsored jointly by the agencies.

There are many areas in which agencies individually and in consort can and must apply the principles of affirmative action. Agencies must extend special treatment to eliminate or circumvent the barriers of past and present social and economic discrimination.

Complaint Procedure

The present complaint procedure, created and put into operation by the Civil Service Commission on July 1, 1969, involves tacit recognition of the fact that totally in-house complaint adjudication is entirely unsatisfactory. The current procedure assures that an equal employment opportunity counselor will be available for each installation to advise complainants on procedures and to attempt to adjust complaints of discriminatory practices informally. If initial attempts fail to provide a satisfactory settlement, the case can be taken before an "independent" appeals examiner.

There are several problems at the initial complaint-and-appeals level which may proscribe effective and fair adjudication. The counselor is appointed by the agency head, and it is not entirely unlikely that an unsympathetic agency head will beget an unsympathetic counselor. It seems likely that an agent elected by the employees who may be affected by subsequent action would provide a greater degree of fairness in the grievance procedure. The principle involved is derived from trade union experience in the grievance process. The major problem with the above proposal is that the counselor's effectiveness may be hampered if the agency head does not approve of that person's selection.

Many sources outside the federal service argue that the concept of an "independent" appeals examiner is impossible to fathom. The same sources argue that the garden has simply been placed in the hands of one billygoat instead of another. The possibility of interdepartmental back-scratching is the major objection to the procedure. Outside observers argue that the new procedure continues the obnoxious practice of insulating federal service employment practices from outside review.

It is my opinion that the new procedures, at the lower levels at least, are better than the former ones and that the major problems with the complaint adjudication exist at a higher level. The Civil Service Commission reports that in the first five months of operation the new procedure of complaint processing resulted in a reduction in formal complaints from 147 to 79 per month. Such evidence is quite inconclusive as to the fairness of the new procedure compared with the old, however. (A sizable number of regional-level equal employment opportunity officers admitted that they were at first enamored with the complaint procedure because of the reduction in complaints. The same individuals now feel, however, that the reduction has been accomplished by a suppression of complaints.) A new method of selection of equal employment opportunity counselors may change the result significantly. However, given the nature of the problems at higher levels of adjudication, it might be wise to assume that the initial levels of grievance adjustment are satisfactory and to look elsewhere for much-needed change.

It has been noted that the agency head may, at individual discretion, accept, reject, or modify the decision recommended by the appeals examiner. It is then up to the individual complainant to appeal his or her case to the Civil Service Commission's Board of Appeals and Review. It is recommended that the responsibility for appealing to this board be completely reversed in such a manner that the agency head must accept the examiner's decision as final or take the initiative for appeal. Such action would eliminate the need for filing civil service suits in a wide variety of cases.

Furthermore, the authority for final appeals and review should be removed from the Civil Service Commission; an independent evaluation team, recommended at an earlier point in this section, should have responsibility for appeals and review. If the authority for a final review is housed in the same place as the authority for evaluation, information derived from inspections could be brought to bear upon the review of individual complaints. (It should be noted that there are a number of precedents in the body of labor law for this type of procedure. For example, evidence concerning an employer's total attitude and action is often admitted when the National Labor Relations Board makes decisions on individual union complaints of "free speech" violations during representation elections.) The inspection-and-review team should also be required to maintain a case reporter to provide the maximum amount of continuity in decisions and policy and to maximize the opportunity for public scrutiny.[17] The establishment of a quasi-judicial board in no way eliminates the need for final recourse in the form of civil action.

The changes in the complaint procedure recommended here are necessary for two reasons: (*a*) to provide the fairest and most effective review of individual complaints, and (*b*) by opening the procedure to independent evaluation and review, to convince the public of the federal government's commitment to equal employment opportunity.

Minority Data

The minority data collection service is perhaps the most valuable contribution the Civil Service Commission performs in connection with equal employment opportunity. The data collection began in 1961, at the behest of the President's Committee on Equal Employment Opportunity, and has continued through the present. Restrictions on keeping personnel records by race have placed severe limitations on the amount and type of data which could be collected within reasonable budget limitations. Although the restrictions have not been eliminated, the Commission has recently been authorized, "for the first time, to maintain minority employment data in automated files. This will permit agencies and the Commission to measure results on a continuing basis and will eliminate both the need and cost of large-scale periodic surveys whose results quickly become outdated" (*Civil Service News*, March 30, 1970, p. 1). The Commission has set down strict rules for the establishment and use of minority data files. For example, it has stated that "the system will at all times be under full control of the director of equal employment opportunity." However, it has not required that agencies maintain certain critical information in their minority files.

The Commission should require that agencies collect data on the educational attainment of federal employees by race. The educational attainment information must be collected and maintained by pay system, agency, and region, just as penetration rates are collected, to be of any use. Educational attainment data not only must be maintained for current employees but also should be collected and maintained for all individuals entering and leaving the federal service. Such data are necessary in order to compare and analyze racial differences in new hires and accessions. Explicit accounts of turnover rates and promotion times by race should also be collected. Data by race should also be collected and maintained, not only on the level of grade and salary aggregations but on within-grade step levels as well. With automated files there is no reason not to collect and maintain such minority data.

An effort must be made to identify "critical" positions within the federal service–those of a policy-making nature and those which have a direct or immediate impact upon the general economic well-being of minority group members. Such a data program is required in order to aim at placing blacks in meaningful public policy posts. In order for employment opportunities for blacks to expand in such areas, minority data by occupation must be available.

The identification of "critical" positions is not an easy task. The Agricultural Research Service, for example, suggests that "insofar as minority group employment is concerned, [the Agricultural Research Service] has no 'critical' occupation . . ."[18] Yet that agency not only conducts research on such matters as "agricultural production, utilization, and marketing; nutrition and consumer use; and control and eradication of pests; and plant and animal diseases" (U.S. General Services Administration, 1969, p. 271); it also has responsibility for communicating the results of its research to farmers. It is difficult to imagine that none of the results of this agency's research would be of use to black farmers. The individuals responsible for communicating the results to the farmers and the individuals deciding the direction of research are certainly in "critical" occupations. The data, when collected, must be organized in such a manner as to maximize their usefulness in terms of analyzing and improving black employment patterns.

Finally, to round out the data collection program, agencies should keep detailed data by race on the types and extent of employee training. Training is perhaps the single most crucial element in determining the occupational advancement of employees, but no data presently are available on the distribution of training by race (see an earlier section of this chapter).

Conclusion

It has been argued that the responsibility for equal employment opportunity in the federal government should be shared. The main actors are the Civil Service Commission, individual agencies, and an independent evaluation team. The Commission's comparative advantage lies in the area of program development designed to eliminate culturally biased barriers, such as the evaluation and hiring processes, to black employment and in the collection and dissemination of data on minority employment. Due to its past and present practices, however, the Commission does not have the ability (or, apparently, the desire) to effectively evaluate equal employment opportunity efforts at the agency level. And it is at the agency level where fundamental changes in personnel procedures need to be made to ensure equal employment opportunity for all job applicants and current employees.

Agencies and their installations, individually and in combination, must extend outreach efforts to black communities and educational institutions. Agencies must seek out and train capable black members of their work forces who have become stagnated in career ladders which do not suit their abilities. The latter effort must be combined with efforts to weed out sources of discriminatory hiring and evaluation among supervisory personnel. Agencies *must* act if equal employment opportunity is to become a reality in the public service. Past actions, however, indicate that they will not do so unless extensive pressure is applied.

Effective pressure must be brought to bear by an independent evaluation agency whose responsibility is not only to pinpoint obviously discriminatory practices but also to scrutinize affirmative action efforts and to publicize good and poor performances. Public accountability is the only kind of pressure, apparently, that will accomplish true equal employment opportunity. The agency must also have responsibility for adjudication of discrimination complaints. It will be able to marshal a great deal of information in the field which is of the highest value in judging complaints. The heart of an effective equal employment opportunity program lies in separating evaluative responsibility from those with vested interests in keeping performance evaluation hidden from view.

Notes

1. Atlanta, Birmingham, Dallas, District of Columbia, Fort Worth, Houston, Jacksonville, Louisville, Memphis, Miami, Mobile, Nashville, New Orleans, Norfolk-Portsmouth, and San Antonio.
2. The sixteen non-South SMSAs are Baltimore, Boston, Chicago, Cincinnati, Cleveland, Denver, Detroit, Indianapolis, Kansas City, Los Angeles, Newark, New York, Philadelphia, Pittsburgh, St. Louis, and San Francisco.
3. The authority for the operation of the program derived from President Nixon's Executive Order 11478 and was codified in P.L. 92-261, Section 717 (Equal Employment Opportunity Act of 1972), signed by the President on March 24, 1972.
4. This information was obtained in an interview with a member of the civil rights staff in the southwest regional office of the Federal Aviation Administration on March 5, 1971.
5. Personal interview with a member of the Equal Employment Opportunity staff of the southwest regional office of the Internal Revenue Service, March 4, 1971.
6. Letter from the director of the Program Development Division of the Bureau of Recruiting and Examining, November 4, 1970.
7. Personal interview with the director of the Office of Agency Consultation and Guidance in the Bureau of Training, Civil Service Commission, September 25, 1970.
8. Letter from the deputy director of the Bureau of Policies and Standards, Civil Service Commission, October 6, 1970.
9. Nearly four years later, President Johnson remarked to me that "we didn't attack the problem on enough fronts–we didn't do enough, son."
10. As of November 30, 1969, there were no blacks employed by the Civil Service Commission in any of its forty-seven positions at GS-16 and above.
11. Letter from William F. Ryan, 20th District, New York, November 24, 1970.

12. Personal interview in the Civil Service Commission, Washington, D.C., March 28, 1969.
13. Personal interview in the Social Security Administration, Dallas, Texas, May 13, 1971.
14. Letter from Wayman E. Register, regional commissioner of the Social Security Administration, to Louis S. Lyon, regional director of the Civil Service Commission, February 26, 1970.
15. Letter from Wayman E. Register, regional commissioner of the Social Security Administration, to Louis S. Lyon, director of the Civil Service Commission, April 30, 1970 (emphasis added).
16. Personal interview with the director of the Office for Civil Rights, Department of Health, Education, and Welfare, Region VI, March 31, 1971.
17. I am indebted to Michael W. Ambrose for this suggestion. Ambrose, now with Community Programs, Inc., is an ex-Civil Service Commission employee in the old equal employment opportunity project office. Prior to his departure from the civil service in the fall of 1968, Ambrose had ample opportunity to review the decisions of the Board of Appeals and Review and recommended that the board itself maintain a reporter.
18. Letter from the director of the Personnel Division, Agricultural Research Service, U.S. Department of Agriculture, July 28, 1969.

References

Donoian, Harry A. 1969. "A New Approach to Setting the Pay of Federal Blue-Collar Workers." *Monthly Labor Review* 92, no. 4 (April).

Educational Testing Service. 1969, 1970. Reports PR-69-5, PR-69-6, PR-70-16, PR-70-17, and PR-70-18. Princeton, N.J.: Educational Testing Service.

Garfinkel, Herbert, and Michael D. Cahn. 1969. "Racial-Religious Designations, Preferential Hiring, and Fair Employment Practices Commission." *Labor Law Journal* 26, no. 6 (June).

Kaufman, Herbert. 1965. "The Growth of the Federal Personnel System." In *The Federal Government Service*, edited by Wallace S. Sayre. By American Assembly. Englewood Cliffs, N.J.: Prentice-Hall.

Krislov, Samuel. 1967. *The Negro in Federal Employment.* Minneapolis: University of Minnesota Press.

National Alliance, March 1971.

Office of the White House Secretary. 1969. "Memorandum from the President for Heads of Departments and Agencies." August 8. Mimeographed.

Reeves, Earl J. 1970. "Making Equality of Opportunity a Reality in the Federal Service." *Public Administration Review* (January–February).

"Report of the Ad Hoc Congressional Committee on Discrimination in Federal Employment and Federal Contractor Employment." *Congressional Record*, September 16, 1970, pp. 32659–32669.

Taeuber, Karl E., and Alma F. Taeuber. 1965. *Negroes in Cities.* Chicago: Aldine Publishing Co.

U.S. Civil Service Commission. 1964. *Study of Minority Group Employment in the Federal Government, 1963.*

———. 1966. *Bulletin No. 713-6* (December 8).

———. 1967*a*. *FPM Installment No.* 272-273 (December 19).

———. 1967*b*. *FPM Supplement Installment No.* 272-273 (December 19).

———. 1968*a*. *Equal Opportunity in Federal Employment* (August-September).

———. 1968*b*. *Study of Minority Group Employment in the Federal Government, 1967.*

———. 1969*a*. *Attachment 2 to FPM Letter No. 713-11* (March 13).

———. 1969*b*. *FPM Letter No. 713-11* (March 13).

———. 1970*a*. *Civil Service News* (March 10, 30).

———. 1970*b*. *FPM Supplement 990-1* (May 29).

———. 1970*c*. *Study of Minority Employment in the Federal Government*, SM70-69B. Washington, D.C.: Government Printing Office.

———. 1970*d*. *Upward Mobility for Lower-Level Employees: Suggested Goals and Action.* Washington, D.C.: Government Printing Office.

U.S. Civil Service Commission, Bureau of Manpower Information Systems. 1964. *Pay Structure of the Federal Civil Service, June 30, 1963.*

———. 1970. *Pay Structure of the Federal Civil Service, June 30, 1969.*

U.S. Department of Commerce, Bureau of the Census. 1970. *1970*

Census of Population, Advance Report. Washington, D.C.: Government Printing Office.

U.S. General Services Administration, National Archives and Records Service. 1969. *United States Government Organization Manual, 1969–1970*. Washington, D.C.: U.S. Government Printing Office (July 1).

U.S. House of Representatives, Committee on Education and Labor. 1970. "Report No. 91-1434" to accompany H.R. 17555, *Equal Employment Opportunities Enforcement Act of 1970*. 91st Cong., 2nd sess. (August 21).

U.S. Post Office Department. 1968. "Report of Findings and Recommendations by the Postmaster General's Task Force on Equal Employment Opportunity" (December 10). Mimeographed.

U.S. Senate, Committee on Labor and Public Welfare, Subcommittee on Labor. 1969. *Hearings on S. 2453, Equal Employment Opportunities Enforcement Act*. 91st Cong., 1st sess. August 11–12, September 10, 16.

Washington Evening Star, July 12, 1971.

Washington Post, April 13, 1969; March 9, 1971.

Wilkins, Roger. 1969. "The Equal Employment Opportunity Posture of the U.S. Federal Government." Ford Foundation. April.

6

Minority Construction Contractors

Robert W. Glover

Improving the status of minority construction contractors has several significant implications for economic conditions of minority groups. Indeed, few industries offer greater upgrading opportunities to them because construction is a growth industry with a relatively large number of blacks already in it, and low capital requirements and ease of entry make the growth of employment and entrepreneurial opportunities for additional minorities relatively easy. Moreover, if they follow the pattern of whites, the growing numbers of minorities who have entered construction apprenticeship programs will become supervisors, business agents, and contractors after they complete their apprenticeship training. In addition, government is heavily involved in improving the economic opportunities of minorities to use their political power to influence public policy in this direction. Finally, construction provides good employment opportunities for males at a time when job opportunities for minority males have declined in many areas. Minority males can enter this industry without the high academic credentials required in other growth occupations.

The topic of upgrading minority construction contractors has drawn the attention of several writers (Debro, 1970, pp. 298–309, and 1971, pp. 70–76; Patterson, 1971, pp. 16–21, 44; Pugh, 1969, pp. 138–150; and Stuart, 1971). However, as of 1972 only two empirical studies had focused on minority construction firms. The first of these was conducted in 1970 by the NAACP under funding from HUD. The findings of this forty-eight–city survey were published in July 1970 as a six-volume registry (U.S. Department of Housing and Urban Development, 1970). It contains names, addresses, and some background information on 2,051 blacks and Spanish-surnamed contractors. In addition to the survey, the NAACP performed a detailed study of contractors in ten cities (U.S. Department of Housing and Urban Development, 1971).

Although the NAACP survey and study were useful in identifying some minority contractors and their problems, they were limited as to both coverage and analysis. In Atlanta and Houston, for example, the survey failed to identify 92 percent of the minority construction firms counted by the Bureau of the Census in 1969 (U.S. Department of Commerce, 1971). A further difficulty with the NAACP study was that, because of an inadequate questionnaire, it was unable to explain certain problems encountered by minority contractors.

The second study was an in-depth survey of minority contractors in the New Orleans area (Shapiro, 1971, pp. 10–12, and 1972). In this study, the author presents a detailed profile of minority contractors in one city; however, because it has no comparative analysis, the study has limited value.

The aim of the present study is to fill some gaps in the available empirical data on minority enterprise in the construction industry. Building on the two studies cited above, I attempted to obtain a profile of minority contractors, a picture of their problems, and some insight into their views toward upgrading in two diverse institutional settings in the South–Houston and Atlanta. These two cities were selected as project cities for several reasons. First, they comprise a significant portion of the construction industry in the South. Together they accounted for 9.7 percent of total contract construction employment in that region in 1969.

Second, both cities have rapidly growing construction sectors. Between 1960 and 1970, employment in contract construction grew in Atlanta at three times the national rate; in Houston it grew at six times the national rate. Third, each city has a large minority population which appears to have a relatively high rate of participation in the construction labor force. According to the 1970 census, blacks composed 51.3 percent of the population of the city of Atlanta and 22.3 percent of the Atlanta SMSA. The city of Houston had a 25.7 percent black population in 1970; the Houston SMSA the same year had a 19.3 percent black and an estimated 6.1 percent chicano population. Moreover, the Bureau of Labor Statistics' urban employment survey of poverty areas in six cities found more than 15 percent of employed non-whites surveyed working in construction in Houston and Atlanta. The comparable percentages for other cities surveyed were Chicago, 5.5; Detroit, 6.3; Los Angeles, 4.9; and New York, 4.7. Similarly 13 percent of black firms in Atlanta counted in *Minority-Owned Business: 1969* were construction enterprises (U.S. Department of Commerce, 1971). In Houston, 22 percent of chicano firms and 10 percent of black firms were construction businesses. Nationally, only 10 percent of all black and chicano firms were in construction.

Finally, Houston and Atlanta offer some interesting institutional contrasts. The Atlanta black community is one of the oldest, best established, and most cohesive in the country. The Houston minority population is composed of two ethnic groups–blacks and chicanos–and is generally far less organized than the black community of Atlanta.

After the cities were selected, an interview instrument was developed and tested, and the task of identifying minority contractors was begun. To locate minority contractors in Houston, a master list was compiled from various sources, including the Urban League, the Magnolia Business Center (a chicano economic development organization), the Mexican American Contractors Association, the Houston Association of General and Sub Contractors, and the NAACP's *Registry of Minority Construction Contractors.* In addition, the Houston telephone book was examined for Spanish-surnamed construction contractors. Suppliers and contractors provided other names. Some of the contractors were spotted on building sites or in minority neighborhoods. Finally, a series of announcements was broadcast on the Spanish community affairs program, "Cita con Carlos," which sought to elicit names of contractors who might wish to be included in the survey.

In Atlanta, names of black contractors were secured from the membership and mailing lists of the Atlanta Associated Contractors and Trades Council, the *Registry of Minority Construction Contractors*, black business directories, and referrals by suppliers, unions, and contractors. The Polk city directory–a reference work which contains cross listings of names, addresses, telephone numbers, and occupations–was used to trace contractors from incomplete references.

An interview sample of contractors was selected in such a way that as complete a cross section as possible could be obtained. Large and small contractors from almost every trade were interviewed. To achieve such a cross section, the sample had to be biased to include a greater than proportional representation of the large firms.

In general, interviews with contractors covered four areas of concern: (*a*) background of the contractor, (*b*) profile of the contractor's firm, (*c*) problems of the firm, and (*d*) the contractor's view of upgrading efforts. Interviews were conducted with a total of 119 active contractors in Houston and Atlanta.

To supplement the information obtained from the contractors, interviews were conducted with 112 additional individuals, including union officials, civil rights leaders, government officials, contractors, association staffs, and other knowledgeable persons. Altogether, 231 interviews were conducted for the study.

Characteristics of Minority Contractors and Their Firms

In comparison with white contractors, minority contractors are relatively few in number, and their enterprises typically are small. According to the Census Bureau report *Minority-Owned Business: 1969*, there were 443 black-owned and 535 chicano-owned firms in the Houston construction market. However, of this number only 76 and 142 enterprises, respectively, had any paid employees. The same report shows a total of 288 black-owned construction firms in Atlanta, of which only 77 had at least one employee. Thus, both cities together totaled 1,266 minority construction firms. Of this number, 407 firms were identified by the various means previously described, and the owners of 119 firms were interviewed. The sample interviewed tended to cover the larger contractors. Of 295 firms with paid employees in both cities, interviews were conducted with 98, or 33 percent. Most are specialty contractors, although proportionally more and stronger general minority contractors exist in Atlanta than in Houston.

The number of minority contractors existing in any given trade is dependent upon several factors, including (*a*) differences in the initial equity capital required (i.e., the "financial entry threshold"), (*b*) differences in the licensing provisions for the trade, and (*c*) differences in the participation of minorities in the trade, which in part reflects the number of minority persons trained for it. Other things being equal, the lower the initial equity required, the less stringent the licensing requirements, and the greater the minority participation in the trade, the greater the number of minority contractors in the trade is likely to be.

Black contractors identified in Atlanta were most numerous in the masonry, painting, and carpentry specialties. Black contractors in Houston were relatively most numerous in plumbing and concrete work. More than a third of the chicano contractors identified were either tile or carpentry contractors. Almost without exception, the specialty contractors had been craftworkers before they became contractors. Most of the general contractors became general contractors after serving as specialty contractors.

Typically, the contractors learned their trade through informal on-the-job training from a relative. However, a large portion of the most successful black general contractors, as well as those in the plumbing and electrical specialties, learned their skills in black colleges, especially Tuskegee Institute in Alabama.

Most of the contractors–both general and specialty–work in the nonunion residential sector, largely in the minority community. However, more than a third work for white customers a majority of the time. The blacks tend to work for black clients more than chicanos do for chicano clients. Whereas 10 percent of the black contractors reported that they work exclusively for black customers, only 2 percent of chicano contractors stated that they work solely in their ethnic community. Furthermore, although many minority contractors perform jobs for whites, the type of work they do then often differs from the type they do for the minority community. For example, one black air conditioning contractor in Houston reported that 90 percent of his service business, but only 5 percent of his installation work, was for white customers.

Generally, the capabilities of the contractors interviewed were limited by their lack of business experience and training. Less than a third had either business training or business experience of any kind before establishing their construction firms. However, there were many exceptions and a wide diversity in experience and capabilities among minority contractors.

All but a handful of minority contractors interviewed had started their own businesses; and as true entrepreneurs, they possess the characteristics which have been attributed to other groups of entrepreneurs by previous studies. Contractors founded their businesses at a relatively young age, the average age being 31.9 years.

Three-quarters of the contractors interviewed had moved to their present locations from other places, mainly rural areas in the South. They tended to be more highly educated than their counterpart minorities in the total population. Although few contractors inherited their businesses and few had fathers in the same type of business, the majority of the contractors had a father who was self-employed. These data confirm the hypothesis that significant role model, who makes the entrepreneurial act credible, is a highly important variable in stimulating entrepreneurial activity.

Many common features were involved in the initiation of the business. First, there was a high incidence of moonlighting. A fourth of the contractors stated that they had first begun their businesses on a part-time basis while they worked on regular jobs. Apparently, moonlighting enables a contractor to gain some experience and test the market before plunging in full time. Second, very few contractors obtained initial capital from outside sources. Less than 5 percent of the contractors had received any assistance with initial financing from banks or savings and loan institutions. Only one contractor interviewed had obtained initial capital from the Small Business Administration loan programs, and this was accomplished only through the intervention of a Manpower Development and Training Act course instructor.

Although other sources–such as customer advances, supplier credit, and loans from family, friends, or previous bosses–were occasionally used, the contractors themselves were by far the primary source of their firms' "start-up" capital. A fifth of the contractors added that they did not need much capital to get into business, although many suggested that they would have required more if they were to "get into business properly" (i.e., properly financed). Third, the decision to form a business was often influenced by common factors: various positive influences, such as the encouragement and support of a builder, or negative influences, such as being denied union membership.

With a few exceptions, most of the minority contractors who were interviewed operated small firms. Only a fourth of the firms had a 1970 gross annual income exceeding $100,000. Only five firms grossed more than a million. On the other end of the scale, 38 percent of the firms had a 1970 gross income of less than $25,000. The employment picture was similar. The six largest firms accounted for 63 percent of all employment for the sample. Only 19 percent of the firms had ten or more employees. On the other hand, 56 percent of the firms had three or fewer employees, and 20 percent had no employees whatsoever. The firms employed predominantly minority-group workers of the same ethnic background; however, as a general rule, the larger the minority firm, the greater was its proportion of white workers.

Minority contractors and subcontractors in most instances are out of the mainstream of the construction industry; this fact is reflected in their lack of participation in trade associations and union work. Only a fifth of the contractors belonged to a majority white contractors' association. In Houston 38 percent of the contractors and in Atlanta

64 percent belonged to minority contractors' associations exclusively. Recently a few of the larger minority contractors have been invited to join such groups as the Associated General Contractors, but few have joined because the majority did not see many benefits to joining; or because membership in these groups cost significant amounts of money; or because one of the major purposes of many of these associations is to negotiate with the unions, and relatively few of the minority contractors have union contracts.

Only 16 percent of the black contractors interviewed in Atlanta and 6 percent of the chicano contractors surveyed in Houston were unionized. Not a single black unionized contractor was located in Houston. Unions state that they are ready and willing to organize the minority contractors, but several factors inhibit the minority contractors from signing a union contract:

1. Most important, minority contractors fear that they will not be able to obtain enough of the larger, better contracts to support union pay rates.
2. Fear of losing job control over selection of their work forces and fear of having inferior workers referred to them by the unions bother many minority contractors.
3. Fear of losing job control, particularly with prejudiced white union workers, disturbs several contractors.
4. Inability to meet certain requirements of the contracts (e.g., performing necessary paper work for fringe benefits) prohibits some contractors from signing.

The survey showed that minority contractors were not unfamiliar with unions. In fact, 39 percent of the contractors had been members of trade unions themselves, and an additional 8 percent had been members of nonconstruction unions.

With some important exceptions, the chief characteristic of the business operations of many of the minority firms was *informality*. Contractors relied on informal channels to obtain labor, most commonly telephoning former employees. Many worked under informal arrangements; one out of five firms used verbal contracts only. Of the firms interviewed, 33 percent carried neither liability nor workmen's compensation insurance. One out of ten contractors interviewed operated without a business registration or permit of any kind. (However, practically all contractors in special trades which require licensing–electrical work, plumbing, and air conditioning–had the required license.)

Minority contractors also tended to train their workers informally. At the time of the interviews, only 17 percent of the firms had ever participated in any formal training effort for their employees. Of the sixteen firms who reported having used formal training, six had participated in union apprenticeship programs.

Obstacles to Upgrading

The minority contractors interviewed expressed considerable interest in expanding their operations. Of fifty contractors interviewed in Atlanta, forty wanted to expand their businesses. Among thirteen black contractors interviewed in Houston, nine wanted to expand; and of forty-nine chicano contractors, thirty-four expressed a desire to grow. However, of the total of eighty-three contractors who wanted to expand, only a fourth aspired to large commercial work.

In general, the contractors who were most interested in expanding their businesses were members of the minority contractors' associations. If this relationship holds true in other cities–and there is every reason to believe it does–the rapid growth of these institutions throughout the country should indicate that the interest of minority contractors in upgrading their firms extends nationwide.

Minority contractors face a multitude of problems in expanding their businesses. They are beset by all the difficulties faced by small entrepreneurs, compounded by all the problems associated with minority status. The two problem areas most often mentioned by the contractors interviewed were lack of financing, particularly interim financing, and difficulties in finding and keeping capable employees. Other major problems were lack of management skills, inability to obtain bonding, debt collection (especially for smaller contractors), inability to obtain jobs (in Houston), and competition (for tile contractors in Houston).

For perspective, the problems of minority contractors can usefully be viewed as a stream. Problems are omnipresent throughout the life of the minority firms, but the composition of the problems changes with the stage of a firm's development. (In using the terms "stages of development" and "advances," I do not mean to imply that one type of business is necessarily better than another. Many contractors are aiming at expanding the volume of their work on small projects. Others prefer to expand by performing larger projects, thus consolidating their operations on fewer work sites. However, the typical expansion course into larger commercial work is through the latter route. Similarly, I do not wish to slight subcontracting in preference to contracting. The largest minority contractor found in the survey did $17 million worth of business annually, most of which came from subcontracting.)

The cross section of the stream, representing the mix of problems which a contractor faces at any given time, is determined by several factors, including length of time in business, volume of work, size of contracts performed, and type of construction (e.g., service rehabilitation and repair or new work; residential or commercial-industrial work). Of course the problems vary by trade; that is, a sheet metal contractor faces a higher financial entry threshold to establish his firm than does a tile contractor. Similarly, a general contractor is more likely to encounter bonding problems than is a specialty contractor.

The width of the stream at any point provides a rough indication of the dimensions of problems a firm faces. Problems are greatest in the beginning (reflected in the high rates of failure in early years, which is typical of businesses in almost every industry) and in the more advanced, expanding stages (e.g., in getting into larger commercial and industrial work). Through any part of the stream, one could take a "slice" which would represent the mix of problems present in that stage of the firm's development.

The characteristics of a problem often change as the firm moves through the various stages of development. For example, whereas lack of management skills in the early stages refers to such matters as bookkeeping, in the latter stages it refers to more complex tasks, such as production scheduling or arrangement of financing. However, the problem of lack of management skills declines beyond some point because certain specialized management talent can be purchased outside the firm. Thus, the survey located a contractor with a third-grade education managing a multimillion-dollar enterprise with a staff which included personnel with master's degrees in business.

In many trades, certain problems intensify as the contractor moves from one type of work to another (i.e., from remodeling work to new work or from residential work to commercial work). In other trades, they do not. In fact in some trades problems diminish as the stage of development advances.

Within the framework of the "problem stream," the difficulties encountered by the minority contractor in a given trade fall into patterns. Financing is generally a problem throughout all stages of development, although it is a crucial entry obstacle in certain trades, such as sheet metal contracting. Labor, on the other hand, obviously does not become a problem until the firm has some employees. Three out of four minority firms in construction have no employee but the owner on the payroll. When the minority firm grows and a work force is hired, a contractor becomes very concerned with keeping the better craftworkers–which usually means they have to be kept busy. As the firm grows larger, the need for skilled craftworkers increases, as does concern for recruiting and training them. If the contractor achieves a more stable level of work and becomes unionized, labor recruitment and training problems diminish because union referral can be used to obtain workers.

Bonding is a problem which affects only the larger contractor because smaller projects often do not require bonding. Both financing and bonding intensify as problems in discontinuous leaps, or "bumps," as the firm grows or as the contractor breaks into a new type of work. For example, when a contractor begins performing commercial work, financial problems are increased due to the fact that commercial work is more commonly contracted on a 10 percent retainage basis than is residential construction.

Certain problems are a greater burden on small or new contractors than on those who have reached large or medium size. For example, finding jobs is likely to be a problem affecting recent entrants into the business or into a particular stage of the business (e.g., commercial work). Debt collection appears to have the greatest impact on small marginal contractors–especially those who can exercise little choice in the matter of selecting customers. Likewise, competition appears to affect the smaller firm more. The smallest firms are under competition from craftworkers who operate illegally as subcontractors on small jobs without carrying insurance or paying sales taxes, social security, or other payroll taxes. "Cheaper competition" characteristically is a problem for contractors in trades with easy entry requirements, such as tiling. Contractors in licensed trades, such as plumbing or electrical work, are protected from this problem. As a firm grows, competition comes from larger contractors who can obtain cheaper building materials because they buy in larger quantities. Also, many of the smaller firms, which can buy supplies only at discounted retail prices, have to compete against larger firms, which have access to supplies at wholesale rates.

Our survey of minority contractors in Houston and Atlanta, which reflected a sample biased to include a greater than proportionate mix of larger firms, showed a definite pattern. A scattering of contractors mentioned problems characteristic of small or new firms. Many more respondents indicated encountering labor and financial problems. Only a few had faced a bonding problem, the problem which receives the most attention from the press (Schorr, 1971, p. 22).

Approaches to Upgrading the Minority Contractor

There are many promising approaches to assisting the minority contractor, but the major vehicles of advancement can be classified in three categories: government assistance, joint ventures and mergers, and minority contractors' associations. Government assistance includes the use of government procurement and contract compliance, as well as direct assistance efforts. Joint ventures and mergers embrace both cooperative efforts with white contractors and pooling arrangements among minority firms. The minority contractors' association is an indigenous uplift effort which involves a wide range of educational and technical assistance activities focused on improving the individual minority contractor. Our study examined all three approaches.

Government Assistance

With respect to government assistance, it was found that neither the traditional programs to assist businesses nor the programs aimed specifically at the minority construction contractor have had much impact in improving the position of the minority contractor. For example, minority enterprise in construction is not well served by such government agencies as the vocational education agencies or the employment services. Few persons in Atlanta and Houston vocational education programs are trained in construction; furthermore, fewer of those enrolled in such programs are minority group members. In addition, vocational education programs generally have little contact with minority contractors.

Since owners of minority enterprises in construction tend to rely on informal rather than formal channels to recruit labor, they have little use for the public employment service. Furthermore, those minority contractors who have used the employment service rated it rather poorly as a source of skilled labor. More minority contractors in Houston made derogatory comments about the employment service than stated they currently were using it.

Similarly, few contractors use the traditional loan programs of the

Small Business Administration (SBA). Only 1 contractor had used this agency's monies to start his firm. Only 7 contractors out of 104 respondents had obtained any small business loans, and 1 of these mentioned that the loan was a hindrance in obtaining bonding because the SBA had required a subordination agreement, giving it first claim to business assets of the firms. This precluded the firm from entering into other bonding agreements which typically include similar provisions. In the interviews, minority contractors offered the following criticisms of the SBA's regular loan programs:

1. The loan application process takes too long.
2. The loan money is available for what the contractors do not need (i.e., to finance establishment of an office or to purchase more equipment) but seemingly never available for what they need (i.e., interim financing to pay for supplies and to meet the payroll).
3. Loans are not large enough to be of any assistance.
4. Too much paper work is involved in obtaining a loan.
5. Loans are not available to those who really need them.

Several SBA programs have recently been specifically directed at the minority contractor, namely, the Action Construction Team project since 1969, the 8 (a) contracting program since 1968, the bonding guarantee program since 1970, and the interim finance program since 1970. Although the action team project was instrumental in initiating many minority contractors' associations, it has become inoperative except in cities where it was funded initially. In Houston and Atlanta, where it was a voluntary effort, the action team was instrumental in establishing minority contractors' associations but accomplished few other tangible results and finally became virtually extinct.

Among other SBA activities, only the 8 (a) program was operational in Houston and Atlanta by the spring of 1971; and as the survey showed, even this program could be termed only "nominally operative." Under the 8 (a) program, SBA is empowered to enter into contracts with other federal agencies and to subcontract these jobs to minority businesses. In Atlanta not a single 8 (a) contract for construction work was located in the survey. In Houston, as of October 15, 1971, only seven minority contractors had been qualified to perform 8 (a) construction work. A dozen contracts had been let for four of these firms–despite the fact that NASA alone had the capacity and contracts to service many more minority contractors. Problems hampering the 8 (a) program in Houston and Atlanta were numerous:

1. Understaffing of the program by SBA
2. Improper allocation of resources
3. Hesitancy in implementing the program
4. Interagency squabbles
5. Inadequate or nonexistent outreach

In addition to the Small Business Administration, several other government agencies and programs could have an impact on improving the position of the minority contractor, namely, Model Cities, the Office of Minority Business Enterprise, the Division of Equal Employment Opportunity of HUD, and the Economic Development Administration. However, none of these agencies or programs had much impact on the minority contractor in either Houston or Atlanta.

The Model Cities program, for example, is covered by the 1969 amendments to Section 3 of the Housing and Urban Development Act of 1968, which requires that, "to the greatest extent feasible, contracts for work to be performed in connection with housing; urban planning, development, or renewal; public or community development be awarded to business concerns, including but not limited to individuals or firms doing business in the field of building construction, rehabilitation, maintenance, or repair, which are located in or owned in substantial part by persons residing in the area of such projects." Presumably, this means using minority contractors, since most of the residents of the Model Cities areas in Houston and Atlanta are members of minority groups. However, only a handful of the minority contractors interviewed had either offices or residences located in the Model Cities areas.

Second, although the Model Cities funding has supported minority contractors' associations in both Houston and Atlanta, little construction work has resulted from the program in either city. In Houston, only demolition contracts have been let, and although they were split into smaller parcels for the benefit of minority contractors, no minority contractors bid on them. In Atlanta, although Model Cities has $5 million worth of housing projects committed to black contractors, the projects are much behind schedule. By the spring of 1971, the only jobs let to minority contractors have been several small contracts for remodeling and repair work.

Only recently, the Office of Minority Business Enterprise has begun operations with field staff in Atlanta. Furthermore, at the time of this study, its staff was out of touch with other government agency operations to assist the minority contractor. Houston had no minority business enterprise field staff in the spring of 1971. HUD's Equal Employment Opportunity agency has been active in attempting to assist minority contractors in some places across the nation but has been largely inactive in others. In the southeast region, this agency has helped organize minority construction contractors' associations in several cities but has done little other than provide information on HUD programs to contractors in Atlanta. No signs of equal employment opportunity activity were found in Houston.

Another government agency, the Economic Development Administration, has funded contractors' association in various cities but has not been active in either Houston or Atlanta. Lack of cooperation–even communication–between these agencies is striking and certainly mitigates their effectiveness. Federal executive boards, composed of agency chiefs over certain areas, have established "minority enterprise committees" in various cities to close the communications gap on this problem, but, unfortunately, at the time of this writing they had had little tangible effect on the status of the minority contractor.

In summary, it can be said that those government programs specifically directed at minority contractors as well as those which are to incidentally assist minority business in construction have resulted in more promise than fulfillment.

Actions taken to integrate the construction industry could have an impact on contractors. Federal contract compliance activities have had little noticeable effect on the minority contractor. However, despite this, a minority of the black contractors interviewed and a third of the chicano contractors had performed at least one small government job. The work was for either federal or local governments; no contractor reported performing any contracts for state government. The federal work was most commonly repair work on repossessed FHA houses or, in Atlanta, rehabilitation work on housing under the Atlanta Model Cities program. Compliance efforts, such as the "Atlanta Plan," have very little impact on the minority contractors because there are virtually no minority contractors in the trades covered by the plan, except in electrical and plumbing work. Thus, the provisions in the plans for the use of minority contractors have had little effect.

Moreover, contract compliance efforts without simultaneous efforts directed at assisting the minority contractor by providing contracts for minority firms will likely have detrimental effects on minority contractors because their most skilled workers will be bid away by white contractors to integrate the predominantly white union business sector. Several minority contractors expressed fear that this might happen.

It has been suggested that upgrading minority firms offers some potential to integrate the building trades. Some advocates of this position reason that, if minority firms could be upgraded to a level where they became a significant bloc of the industry, such white institutions as unions and contractors' associations could not afford to ignore them. However, upgrading minorities is not likely to lead to sizable increases in the number of minority construction workers, at least in the immediate future, for the following reasons:

1. In trades in which unions have the fewest minority members, minority contractors are also generally scarce.
2. Minority contractors currently employ less than 10 percent of the minority work force in Houston or Atlanta.
3. Although three-quarters of the minority contractors want to expand their businesses, only a fourth of these firms aspire to work in the unionized (large commercial and industrial construction) sectors in Houston and Atlanta.
4. The larger a minority construction firm grows, the smaller the proportion of minority workers it tends to employ.

A few firms presently operate under union contract, and, if upgraded, many others would not be adverse to signing union contracts. However, the result would not be significant enough in itself to integrate the trades in Houston and Atlanta. Efforts still need to be made through other approaches, such as apprenticeship outreach programs.

Joint Venturing

There are many varieties of joint ventures, for example, minority-majority or minority-minority. Moreover, there is a continuum in the form of possible combinations, ranging from temporary schemes for one project only to full-scale limited mergers. Minority contractors might "joint venture" for any of a variety of reasons: to pool work, to obtain contracts beyond their capacity, to gain experience, or to gain something essential to the winning or performance of a contract.

The anticipated benefit might not always be gained, however. Especially with respect to minority-majority combinations, it was found that, although this technique offers upgrading potential for minority contractors, it is a complicated matter and should be undertaken by a minority contractor only with certain precautions. According to John Brown,[1] secretary of the National Association of Minority Contractors, a joint venture has the possibility of being fruitful to the minority contractor only under certain conditions, namely:

1. The contractors must mutually participate in all phases of the project.
2. The arrangement should benefit both contractors.
3. In general, separate corporations should not be established for joint venturing.
4. Joint ventures should be undertaken only under written contract and with the counsel of a qualified lawyer.

Although cases of successful joint ventures between minority and white contractors were found in other places, no such ventures were found in either Houston or Atlanta. White contractors apparently joint venture with minority contractors in other cities in order to gain access to work in the minority community. But it appears they encounter little difficulty gaining access to such work in Houston or Atlanta. In these two cities, the arrangement closest to joint venturing found was a contract for which a white contractor had put up a bond for the black contractor; however, the black contractor was charged three times the market rate for obtaining the bond. In Houston and Atlanta, several minority contractors interviewed had joint ventured with a fellow minority contractor. Although most of these were small undertakings, one black merger in Atlanta, Bankhead West, had been promised $5 million in work on Model Cities housing projects.

The Minority Contractors' Association

Upgrading efforts through the minority contractors' associations represent in a sense the trade association approach to minority economic development (Venable, 1972). Minority construction contractors' associations have reportedly been successful in other cities, such as Oakland, where the General and Specialty Contractors Association was initially supported by the Ford Foundation, the Economic Development Administration, and the Labor Department's projects.

Minority contractors have largely been an invisible group. Most work out of their homes and do little advertising. For the present, minority contractors' associations offer virtually the only route of access for assistance efforts to many minority contractors. Most minority contractors have not even been identified. As previously mentioned, even the HUD-sponsored NAACP survey of minority contractors in 1970 missed more than nine out of ten of the minority contractors in Houston and Atlanta, as counted in the Bureau of Census publication *Minority-Owned Business: 1969*.

In one sense, the minority contractors' association is a rare development: it offers an example of successful community organization. Several government agencies and civil rights organizations (including the Small Business Administration, the Interracial Council on Business Opportunity, the NAACP, the Urban League, the National Business League, the Equal Employment Opportunity division of HUD, and the League of United Latin American Citizens) have initiated local associations. However, in almost every case, the outside party either has withdrawn or has faded out, leaving the association in the hands of the contractors themselves. In another sense, however, the minority contractors' association is not a unique phenomenon, because it occurs in what is one of the most highly organized and unionized industries in the nation.

Nationally, black contractors are organized into two federations, the NAACP-supported Afro-American Builders and the National Association of Minority Contractors. Chicanos are organized into a separate federation, the Southwest Association of Minority Contractors, which is supported by the League of United Latin American Citizens. Local groups are usually affiliated with one of these federations.

In both Atlanta and Houston, the minority contractors are organized into associations. In Atlanta the contractors have formed a nonprofit corporation, the Atlanta Associated Contractors and Trades Council Inc. In Houston the black contractors are organized in the Houston Association of General and Sub Contractors. Originally this group included both black and chicano contractors; however, in April 1970 the chicano contractors split off and formed their own group, the Mexican American Contractors Association. It perhaps is regrettable and illogical that blacks and chicanos are organized separately, but it may be the only feasible approach. In every city where both minorities are present in significant proportions and minority construction contractors are organized (as in Los Angeles, Denver, and Houston), they are organized into separate groups. In Houston, the chicano and black contractors' groups had failed to communicate with one another more than a year after the split.

The Atlanta contractors are supported by Ford Foundation funds, as well as funds from the Minority Contractors Assistance Project, which has funded similar organizations for providing a revolving loan fund and bonding assistance on a pilot basis in three other cities–Los Angeles, Detroit, and New Orleans. The assistance project lends insurance company funds to the contractors' associations, who in turn lend the monies to their members. Unfortunately, the initiation of the Minority Contractors Assistance Project was delayed for more than a year over the renegotiation downward of the interest rate for the loans. In addition to the aforementioned support, each association in both cities receives some financial support from the Model Cities program.

The minority contractors associations have potential for assisting contractors in numerous ways, including:

1. Bringing minority firms into contact with the mainstrean construction industry, by generally making the contractors more visible
2. Offering managerial and technical assistance to and educating owners of minority firms to enable them to better operate their businesses by:
   a. Helping to improve their accounting systems
   b. Providing assistance with bidding and estimating
   c. Helping with loan packaging and teaching contractors the procedures involved in obtaining loans
   d. Helping with surety bond packaging and teaching contractors the bonding procedures involved
   e. Encouraging journeymen to become qualified to start their own firms and helping them become properly established at the outset with such matters as licensing and tax registration
   f. Assisting minority owners in locating jobs by serving as a clearinghouse to gather information on upcoming jobs from such informal sources as personal contacts, as well as such formal sources as the *Dodge Reports*,[2] and by serving as an outreach function for white general contractors who want to work with qualified minority subcontractors
   g. Assisting minority contractors to negotiate joint ventures
3. Helping focus community resources on minority firms by:
   a. Prodding government agencies to better implement programs authorized by Congress
   b. Helping to provide outreach to ensure participation of minority contractors in such programs as the SBA 8 (a) pro-

gram and to seek out qualified minority contractors to perform construction contracts available under the Model Cities program, urban renewal, and other government efforts involving construction work

   c. Acting as "ombudsmen" to help minority contractors through the maze of procedures involved in dealing with governmental programs
   d. Administering labor training programs for member contractors and providing the institutional component of the programs
   e. Administering revolving loan funds
   f. Bringing contractors in touch with community experts from local universities, contractors' associations, and professional associations (such as certified public accountants) to advise and tutor individual contractors and to speak at association meetings
   g. Providing information to contractors on matters of concern to their businesses, such as new technological or legal developments, for example, the Williams-Steiger Occupational Health and Safety Act of 1970
4. Providing various useful services to contractors, such as:
   a. Making available an office center with secretarial and bookkeeping services
   b. Helping member contractors to compete with larger contractors by arranging to buy materials or equipment in greater volume at discount

According to minority contractors' association officials interviewed for the study, a successful association requires several ingredients, including community backing; an active, talented staff; start-up funding; and the solid support of member contractors. All the associations hope eventually to achieve a position of self-sufficiency. However, by 1978, none of the associations in Houston or Atlanta had become self-supporting.

Summary and Conclusions

Minority construction contractors comprise a significant portion of total minority enterprise. Nationally, one out of ten existing minority businesses is a construction firm. In the black community of Atlanta and the chicano community of Houston, construction business is even more important relatively. Construction contractors comprise 13 percent of all black enterprises in Atlanta and 22 percent of chicano enterprises in Houston.

Houston and Atlanta offered natural sites for our study because together they accounted for one out of every ten jobs in contract construction in the South in 1969 and because they have rapidly growing construction sectors. They also have large minority populations which have relatively high rates of participation in construction, and they offer some interesting institutional contrasts.

The present study examined characteristics of existing minority construction contractors and their firms in the two cities, obstacles the contractors face in expanding and improving their businesses, and promising approaches to upgrading the minority construction contractor. With some important exceptions, minority construction contractors operate small proprietorships which usually employ three or fewer workers and work in residential construction, largely within the minority community. Most minority contractors are specialty contractors, although there exists a relatively large and strong contingent of general contractors in Atlanta. Black contractors identified in Atlanta were most numerous in the specialties of masonry, painting, and carpentry work. In Houston, black contractors were most numerous relatively in plumbing and concrete work, whereas chicanos were either tile or carpentry contractors.

Most minority construction contractors are largely out of the mainstream of the construction industry. Only a fifth of the contractors interviewed belonged to a majority white contractors' association. In Atlanta 16 percent of the black contractors surveyed, but only 6 percent of Houston's chicano contractors, were unionized. Not a single black unionized contractor was located in Houston.

Minority contractors' business operations tend to be highly informal. Labor is recruited through informal procedures and workers are trained informally on the job. Most minority contractors have never applied for a bank loan or bond. One out of five firms surveyed work under verbal contracts only. A third of the contractors carry neither liability nor workmen's compensation insurance. Many of the contractors work as craftworkers on the job site with their employees. Most contractors operate out of their homes and usually do not advertise, preferring to obtain customers through word-of-mouth. As a result of their small size and the informal nature of their business operations, minority contractors are largely invisible–even to government agencies and other groups who aspire to assist them.

Regarding the personal characteristics of the contractors–the specialty contractors become "specialized" after having been skilled craftworkers, most commonly in carpentry, masonry, and (for chicanos) tilesetting. Typically, contractors in most trades received their training informally on the job from a relative; however, a large portion of the most successful black general contractors, as well as those contractors in plumbing and electrical work, learned their skills in black colleges. Although the minority contractors interviewed tend to have more formal education than their counterparts in the population, their capabilities are limited by their lack of business experience and training. Less than a third had any business training or business experience before establishing their construction firms. However, there are many exceptions, and there exists a wide diversity in quality of talent among minority contractors.

Three-quarters of the minority contractors interviewed expressed a desire to upgrade their businesses. However, only a fourth of these aspired to perform larger commercial jobs. A minority contractor faces a multitude of problems in expanding business operations. The two problem areas of foremost concern to the contractors interviewed were lack of financing, particularly interim financing, and difficulty in finding and keeping capable workers. Other problems of major concern to the contractors were lack of management skills, inability to obtain bonding, debt collection (especially for smaller contractors), inability to obtain jobs (in Houston), and competition (especially for tile contractors in Houston).

Three approaches to upgrading minority contractors were examined: government assistance, joint venturing, and the minority contractors' associations. With respect to government assistance, it was found that, although several government programs aim specifically at assisting the minority contractor, these programs have resulted in more promise than fulfillment. Furthermore, minority contractors appear not to be well served by any government programs, including the employment service, vocational education programs, and contract compliance endeavors, such as the "Atlanta Plan."

With regard to joint venturing–it was found that, although this technique offers upgrading potential for minority contractors, it is a complicated matter and should be undertaken only with certain precautions. Finally, the minority contractors' association can assist member contractors by helping to bring them into contact with the mainstream construction industry, to educate and train them to better operate their businesses, and to focus community resources upon them.

Notes

1. Personal interview, Los Angeles, December 30, 1970.
2. These are listings of upcoming construction projects which are published daily by McGraw-Hill Publishing Company in major construction areas across the country.

References

Debro, Joseph. 1970. "The Minority Builder." *Labor Law Journal* 25, no. 5 (May).

———. 1971. "Financing Minority Contractors." *Bankers Magazine* 154, no. 1 (Winter).

Patterson, Pat. 1971. "Construction Opportunity on the Rise." *Black Enterprise* (March).

Pugh, Douglas G. 1969. "Bonding Minority Contractors." In *Black Economic Development*, edited by William F. Haddad and Douglas G. Pugh. Englewood Cliffs, N.J.: Prentice-Hall.

Schorr, Burt. 1971. "Black Construction Contractors Find Selves Cut Out in Lucrative Long-Term Contracts." *Wall Street Journal* (May 7).

Shapiro, Theresa R. 1971. "Black Builders in Greater New Orleans." *Louisiana Business Survey* 2, no. 3 (July).

———. 1972. *Black Construction Contractors in New Orleans*. New Orleans: University of New Orleans, Division of Business and Economic Research.

Stuart, Reginald. 1971. *Black Contractors' Dilemma*. Nashville: Race Relations Information Center.

U.S. Department of Commerce, Bureau of the Census. 1971. *Minority-Owned Business: 1969*. Washington, D.C.: Government Printing Office.

U.S. Department of Housing and Urban Development, Office of the Assistant Secretary for Equal Opportunity. 1970. *Registry of*

Minority Construction Contractors. Vols. I–VI. Washington, D.C.: Government Printing Office.

———. 1971. *A Survey of Minority Construction Contractors*. Washington, D.C.: Government Printing Office.

Venable, Abraham S. 1972. *Building Black Business: An Analysis and a Plan*. New York: Earl G. Graves Publishing Co.

7

Some South and Non-South Comparisons

Ray Marshall and Virgil L. Christian, Jr.

The structure of black employment in the South remained sharply different in 1970 from that of the rest of the country. Some of the reasons are historical, tracing to blacks' beginnings on southern plantations; some are demographic, originating in the heavier rural concentration of the population in the South; some are sociological, resulting from traditional attitudes about the "place" of blacks in all phases of southern life and culminating in the concept of low-pay, low-status "Negro jobs"; some are institutional, typified by the segregated and inadequate school system afforded black southerners until the recent past; some are political, relating to the blacks' lack of voting power and its effects on public decision making; and some are purely economic, deriving from characteristics of southern industry and the impact of those characteristics on both sides of southern labor markets. The net result is that black per capita incomes, taken state by state or averaged over the entire South, are lower than white per capita incomes and lower than black incomes elsewhere, which in turn suggests–at least on the surface–that racial factors remain greater barriers to black progress in the South than elsewhere.

Nevertheless, several factors independent of overt labor market discrimination partially account for blacks' income disadvantage in the South. First, southern blacks are still heavily concentrated in agriculture, which remains by a wide margin the industry that is the largest employer of black males, while few blacks outside the South are on the farm. Agriculture is a low-income industry, for both wage workers and small operators; black per capita income in the South therefore suffers from this, both in the absolute and relative to nonsouthern blacks. No quite so obvious, however, is this factor's influence on national income comparison. Agriculture pulls down both white and black incomes in the South, but only white incomes in the non-South, thus closing the racial income gap in those nonsouthern states where agriculture is important for whites.

Second, a much larger proportion of southern blacks make their homes in smaller urban centers or in rural nonfarm areas than is true in the remainder of the country. Data from the 1970 census show that nearly nineteen of every twenty blacks in the non-South live in metropolitan areas and nearly four in five live in central cities, whereas roughly half of the black population in the South lives outside SMSAs (Table 7-1). Since metropolitan wage and salary incomes throughout the country are higher than nonmetropolitan incomes, blacks are helped absolutely and relative to whites in the non-South by virtue of their urban concentration. (As an aside: It can be noted that the pool of low-skill, displaced, agricultural labor concentrated in the nonmetropolitan South is heavily weighted with blacks and that the blacks caught in these rural nonfarm labor markets are low-wage workers indeed.)

Third, the industry mix of the South, as compared with the non-South, is oriented toward low-wage, labor-intensive industries that are losing their share of total employment. The South's competitive performance in those industries is not bad. The problem is not that southern firms, within industries, are not doing well; it is that the South is prominent in industries that are themselves losing ground (Maddox, 1967, pp. 52–79). The industries that are oriented toward low-wage, labor-intensive standard industrial codes (SICs) are precisely those which the blacks have penetrated most successfully, although at the lowest occupational levels. Hiestand tells us, "Most commonly the employment of Negro men declined in industries that were growing overall, while the common pattern in the occupations was that Negro male employment grew in many fields that were declining" (1964, pp. 70–71). The quote relates to the entire nation; the conclusion is doubly true for the South. On the other hand, many of the region's rapidly growing industries are manned by highly skilled, highly educated work forces, mostly white and recruited in part from outside the South. The result has been a widening of the gap between black and white incomes in the South.

On the other side of the coin, it should be pointed out that the concentration of the nonsouthern black population in rigidly bounded neighborhoods within huge metropolitan areas has created a set of employment problems that are distinctly different from those in the

TABLE 7-1. Urban and Rural Distribution of Black Population, South and Non-South (1970; thousands)

Place of Residence	Number: South	Number: Non-South	Percent: South	Percent: Non-South
Inside SMSAs				
Inner city	4,505	8,082	36.8%	76.5%
Suburban ring	1,797	1,739	14.7	16.5
Total	6,302	9,821	51.5	93.0
Outside SMSAs	5,942	743	48.5	7.0

Source: U.S. Department of Commerce, Bureau of the Census, 1970.

South. Some of these problems are serious in that their resolution involves fundamental institutions that are difficult to change; collectively, they pose a real threat to the blacks' drive for equality of opportunity.

For example, Kain (1968) and Mooney (1969) have found that segregated housing, concentrated in the inner cities on the one hand, and industrial growth, centered in the suburban rings on the other, have a pronounced effect on black employment in most nonsouthern cities. This turned out to be an inconsequential factor in most of the southern cities included in this study: they show small concentrations of blacks well scattered through the cities, and "salt and pepper" neighborhoods are not uncommon. Black concentrations in northern ghettos probably account for the finding that black migrants from the South have better employment and earnings records than northern-born blacks in the same places and with the same characteristics (Masters, 1970).

Although a test of this hypothesis is beyond the scope of the present study, it is likely that demand-and-supply conditions account for the higher earnings of southern-born blacks. As compared with those born in ghettos outside the South, the southern-born migrants probably are more willing to take low-wage jobs and may be preferred by employers to ghetto-born blacks. If this hypothesis is correct, the migrants might have better employment records, but their children will be caught up in the ghetto syndrome unless something is done about the ghettos and the conditions they breed.

Another factor of great potential importance is that the drive for educational equality seems increasingly to fare better in the South than elsewhere. The region suffered its agony in the 1950s and early 1960s, but after incurring costly economic and social disruptions in futile resistance to de jure segregation, it seemed to sense that the price was too high. Substantial progress toward desegregation followed, with the result that racial separation in northern schools, generated by housing segregation and fueled by strong resistance to bussing, is in many places more pronounced than in the South. In fact, school segregation in 1971 was more pronounced in the North than in the South. Moreover, since northern segregation involves discriminatory housing and rights in real property, it may well prove more intransigent than was true in the South.

Finally, blue-collar areas of northern industrial SMSAs–Detroit, Cleveland, Gary, and southside Chicago, which are populated by well-defined ethnic minorities–are confronting blacks with overt racial hostility of the same strength and virulence they faced for centuries in the South. Southern blacks had institutions which they controlled, and they held the better jobs in black neighborhoods, but that is less likely to be true in the North. As a result, blacks are in many ways better off in the South than they are elsewhere.

Moreover, since blacks have made more relative visible progress in the South than elsewhere, they probably are more optimistic about the future than their northern counterparts, as Rungeling and Ignatin demonstrate in their study of psychological factors affecting black employment. The cumulative thrust of these forces is to close the South–non-South gap for the wrong reason: to bring blacks outside the South back to the same relative position in the social structure that they hold in the South, with blacks in both places losing ground to the rest of society.

Scope and Method

A most useful summary measure of the disadvantagement for minorities in a labor market is the extent of wage and salary discrimination against them. Such measures, nationwide and by region, were made by Formby (1968), wherein his estimates permit rough comparison of the income positions of blacks in the South with those in the non-South and show, given the validity of his assumptions, disadvantages of nonwhites vis-à-vis whites, both within and outside the South. The comparisons are rough proxies for income comparisons because they omit certain categories of income. The article, however, has a lengthy discussion on the data problem inherent in this type of study.

The purposes of the present study, however, are quite different: they relate to industry penetration and occupational status rather than to income. Specifically, they are to use EEO-1 data (which give occupation by race and sex) to find which southern industries (two-digit SICs) provide southern blacks with employment and which do not; and they combine occupational distribution generated by EEO-1 data with census income data, by occupation, to calculate indices of occupational position, by race and sex and SIC, to find out which industries have allowed blacks to move upward in the occupational structure. Comparative incomes do not enter the picture directly– and indirectly only to the extent that the index of occupational position is an adequate proxy for income.

Sections which follow outline the positions of blacks (*a*) in manufacturing and (*b*) in the South's ten leading industries and present tables showing participation rates and occupational distributions aggregated over the entire region. The chapter continues with a brief review of the importance of agriculture as an employer of black males, adds a comparison of the income position of farmers who left southern agriculture and remained in the South with that of those who left agriculture and also left the South, and concludes with the results of some regressions which relate penetration rates and indices of occupational position to economic and institutional variables associated with them. Two-digit SIC comparisons are based on 1966 EEO-1 data to provide a benchmark from the first year of reporting against which changes might be measured. Regional aggregations of 1969 show only slight change from similar aggregations of 1966 data and imply that the statements made from 1966 data were still valid in 1969.

Blacks in Manufacturing Industries

Tables 7-2 and 7-3 show some of the basic relationships between the employment positions of blacks and whites in manufacturing, by sex. Although absolute employment of white and black males in the South is concentrated in much the same industries (the rank coefficient or correlation is 0.67), there are some significant differences.

The industries in which the greatest disparities in absolute employment are found are lumber and wood products–such employment is third for black males and fifteenth for white males; primary metal industries–fourth for blacks and ninth for whites; machinery other than electrical–sixth for whites and eleventh for blacks; and electrical machinery and equipment–fifth for whites and thirteenth for blacks. In other words, in absolute terms black males are overrepresented compared to whites in food and kindred products; tobacco manufacturing; lumber and wood products; stone, clay, and glass products; and primary metals industries. Black males are noticeably underrepresented, compared to whites, in absolute terms in chemicals and allied products, petroleum refineries, machinery other than electrical, electrical machinery and equipment, and transportation equipment.

Southern black and white females are also concentrated in essentially the same industries (the rank coefficient of correlation between these variable is 0.73), although the tobacco, wood products, and furniture industries were relatively much more significant for black women.

The indices of occupational position for black and white males demonstrate some significant consistencies. Those of black males in the South are consistently below those of black males in the non-South, both relatively and as a percentage of the white male indices of occupational position. Indeed in all but three cases–printing and publishing, petroleum refining, and instruments–black males in the non-South occupied higher positions than white males in the South. However, there is a strong correlation (0.86) between the black percentages of the white indices in the South and in the non-South. There also is a very strong correlation (0.84) between the indices of occupational position of black males in the South and in the non-South, indicating that the occupational positions are relatively similar, though uniformly higher in the non-South.

It will also be observed that black women outside the South have indices of occupational position consistently larger than either black or white women in the South. Moreover, the index of occupational position for black women in the non-South is a much higher percentage of the white female index than the percentage the black female index is of the white female index of occupational position in the South. And in one case, the leather industry, black women in the non-South have a larger index of occupational position than white women. Compared to white women, black women in the South have the lowest indices of occupational position in petroleum refining and primary metals, reflecting the concentration of black women in menial jobs in those industries, while white women are employed primarily in white-collar occupations.

Although the black male indices are strongly correlated with those of the white males in the South and the non-South, there is no significant relationship between the black and white female indices in the South (r = 0.35). Black women have a higher index of occupational position in apparels than in any other industry, but this industry ranks thirteenth for white women. Similarly, petroleum refining ranks first for white, but fifteenth for black women; primary metals ranks second for white, but twelfth for black women. In all these cases, blacks are apparently restricted to menial jobs, while whites are in white-collar occupations.

Although the correlation between the black and white female indices of occupational position was not significant in the South, these variables are highly correlated in the non-South (0.97). Outside the South, the indices for black and white women are highest in the petroleum refining, transportation equipment, printing and publishing, and chemical industries. Indeed the only significant differences for female employment in the non-South were in the apparel, furniture, paper, and leather industries. The textile industry indices for black and white women were relatively more significant in the South than elsewhere. The index for black women in the apparel industry was comparatively higher in the South than for white women in the South or non-South, or for black women in the non-South.

TABLE 7-2. Black Participation in Southern Manufacturing (1966)

Types of Manufacturing	White Males	Black Males	Total* Males	Percent Black Males
Food and kindred products	147,390	43,715	202,554	21.58%
Tobacco manufacturers	30,052	10,716	41,213	26.00
Textile mill products	290,911	39,910	331,918	12.02
Apparel & other textile products	45,087	5,677	52,877	10.74
Lumber, wood products, not furniture	39,132	30,334	70,932	42.76
Furniture and fixtures	83,907	17,167	103,038	16.66
Paper and like products	99,615	15,870	116,194	13.66
Printing, publishing, etc.	45,033	3,596	50,091	7.18
Chemicals, etc.	190,594	21,951	214,054	10.25
Petroleum refining	57,509	4,362	63,265	6.89
Rubber and miscellaneous plastic products	30,100	3,876	34,697	11.17
Leather and its products	19,533	1,835	21,993	8.34
Stone, clay, and glass products	50,603	16,603	70,066	23.69
Primary metals industries	85,686	24,772	114,515	21.63
Fabricated metal products, not ordinance or transportation	88,891	12,987	105,421	12.32
Machinery, not electrical	102,124	12,167	116,305	10.46
Electrical machine equipt. not supplies	118,173	6,834	126,297	5.41
Transportation equipment	187,132	21,415	211,819	10.11
Instruments	24,809	1,064	26,585	4.00

Source: Equal Employment Opportunity Commission data, 1966.

*Includes other.

White Females	Black Females	Total* Females	% Black Females	Total Employees	Total Black	Percent Black
52,370	11,999	69,910	17.16%	272,464	55,714	20.44%
18,957	5,145	24,745	20.79	65,958	15,861	24.04
251,003	11,091	263,350	4.21	595,268	51,001	8.57
243,672	21,721	275,944	7.87	328,821	27,398	8.33
4,519	2,724	7,341	37.11	78,273	33,058	42.23
18,799	3,276	22,446	14.60	125,484	20,443	16.29
19,230	774	20,170	3.84	136,364	16,644	12.20
19,012	527	20,122	2.62	70,213	4,123	5.87
35,335	1,584	37,064	4.27	251,118	23,535	9.37
7,748	79	8,004	0.99	71,269	4,441	6.23
9,398	725	10,301	7.04	44,998	4,601	10.22
24,917	1,230	26,829	4.58	48,822	3,065	6.28
9,442	412	10,018	4.11	80,084	17,015	21.24
6,105	248	6,422	3.86	120,937	25,020	19.47
13,944	747	14,991	0.50	120,412	13,734	11.07
15,586	680	16,494	4.12	132,799	12,847	9.67
72,633	4,262	77,425	5.50	203,722	11,096	5.44
19,194	763	20,125	3.79	231,934	22,178	9.62
22,702	3,379	26,590	12.71	53,175	4,473	8.41

TABLE 7-3. Black and White Indices of Occupational Position, South and Non-South (1966)

Types of Manufacturing	Males in South			Males in Non-South		
	Black	White	% White	Black	White	% White
Food & kindred products	2,604	3,768	69.1%	4,293	5,008	85.7%
Tobacco manufacturers	2,354	3,699	63.6	3,976	5,149	77.2
Textile mill products	2,422	3,347	72.4	4,291	4,747	90.4
Apparel & other textile products	2,748	3,482	78.9	4,451	5,190	85.8
Lumber, wood products, not furniture	2,329	3,298	70.6	4,292	4,775	89.9
Furniture and fixtures	2,505	3,241	77.3	4,535	4,950	91.6
Paper and like products	2,536	3,630	69.9	4,352	4,982	87.3
Printing, publishing, etc.	2,861	4,400	65.0	4,356	5,414	80.5
Chemicals, etc.	2,694	4,344	62.0	4,545	5,580	81.5
Petroleum refining	2,868	4,767	60.2	4,524	5,685	79.6
Rubber and miscellaneous plastic products	2,719	3,627	75.0	4,584	5,220	87.8
Leather and its products	2,789	3,404	81.9	4,416	4,659	94.8
Stone, Clay, and glass products	2,547	3,737	68.2	4,327	5,013	86.3
Primary metals industries	2,747	3,926	70.0	4,459	5,043	88.4
Fabricated metal products, not ordinance or transportation	2,793	3,778	73.9	4,542	5,203	87.3
Machinery, not electrical	2,816	4,022	70.0	4,700	5,384	87.3
Electrical machinery, not supplies	2,905	4,184	69.4	4,839	5,725	84.5
Transportation equipment	3,011	4,225	71.3	4,753	5,442	87.3
Instruments	2,861	5,021	57.0	4,738	5,683	83.4

Source: Equal Employment Opportunity Commission data, 1966.

Females in South			Females in Non-South		
Black	White	Percent White	Black	White	Percent White
1,489	1,830	81.4%	2,208	2,424	91.1%
1,593	2,016	79.0	2,401	2,560	93.8
1,975	2,174	90.8	2,446	2,531	96.6
1,998	2,064	96.8	2,525	2,533	99.7
1,517	2,099	72.3	2,487	2,537	98.0
1,668	2,078	80.3	2,397	2,702	88.7
1,644	2,151	76.4	2,362	2,564	92.1
1,903	2,347	81.1	2,679	2,901	92.4
1,868	2,347	79.6	2,615	2,915	89.7
1,660	2,733	60.7	3,074	3,131	98.2
1,806	2,076	87.0	2,482	2,585	96.0
1,864	1,979	94.2	2,434	2,373	102.6
1,724	2,096	82.2	2,501	2,654	94.3
1,705	2,505	68.1	2,572	2,812	91.5
1,756	2,160	81.3	2,570	2,711	94.8
1,853	2,289	81.0	2,564	2,830	90.6
1,962	2,084	94.0	2,551	2,648	96.4
1,983	2,470	80.3	2,724	2,946	92.5
1,685	1,935	87.1	2,536	2,724	93.1

TABLE 7-4. Racial Employment in Ten Major Southern (1966)

Types of Manufacturing	White Males	Black Males	Total** Males	% Black Males
Wholesale trades	160,659	27,797	193,391	14.37%
Textile mills	290,911	39,910	331,918	12.02
Food and kindred products	147,390	43,715	202,554	21.58
Chemicals and so forth	190,594	21,951	214,054	10.25
Transportation equipment	187,132	21,415	211,819	10.11
Railroad transportation	117,584	21,149	141,397	14.96
Paper and allied products	99,615	15,870	116,194	13.66
Electrical equipment and supplies	118,173	6,834	126,297	5.41
Machinery, except electrical	102,124	12,167	116,305	10.46
Furniture and fixtures	83,907	17,167	103,038	16.66

Source: Equal Employment Opportunity Commission, 1966

*These were the ten southern industries reporting the

**Includes other.

Blacks in the South's Ten Largest Industries

Table 7-4 shows the relationship of black to total employment in the South's leading industries. There is a very high correlation between the employment of blacks and whites in these ten industries. However, the ten leading industries for black male employment would in-

Industries*

White Females	Black Females	Total** Females	% Black Females	Total Employ-ees	Total Black	% Black
38,296	6,935	46,456	14.93%	239,847	34,732	14.48%
251,003	11,091	263,350	4.21	595,268	51,001	8.57
52,370	11,999	69,910	17.16	272,464	55,714	20.44
35,335	1,584	37,064	4.27	251,118	23,535	9.37
19,194	763	20,125	3.79	231,944	22,178	9.62
5,480	285	5,787	4.92	147,184	21,434	14.56
19,230	774	20,170	3.84	136,364	16,644	12.20
72,633	4,262	77,425	5.50	203,722	11,096	5.44
15,586	680	16,494	4.12	132,799	12,847	9.67
18,799	3,276	22,446	14.60	125,484	20,443	16.29
		TOTALS		2,336,194	269,624	18.94

argest number of employees.

clude lumber and wood products and heavy construction contractors as third and tenth, respectively, rather than machinery and electrical equipment, which are more important for whites than for blacks. Although the food industry is more important for blacks than for whites, the difference is much greater for black men than for black women.

Table 7-5 shows the indices of occupational position of blacks com-

TABLE 7-5. Black and White Ratio for Index of Occupational Position in Ten Major Southern Industries

Type of Manufacturing	Male		Female	
	South	Non-South	South	Non-South
Textile mills	0.724	0.904	0.908	0.966
Chemicals and so forth	0.620	0.815	0.796	0.897
Transportation equipment	0.713	0.873	0.803	0.925
Food and kindred products	0.691	0.857	0.814	0.911
Wholesale trades	0.632	0.819	0.583	0.919
Railroad transportation	0.589	0.810	0.514	0.742
Electrical equipment and supplies	0.694	0.845	0.941	0.964
Machinery, except electrical	0.700	0.873	0.810	0.906
Paper and allied products	0.699	0.873	0.764	0.921
Furniture and fixtures	0.773	0.916	0.803	0.887

Source: Equal Employment Opportunity Commission data, 1966.

pared to whites in the South and non-South for the ten industries. The relative black position is better elsewhere than in the South in every case. The relative position of black men is highly correlated by industry; a similar but weaker relationship is present for black women. Blacks occupy a lower position in railroad transportation in the South and non-South, but their relative index of occupational position is especially low in the South, probably reflecting the long history of racial discrimination in that industry. It is also noteworthy that the lowest relative position of black men in the non-South is higher than the highest relative position in the South, although this conclusion does not hold for women.

Participation Rates and Occupational Distribution in the South and Non-South

Tables 7-6 through 7-9 give additional evidence of the occupational position of blacks in the South and elsewhere. Although blacks constituted 14.2 percent of total employment in southern industries, they accounted for less than 1 percent of the managerial and professional categories in 1966 and only 1.9 percent of sales and technical employment. Blacks were greatly underrepresented in the sales, clerical, craftworker, and operative categories and greatly overrepresented in the laborer and service categories, 58 percent of black men falling in the last two groups.

The tables show some improvement in black participation in white-collar operative jobs between 1966 and 1969. Compared to those outside the South, southern black men had a greater share of managerial, professional, technical, craftsmen, and operative jobs in 1966 and 1969. However, black men also were more heavily concentrated in laborer and services categories, compared to elsewhere and compared to white men in the South. Although the proportion of black men in the laborer and services categories declined in the South between 1966 and 1969, nearly half of the black men, but only slightly more than 10 percent of the white men, were in these categories. The employment patterns of white men were very similar in both the South and non-South.

Black women's share of all jobs increased markedly in the South between 1966 and 1969–from 9.37 to 13.39 percent, as compared with an increase of 7.40 to 9.25 percent elsewhere. Southern black women made particularly significant gains in their share of managerial, technical, sales, clerical, craftworker, and operative positions. Nevertheless, in 1969, 41 percent of black women in the South–but only 12 percent of white women–were in the laborer and services categories. Outside the South, 35 percent of black and only 15 percent of white women were in these categories.

Some Inferences from EEO-1 Data

The inferences presented here relate to six general topics concerning the relationship between black employment in the South and certain economic and institutional variables. The inferences are not as formal

TABLE 7-6. Black and White Male Participation Rates in th

	South			
	% Black		% White	
Position	1966	1969	1966	1969
Managerial	0.84	1.30	98.13	97.41
Professional	0.66	1.17	97.82	96.95
Technical	1.95	3.17	96.07	94.24
Sales	1.87	4.06	95.88	92.78
Clerical	3.25	5.73	94.58	91.12
Craftworker	4.48	6.75	93.56	90.53
Operative	16.61	21.31	80.58	74.83
Laborer	42.90	42.85	52.51	50.98
Services	37.12	44.12	57.83	49.55
TOTAL	14.17	15.23	83.17	81.35

Source: Equal Employment Opportunity Commission data,

TABLE 7-7. Black and White Male Occupational Distributio

	South			
	Black		White	
Position	1966	1969	1966	1969
Managerial	0.62%	0.99%	12.35%	13.96%
Professional	0.30	0.56	7.65	8.70
Technical	0.49	0.85	4.08	4.70
Sales	0.86	2.14	7.49	9.18
Clerical	1.25	2.00	6.18	5.96
Craftworker	6.38	9.07	22.70	22.76
Operative	32.00	37.07	26.46	24.37
Laborer	40.94	33.73	8.54	7.51
Services	17.17	13.58	4.56	2.85

Source: Equal Employment Opportunity Commission data,

outh and Non-South (1966 and 1969)

Non-South			
% Black		% White	
1966	1969	1966	1969
0.70	1.26	98.27	97.59
0.88	1.46	96.94	95.65
2.22	3.45	95.41	93.32
1.43	3.14	97.15	94.75
3.31	5.95	93.94	89.97
3.04	4.05	94.44	92.52
10.03	11.46	86.23	83.43
15.30	16.05	76.53	74.08
19.17	22.96	74.54	68.50
6.58	7.38	90.02	88.25

966 and 1969.

ates in the South and Non-South (1966 and 1969)

Non-South			
Black		White	
1966	1969	1966	1969
1.15%	2.09%	11.85%	13.48%
1.19	2.01	9.50	11.05
1.61	2.41	5.05	5.48
1.41	3.23	6.73	8.19
3.57	5.38	7.42	6.84
8.87	10.25	20.15	19.68
40.71	37.39	25.62	23.48
23.17	20.29	8.48	7.82
18.31	15.95	5.21	3.98

1966 and 1969.

TABLE 7-8. Black and White Female Participation Rates i

	South			
	Black		White	
Position	1966	1969	1966	1969
Managerial	1.96	3.00	96.29	94.99
Professional	5.66	5.64	92.23	91.65
Technical	11.13	14.84	85.79	80.82
Sales	3.37	5.52	92.67	90.47
Clerical	1.56	4.07	96.77	93.46
Craftworker	6.63	11.60	89.21	84.03
Operative	8.77	15.86	88.97	80.52
Laborer	24.52	28.75	69.93	65.91
Services	33.89	41.44	61.29	53.15
Total	9.37	13.39	87.85	83.05

Source: Equal Employment Opportunity Commission data,

TABLE 7-9. Black and White Female Occupational Distributio

	South			
	Black		White	
Position	1966	1969	1966	1969
Managerial	0.45%	0.51%	2.35%	2.62%
Professional	1.26	1.57	2.19	4.12
Technical	4.09	3.06	3.36	2.69
Sales	2.78	3.92	8.14	10.37
Clerical	5.01	9.31	33.14	34.51
Craftworker	3.15	3.67	4.52	4.29
Operative	31.67	37.00	34.27	30.30
Laborer	18.76	16.20	5.70	5.99
Services	32.84	24.74	6.33	5.12

Source: Equal Employment Opportunity Commission data,

:he South and Non-South (1966 and 1969)

Non-South			
Black		White	
1966	1969	1966	1969
2.11	3.63	96.64	94.44
3.75	4.29	93.33	92.14
7.49	11.54	82.62	84.84
3.59	4.74	94.22	92.70
4.08	7.34	93.54	90.17
6.01	9.15	89.16	85.42
8.79	10.52	86.58	83.45
12.08	13.39	81.00	77.69
19.64	22.35	76.76	72.95
7.38	9.09	89.30	86.65

1966 and 1969.

Rates in the South and Non-South (1966 and 1969)

Non-South			
Black		White	
1966	1969	1966	1969
0.77%	1.11%	2.74%	3.03%
1.69	2.91	3.34	6.56
4.80	4.25	4.74	3.28
4.36	5.49	9.48	11.26
22.35	29.83	43.04	42.60
2.17	1.94	2.34	2.23
22.44	19.35	18.22	16.12
12.28	10.99	6.70	6.67
29.14	24.13	9.42	8.25

1966 and 1969.

as those generated by regression models invarious of the city studies, but they involve the following interesting questions:

1. How do blacks fare in the growing versus the declining industries?
2. How is the occupational status of blacks affected by the average income level (as proxy for skills level) of the industry?
3. How does the occupational status of blacks relate to their participation in the industry work force?
4. How does the fact that blacks attain lower median educational levels affect their occupational status?
5. How strong is the association between the black participation rate in particular industry and the joint variable of (*a*) black proportion in the population and (*b*) income level of the industry?
6. Are blacks better off, compared to whites, in the occupational structure in SMSAs than they are in more rural areas?

The first question is an outgrowth of the work of Hiestand (1964) and can be decategorized into two more directly answerable ones:

1. Is the proportion of blacks in the work force larger in the declining rather than in the expanding industries?
2. Do blacks achieve a significantly different occupational status in the two cases?

The answer to the first question is definitely yes; the answer to the second is that there seems to be very little difference.

The seven southern industries exhibiting the poorest growth characteristics are (1) agriculture, (2) sawmills and planing mills, (3) tobacco products manufacturing, (4) mining, (5) personal services, (6) textile mills products manufacturing, and (7) forestries, fisheries, and logging (Maddox, 1967, p. 56).

The seven most rapidly expanding southern industries are (1) electrical machinery manufacturing, (2) transportation equipment manufacturing, (3) rubber products manufacturing, (4) apparel products manufacturing, (5) nonelectrical machinery manufacturing, (6) paper and allied products, and (7) metals industries manufacturing (Maddox, 1967, p. 56).

In declining industries (1), (2), and (5) above, blacks make up 34.13, 42.23, and 44.04 percent, respectively, of the industry work forces; the mean for the seven is 25.25 percent. On the other hand, the largest black representation in the expanding industries is 14.32 percent in paper and allied products; the mean for the seven is 10.18 percent. The mean occupational index for blacks (compared to whites) is higher in the expanding industries, 0.726 as opposed to 0.708 for whites. The difference, however, is numerically small and is not statistically significant at any of the conventional levels.

The second question originates with the widely held notion that blacks–disadvantaged because of their environs, their inadequate opportunities for education, and their lack of technical skills–are less likely to move upward in the occupational structure in sophisticated, high-income industry than in standard industrial classifications having a more blue-collar work force. The EEO-1 data do not strongly support this idea: there is little evidence that the occupational status of blacks is affected by the income level of the industry. (We should emphasize that this discussion relates to relative occupational position, *not* penetration.)

When the black/white ratio of indices of occupational position was correlated with the white index itself, the latter being a proxy for the income level of the industry, the value in each case was extremely small–0.111 for men and 0.0223 for women. The regression coefficients were also small. Although both correlation and regression coefficients were statistically significant because of the large number of observations, they indicate minimal relationship. The implication is clear: if blacks penetrate higher-income SICs, they move up in the occupational structure about as well as they would in lower-income industries.

The third question can be answered unequivocally: there is scant evidence that the occupational position of blacks, compared to whites, is adversely affected by blacks' being a larger proportion of the industry work force. When the black/white ratio of the indices was correlated with the proportion of blacks in the work force, the r^2 was somewhat low for both males and females. (The thorny issue of determining boundaries of labor markets has been sidestepped. Our correlations are across states and SMSAs.)

The data also provide considerable evidence that the relative educational attainment of blacks adversely affects their occupational status. Of the occupational discrepancy between black and white men, 22 percent can be attributed to the failure of blacks to achieve the same medial years of schooling, and if an adjustment is made for quality of education, the figure rises to 53 percent. For women, the figures

TABLE 7-10. Indices of Occupational Position for Metropolitan Employment by Race, Sex, and Region* (1969 and

Sex and Region	Index of Occupational Position for 1969 Black (1)	White (2)	Black Compared to White (1)÷ (2)
Male employment			
South			
Metropolitan	$4,996	$6,900	72.4%
Nonmetropolitan	4,872	6,502	74.9
Non-South			
Metropolitan	5,374	6,831	78.7
Nonmetropolitan	5,290	6,460	81.9
Female employment			
South			
Metropolitan	2,792	3,318	84.2
Nonmetropolitan	2,840	3,140	90.5
Non-South			
Metropolitan	3,010	3,336	90.2
Nonmetropolitan	2,889	3,188	90.6

Source: Calculated from EEO-1 reports using 1966 U.S.

*U.S. Median incomes, by occupation, are higher than for For this reason, in addition to several others, the index proxy for median income, and the difference between the affects both races, however, but affects the ratio hardly

indicate that 65 percent of the discrepancy is wiped out at equal schooling and more than 100 percent is explained if an adjustment for quality is made! The adjustment, based on the Coleman study (1966), treats one year of southern white schooling as the equivalent of 1.37 years of black schooling. This means of course that black and white women are disadvantaged compared to their units of educational attainment but that the disadvantage of white women is relatively greater.

There is some evidence–but not overwhelming–that the black proportion of an industry's work force is positively related to the proportion of blacks in the population and negatively related to the median

and Nonmetropolitan Private Nonagricultural
1966)

Black (3)	White (4)	Black Compared to White (3) ÷ (4)
$4,679	$6,719	69.6%
4,632	6,399	72.4
5,154	6,671	77.3
5,083	6,364	79.9
2,686	3,289	81.7
2,740	3,131	87.5
2,892	3,296	87.7
2,839	3,209	88.5

(Column group heading: Index of Occupational Position for 1966)

ncome weights.

the South and lower than for the Non-South.
of occupational position is an inadequate
South and Non-South is understated. This
at all.

income (the white index of occupational position as a proxy) level of the industry. Both regression coefficients are statistically significant: the first being positive, as we would expect; the second, negative, also as we would expect. However, the coefficient of multiple determination–r_{12}^2–is only 0.14, which means that much that is important in the causative system has been omitted.

Finally, the question regarding the relative occupational position of blacks in nonmetropolitan as opposed to metropolitan industry can be answered without equivocation: for both men and women, in both the South and elsewhere, blacks are comparatively better off in nonmetropolitan areas (Table 7-10). However, in absolute terms–the occupational index itself rather than its ratio to the white index–black men seem to be better off in metropolitan than in nonmetropolitan employment, both in the South and elsewhere, presumably reflecting the more sophisticated character of urban industry. Apparently, blacks–caught at the lower end of the occupational structure, regardless of the character of the industry–suffer less than whites in the shift to lower-skills-level industry in nonmetropolitan areas.

References

Coleman, James S., et al. 1966. *Equality of Educational Opportunity*. Report to the U.S. Office of Education. Washington, D.C.: Government Printing Office.

Formby, John. 1968. "The Extent of Wage and Salary Discrimination against Nonwhite Labor." *Southern Economic Journal* (October).

Hiestand, Dale L. 1964. *Economic Growth and Employment Opportunities for Minorities*. New York: Columbia University Press.

Kain, John. 1968. "Housing Segregation, Negro Employment, and Metropolitan Decentralization." *Quarterly Journal of Economics* 82, no. 2.

Maddox, James G. 1967. *The Advancing South: Manpower Prospects and Problems*. New York: Twentieth Century Fund.

Masters, Stanley H. 1970. *A Study of Socioeconomic Mobility among Urban Negroes*. New Brunswick, N.J.: Rutgers University Press.

Mooney, Joseph. 1969. "Housing Segregation, Negro Employment, and Metropolitan Decentralization." *Quarterly Journal of Economics* 83, no. 2.

U.S. Department of Commerce, Bureau of the Census. 1970. *Current Population Reports*. Washington, D.C.: Government Printing Office.

8

Economics of Employment Discrimination

Ray Marshall and Virgil L. Christian, Jr.

A major objective of this study has been to establish some basic principles or consistencies concerning black employment patterns in the South and in the nation. We have therefore reviewed many other studies to determine the extent to which their findings seem to conform to ours. We also have attempted to relate our work to theories of discrimination in order to determine the extent to which these theories seem to explain the basic causal forces at work as we see them on the basis of our studies. We are concerned with theory because of our conviction that effective policies to deal with black employment problems require adequate attention to a conceptual framework which will make it possible to separate the important from the unimportant causes and the real from the apparent causes.

Our primary objective has been to account for racial differentials in *employment*, rather than in *income*, which is the objective of many works dealing with the economics of discrimination, and to set forth the conceptual framework we have found to be must useful for understanding the causes of black employment patterns.

A Review of Other Studies

Gary Becker, in a pioneering study (1957), concerned himself primarily with direct or overt discrimination, which manifests itself as unequal treatment in the labor market. He believed that employers with a "taste for discrimination" would hire whites instead of blacks at the same wage if they had equal productivity, implying that blacks of equal productivity would receive less than whites. The difference between white and black wages, expressed as a proportion of the white wage, he called the "discrimination coefficient," and he believed that actual wage differentials showed this to be large. Since the discriminating employer would be at a disadvantage in acquiring a work force, as nondiscriminating competitors could acquire the same quality labor at lower wages, the discriminator could not survive indefinitely under conditions of perfect competition. Thus Becker argues that the existence of discrimination is evidence of elements of monopoly in product markets and implies that an effective way to combat direct employer discrimination would be to make product markets more competitive.

In his attempt to get at these matters quantitatively, Becker developed an index of occupational position. He calculated the index for each race by multiplying the median income for each occupation by the proportion of the work force of each race in that occupation. Median incomes were assumed to be the same for both races; differences in the index between the races therefore reflected different occupational distributions rather than concentration within low-wage sectors in each occupation.

Black concentration in the lowest-income occupations led to a low index for them; if blacks were paid less than their white counterparts at a given occupational level, black income disadvantages would be even greater than that suggested by the indices. Using this index, Becker concluded that blacks gained little ground in the job levels between 1910 and 1950 and noted that they were relatively worse off in the South than elsewhere throughout this period.

With the assertion that "the average occupational position of Negroes relative to whites has been remarkably stable since 1910," Becker seemed to put himself in opposition to Eli Ginzberg (1956), who believed that "the Negro has made truly spectacular gains [in the fifteen years between 1941, World War II beginning, and 1956] in the civilian economy, both in the North and South." However, Ginzberg was talking about absolute gains, while Becker meant black gains, compared to white gains, in terms of improvements in occupational position alone.

The argument was taken up by Elton Rayack (1961), who attempts to answer two questions raised by the different points of view:

1. Has there been an advancement in the occupational position of blacks since 1940?
2. If so, is the advancement attributable to a reduction in discrimination?

Rayack, using Becker's own device, the index of occupational position, argues that blacks have closed the gap. But he does not fix the weights through time in the way that Becker does. Becker used constant weights in all years for which he made the calculations; thus, changes in his index measure actual occupation shifts.

Rayack changes the weights from year to year, using as the weight in each year the median income for the given occupation for that year; thus, his index is as much an indicator of relative earnings as an index of occupational position. For example, suppose that, in the three occupational categories used by Becker, blacks and whites maintained exactly the same percentages among the occupations in the first and second years: for whites, 10 percent unskilled, 50 percent semiskilled, 40 percent skilled; for blacks, 60 percent unskilled, 30 percent semiskilled, 10 percent skilled.

Since Becker uses the same weights in calculating the index of occupational penetration for the two years, he would show exactly the same indices of occupational penetration for both races in both years and would conclude–correctly–that blacks have made no advance at all, comparatively, in the occupational structure. However, suppose further that, for some reason, income differentials were wiped out among the three skill categories by the last year: all three groups have the same median incomes. Then Rayack would show the same index for both races in that last year, even though the occupational distributions are different. Then he would show–correctly–that the income differential had been wiped out but for a reason having nothing to do with occupational upgrading.

Rayack's method shows an improvement in the occupational index of blacks compared to whites, when either (*a*) they move up in the occupational structure or (*b*) there is a decline in the income gap between high- and low-skill occupations. Which of the two is better in a given case depends entirely upon the purpose of the user. Rayack overstates his case in accusing Becker of error when the latter uses constant weights, since Becker must use constant weights to achieve his purpose of measuring occupational upgrading. But Rayack does have a point in maintaining that an index calculated with constant weights does not measure changes in relative income positions if there has been a shift in median incomes among occupations, by race.

On the other hand, Rayack's assertion that "the present [1962] occupational position of the Negro relative to the white is substantially better than it was prior to World War II" is distinctly questionable; the gains blacks had made were not due to occupational upgrading but to a shift favorable to lower-status occupations in relative occupational incomes. Finally, Rayack agrees with Becker that there has been little decline in the "taste for discrimination" in recent decades, attributing most black gains to tightness in labor markets in the World War II and early postwar years.

Finis Welch (1967), using an analytical mechanism somewhat similar to Becker's, hypothesizes that workers have strong preferences for working with members of their own race, so that the "taste for discrimination" runs from employee to employer, rather than from employer to employee. If one assumes an indifference map for typical workers–one having the property that, on a given indifference curve, the wage to these workers is a decreasing function of the proportion of their race in the firm's labor force (i.e., they will work for less the higher the percentage of their race in the firm's labor force)–then it is possible to show that cost minimization at each output requires totally segregated employees within firms. That is, a given firm will use either all white or all black labor.

There is another interesting implication of this analysis: wages for whites and blacks must be equal at given skill levels (black labor and white labor are perfect substitutes) for competitive equilibrium to exist. However, Welch notes that there are substantial differences in educational levels between the races, which creates complementarities where blacks and whites work in different or related occupations, rather than as perfect substitutes, and leads to integrated work force and wage differentials.

Robert Strauss (no date) defines discrimination pragmatically in terms of "expected" and "unexpected" employment patterns for blacks, looking at the specific question: Where, occupationally and industrially, are black males employed, and how does this compare with where, in the absence of discrimination, we would expect them to be employed? The procedure involved adjustment for the proportion of blacks available in a given labor market at the skill level required for that occupation in the market, calculation of "expected" employment, and comparison with actual employment.

Strauss compares occupations among firms within small labor markets, by assuming well-defined job search patterns in the market, in order to pinpoint firms that apparently discriminate against blacks. He also uses national employment statistics to compare the ratio of actual to expected black employment, by occupation, across industries and finds that the majority of industries have a low percentage of black male employees but that those which hire more than the average percentage of blacks are very large employers indeed. Industries with few blacks tend to have few in all occupations. His work leads him to conclude that:

1. Southern blacks are more excluded from middle-skill occupations than are blacks in other regions.
2. Unionization is a strong bar to equal employment opportunity.
3. Large corporations are more inclined to use few blacks than small firms.

His third conclusion, he believes, is probably due to unionization which goes with large firms. This aspect of his work seems to support Becker's "taste for discrimination" thesis. Oligopolistic firms have sufficient market control to exercise this "taste" and still survive; more competitive firms cannot.

The useful summary measures that Strauss uses are those in which he develops "expected" black male employment by holding constant regional location and the relative number of black workers and of qualified black workers available for each occupation and the relative numbers of qualified black workers available within an occupation on the basis of job-search patterns. His work is not greatly dissimilar in either concept or objective from that done by Robert McKersie (1971) in that each has tried to develop a technique for identifying problem industries, and problem firms within industries, in specific labor markets.

However, McKersie's treatment of the impact of unions on black employment is not nearly so broadly based as that of Ray Marshall (1965 and 1967), who finds great diversity among the policies of national and international unions and among locals within the larger organizations, and Orley Ashenfelter (1971), who has made an ingenious attempt to measure econometrically the effect of unionism on the average wage of black compared to white labor. The evidence generated by Ashenfelter's model leads him to conclude that, in the absence of offsetting discriminatory effects, the effect of unionism has been to raise the average black/white ratio relative to that in nonunion markets. However, when he examines differences between craft and industrial unions, he finds–not surprisingly–that industrial unions have narrowed the intraindustry black-white wage gap but that craft unions, which are likely to concentrate blacks in low-skill occupations, may actually have increased it.

Harry Gilman argues: "The proposition that members of minority groups are 'the last to be hired and the first to be fired' has gained wide acceptance. This proposition will be interpreted here as saying that the burden of short-time layoffs and unemployment will fall disproportionately on workers, such as nonwhite workers, who are members of minority groups" (1965, pp. 1077–1096). Following this, he sets out to categorize the causes for the difference between white and nonwhite unemployment rates into objective labor market factors and an unexplained residual, with the residual attributable, presumably, to discrimination in the market. He considers several hypotheses that look reasonable a priori: nonwhites may be concentrated in occupations that are characterized by high unemployment rates in normal years and are particularly sensitive to cyclical pressures; they have lower educational attainment, on the average, even after standardization for occupation; they are disproportionately concentrated in industries having chronically high levels of unemployment; and their employment is less concentrated in the prime working years, 25 to 44.

Gilman's method of analysis–basically multiple regression–involves standardization for these variables and leads him to conclude that only roughly half of the difference in white and nonwhite unemployment rates is accounted for by these factors, leaving a possible racial differential to account for at least part of the remainder. He recognizes, however, that social attitudes toward nonwhites may reflect themselves in these so-called objective factors and refers at some length to their impact on both the quantity and quality of nonwhite education. In other words, these so-called objective factors might themselves be strongly influenced by discrimination.

Randall Weiss (1970) has studied in detail the effect of educational achievement on earnings of blacks and whites and cautions against assuming that educational upgrading of blacks will automatically reduce by very much the income advantage held by whites (p. 150). His regression model, which takes annual earnings in 1959 as the dependent variable, shows a strong positive relationship between educational achievement and earnings for whites but a much weaker relationship for blacks. Specifically, the size of the regression coefficient for the education variable is only a fourth as much for an additional year of education achievement as it is for whites. Weiss uses educational achievement rather than years of schooling in his regression coefficients. Recognizing that black schools have been generally inferior, he uses data from Coleman (1966) to modify raw years of schooling to a comparable basis for the races. Following development of his regression coefficients, he develops a recursive model that seeks to break the effect of increased education into two components:

1. Gains in the average number of weeks worked per year
2. Gains in occupational levels

He finds that his model works well for whites in that additional education is strongly associated with both more work per year and higher occupational levels but that the fit is not at all good for blacks. He regretfully concludes that educational advances do not seem to be the answer for blacks, closing with the rather dramatic statement that "given a labor market that distributes rewards among blacks without regard to their education, the solution to the black poverty problem seems to be outside the classroom." He does not deny that educational upgrading might alter social attitudes about blacks that would ultimately be reflected in the labor market–nor does he affirm it. This aspect of the problem lies outside the scope of his investigation.

The impact of segregated urban housing on black employment has been investigated by John Kain (1968) and Joseph Mooney (1969). Noting the increasing concentration of blacks in inner city ghettos, on the one hand, and the declining importance of the central city as a source of jobs, on the other, these researchers raise serious questions about the number and kinds of jobs accessible to the black community. Mooney finds that the sectors which are growing in importance in the central city–selected services and finance, insurance, and real estate–fill 52 percent of their jobs with women, whereas the manufacturing sector, much more important for men in general and for black men in particular, has moved steadily toward the suburbs, far away from concentrations of blacks.

Both Kain and Mooney developed regression models which show a statistically significant negative relationship between the suburban ring as a source of jobs and the inner city as the center of black housing, although Mooney's study shows SMSA unemployment rates to be much more important. However, he is not surprised at this and even suggests the reason: Recently constructed plants in outlying areas are likely to use newer, more sophisticated, and more capital-intensive methods and lose employment less rapidly in slack times. Their largely white work force is therefore less vulnerable to slack employment than the more heavily black work forces of older, more labor-intensive, core industry. Hence the two variables–unemployment rate and decentralization of industry relative to black housing concentrations–are separate manifestations of a common cause.

Dale Hiestand (1964) and James Tobin (1965) are convinced that little progress can be made in upgrading the job status of blacks unless labor markets are kept tight. They take a macroeconomic view of the problem, concentrating on the relative disadvantage of blacks at differing levels of economic activity, rather than specific causes of that disadvantagement. Hiestand thinks that blacks, as immigrant white minorities before them, make sizable advances only when employers have recruitment problems due to tight labor markets. White males are the preferred source of manpower–they are first in the hiring queue–and minority groups form a reserve labor supply that will be nearly exhausted only when the demand for manpower is great.

Blacks, on the other hand, move into an industry and then upward in the industry as whites move to better alternatives. Thus, blacks are more likely to be found in declining, labor-intensive industries than in growth industries calling for a sophisticated, highly skilled work force. Apparently, in Heistand's view, blacks will continue to have an occupational disadvantage in the foreseeable future; they can avoid high unemployment rates as well only if there is a steady general advance of the economy.

Tobin's position is somewhat similar. He observes that "Negro unemployment rates are multiples of the general unemployment rate. This fact reflects both the lesser skills, seniority, and experience of Negroes and employers' discrimination against Negroes. These conditions are a deplorable reflection on American society, but as long as they exist Negroes suffer much more than others from a general increase in unemployment and gain much more from a general reduction" (p. 881). Noting that aggregate spending in the economy can be controlled by monetary and fiscal policies, he points to the obsessive national fear of inflation and balance of payments deficits as the reason why this "relatively simple way out" has not been adopted. (He also has some interesting observations about the relationship of the existing welfare system, and various welfare proposals, to poverty among blacks, but that lies a bit outside the scope of this section.)

Yet not all manpower economists are persuaded that the "tight labor markets" hypothesis is correct. Charles Killingsworth says: "Whatever may have been the merits in earlier years of the advocacy of the 'tighter labor markets' as the 'single most important step' to remedy Negro disadvantage, further pursuit of that course is now obviously inappropriate. . . . Recent experience has confirmed–at least with regard to Negroes–the research finds of the past decade or so which emphasized the imperfections, rather than the homogenizing power of the labor markets. . . . I have *never* seen a peacetime example of a job being redesigned so that it could be filled with unskilled rather than skilled labor" (1967). Killingsworth gives a more detailed discussion of this point in a subsequent volume (1968).

Lloyd Atkinson (1970), in this same vein, takes sharp issue with the methodology of Harold Guthrie (1970), who finds a strong dependence of the growth rate of black and white incomes on the level of employment. Atkinson argues that Guthrie's results are a consequence of treating unemployment rates during cyclical movements when unemployment is changing as though they were constant over long-term periods. High unemployment rates are associated with the down phase of the cycle, says Atkinson, and annual income growth is relatively low during that phase. Similarly, in most years of low unemployment, the economy is experiencing a recovery, and the growth in income is well above that which would be sustained on a secular basis at the same unemployment rate. Thus, he says, "including such years in the regression means that one is bound to exaggerate the effect on secular growth rates of the level of the unemployment rate" (p. 3).

Barbara Bergmann (1970), making use of Becker-type theoretical constructs, divides the labor market into two occupations–one prestigious, one menial–and assumes a crucial differential, for each occupation, between black and white wages which will make employers indifferent to whether they choose black or white workers. She then shows that occupational segregation will be stable if the difference between marginal productivities in the prestigious and menial occupations lies between the crucial differences in wage rates for two occupations. Should the marginal productivity of blacks in the prestigious occupation rise to the point where it exceeds that in the menial occupation by more than the crucial differential between black and white wages for the prestigious occupation, then blacks will be hired into the prestigious occupation, lowering the demand curve for white labor in it.

Thus, blacks gain by increases in marginal productivity in prestigious occupations if the gain is sufficient to allow some of them to enter it, as there is a wage increase both for those who enter and for the reduced supply who remain in the menial occupation. White wage losses will be small if whites are a big majority in the total labor force. She also argues that, if employers are able to exercise monopolistic power in buying their labor, or if they can arrive at easily policed "gentlemen's agreements" to restrict blacks and women to jobs for which they "fit," employers' profits may be increased by discrimination. In further work along these lines (Bergmann, 1971), she uses a variant of the constant elasticity of substitution (CES) production function and estimates aggregate output and relative black and white wages, assuming (*a*) rigid segregation of the races in two occupations and (*b*) complete mixing of the labor force and assignment to occupations without regard to race. Her calculations indicate strong positive gains in aggregate output and in black wages when discrimination stops and also indicate very mild negative effects on white wages.

In a more empirical vein, Bergmann joins with Jerolyn Lyle (1970) to examine differences among metropolitan areas and among industries in the occupational standing of blacks and finds that variables often taken by other researchers to be of great importance on black occupational levels–education, locational elements, establishment size, skill level of the work force–are not nearly so important as the general attitude toward blacks in the community. Using the vote for George Wallace in the 1968 presidential election as a proxy for the attitudinal variable, they find that it dominates the regressions: "The Wallace vote explains a major portion of the variance among area scores. This result does not conflict with our expectation that within an area a better educated Negro is probably going to do better than a poorly educated one. But it does provide some evidence that efforts to encourage nondiscriminatory behavior of employers will have a bigger payoff than efforts to improve education, transportation, and all the rest" (p. 16). However, the conclusion of Bergmann and Lyle can be only tentative at best because there is no demonstration that the Wallace vote represented racial prejudices that cause employment discrimination. Many white ethnic groups who supported Wallace did so because of his economic as well as his racial views. Nor does it follow that institutional or overt discrimination can be changed by changing employer attitudes, a point that will be elaborated upon later in this chapter.

In another Maryland project study, Bradley Schiller (1970) attempts to decompose discrimination against poor blacks into two parts: first, that associated with coming from poverty backgrounds and, second, that associated with race. He derives a numerical index of occupational status and estimates that poor blacks–the sons of the Aid to Families with Dependent Children–would have reached a mean index some 25 percent higher than they actually reached had they not been black. He thinks that equal educational opportunity is denied all those coming from deprived backgrounds and that whites as well as blacks suffer loss in occupational status due to earlier inadequate schooling.

However, blacks suffer additional direct racial discrimination in occupational attainment, leading to the difference of 25 percent. Black sons of the dependent-children aid program "suffer the double encumbrance of being both poor and black."

The series of studies on black employment in American industry and in southern industry made by Herbert Northrup and his associates at the Industrial Research Unit of the University of Pennsylvania (1971*a*, *b*) provides some important insights and current data on racial employment patterns in industry. The industries covered include most of the nation's largest employers–automobile, steel, aerospace, hotel, petroleum, rubber tire, and chemical (and in the South, paper, lumber, tobacco, bituminous coal mining, and textiles)–and there is a final summary and comparative analysis.

The project attempts to determine why some industries, and some firms within industries, are more hospitable to minority group employment than others; explanation of minority employment patterns is sought in the light of key hypotheses relating to both sides of the labor market: the demand for labor, the nature of work, the time and nature of the industry's development, the mores of the community, the relationship of racial employment policies and consumer market orientation, the concern of the industry about its image, the ethnic group orientation of management, community crises, the nature of union organization, the impact of technology, the services industry situation, industrial location, the role of government, and managerial action and policy. The ultimate objective is, of course, to propose appropriate policy measures for improving black employment opportunities.

The factors discussed by Northrup et al. as influencing black employment patterns include (*a*) the demand for labor, which shows that tight labor markets facilitate black employment while rising unemployment levels and technological changes tend to displace labor, and (*b*) the nature of the work–the position of blacks increases as the jobs become less attractive (Briggs, 1970). In the southern industries studied (lumber, paper, coal mining, tobacco, and textiles), Northrup and others found blacks to be almost nonexistent in the officials and managers category, although blacks sometimes supervised blacks. These writers also found white-collar discrimination to be more vividly demonstrated in sales than any other category, a finding they attribute to the employer's fear of losing white customers.

Historically, Northrup et al. found, black men have been hired primarily in hot, dirty, heavy, blue-collar jobs; only 2 or 3 percent are hired in the skilled craftsmen categories. However, they conclude, blacks made significant gains in the operatives category, especially in textiles, in the period 1966 to 1968, primarily because of pressures from the federal government and tight labor markets. Despite some upgrading of black women into white-collar work, they were still heavily concentrated in the services categories.

Kenneth Arrow makes some improvements on the discrimination models developed by Becker and Welch. His basic aim is

> . . . to use as far as possible neoclassical tools in the analysis of discrimination. . . . even though the basic neoclassical assumptions of utility and profit maximization are always retained, many of the usual assumptions will be relaxed at one point or another: convexity of indifference surfaces, costless adjustments, perfect information, perfect capital markets. . . . I believe there are many other economic phenomena for the explanation of which each of these assumptions must be abandoned so that the steps proposed here are not ad hoc analyses for the case at hand but should be important elements of social factors on economic behavior without either lumping them into an uninformative category of "imperfections" or jumping to a precipitate rejection of neoclassical theory with all its analytic power. (1971*b*)

Arrow's model assumes black (B) and white (W) workers to be equally productive. He defines discrimination as where some economic agent has negative or positive valuations of workers for which he is willing to pay. He also assumes that, "given the tastes, the markets work smoothly. General equilibrium requires full employment of both B and W workers; the wages of both will adjust to clear the market, and the discriminatory tastes will be reflected in wage differences."

In the simplest case, employers maximize a function where they equate the marginal product of each unit of black labor (MP_B) with the wage of black workers (W_B) or white workers (W_W) and their marginal products (MP_W) *plus* the discrimination coefficient (d_B) or (d_W), which is defined as "the price the employer is willing to pay, in terms of profits, for reducing his B labor force (or increasing his white labor force) by one." In this simplest case, all employers are assumed to have equal tastes for discrimination. Therefore,

$$W_B = MP_B - d_B$$

and black workers will be paid less than their marginal products. Similarly,

$$W_W = MP_W + d_W$$

so that whites are paid more than their marginal products, assuming that the employer prefers whites to blacks. Under these restrictive assumptions, black workers lose by discrimination and white workers gain. Moreover, under what Arrow calls the "plausible hypothesis" that employers' satisfactions depend only on the ratio of B to W workers, so that

$$d_W W + d_B B = 0,$$

employers neither gain nor lose, white workers gain, and black workers lose relative to their marginal products.

However, when Arrow relaxes the assumption that employers have equal tastes for discrimination (or that utility functions are identical between firms), it is difficult to support the conclusion that firms will hire the same proportions of B and W workers in the long run; in this case, the long-run trend is toward segregated work forces if there is a discrimination coefficient either against blacks or in favor of whites, and those firms which are least discriminatory will get larger. In the long run, capital will flow to these firms, and competition makes it possible for only the least discriminatory firms to survive. But, Arrow observes, "since in fact racial discrimination has survived for a long time, we must assume that the model just presented must have some limitation" (p. 9). However, Arrow might have followed Becker's example and attributed the persistence of discrimination to imperfect product market competition.

Arrow also considers the apparent contradictions between the Becker-Arrow neoclassical model and the observed employment patterns which seem to contradict that model. The implicit contradictory observed patterns are for wages to be equal for workers in the same classifications on the same job and for black workers (or women) to be excluded from certain occupations and departments within a firm. Traditional neoclassical analysis requires convexities in indifference curves between such variables as "wages" and "preference ratios" of white and black labor, which assumes that black and white workers are substitutes and therefore will be used in combination, depending

different behavior from the physical distance assumption; namely, whites do not avoid physical association with blacks but attempt to ensure that the association is such that whites have higher status.

The differences between Becker's and Thurow's concepts of discrimination have important policy implications. Under Becker's model, blacks or government can do little to end discrimination other than making product markets more competitive and demonstrating to whites that they suffer economic losses from discrimination. Under Thurow's theory, there are "many actions which governments and Negroes can take to end discrimination." Many of the effects of discrimination "rest on monopoly and monopoly powers of whites. Governments and Negroes can attempt to break down these powers of government, labor, and business institutions."

As Thurow emphasizes, neoclassical economic theory can demonstrate that whites gain and blacks lose from discrimination, but it cannot tell us whether employers or white workers gain. Moreover, empirical data, given the validity of the assumptions and the correctness of the specifications in his model, suggest to Thurow that black losses and white gains from discrimination are about $15 billion a year. Furthermore, he tells us, "discrimination causes a large reduction in the potential level of output of the American economy" and black economic resources are "inefficiently utilized as a result of discrimination. Efficiency losses amount to approximately $19 billion a year" (p. 158). Thus, discrimination causes whites to gain, but not as much as blacks and the nation lose.

Comments on the Theory of Discrimination

Explicit and implicit definitions of discrimination used in a theory or conceptual framework have important implications for policies to combat discrimination. Becker, Arrow, and Welch consider discrimination to be based on attitudes or prejudices which cause people to want to avoid associating with or hiring particular individuals. Thus Becker and Arrow speak of a "taste for discrimination" for which maximizing agents are willing to pay. Moreover, in Becker's theory whites are concerned about physical distance from blacks and are willing to pay a premium not to associate with them.

We have found the neoclassical definition and formulation of discrimination to have very limited value either in understanding the employment disadvantages of blacks or in prescribing policies to eliminate them. We have also found it important to distinguish institutions, from the specific, overt discriminatory actions of particular decision makers. We have therefore found *behavior models* (which look at the behavioral characteristics of employers, unions, white workers, black workers, government agencies, and their interactions with each other and the environment within which they operate) to be more useful than the narrow formulations of the neoclassical model.

Moreover, we consider it important to formulate different models for men and women, for various categories of discrimination (i.e., employment, occupation, income, housing, capital markets, product markets, education, and so forth), and for each distinct geographic entity and decision-making agent. Our studies also lead us to the conclusion that *social* rather than *physical* distance is the main concern of prejudiced white workers. In our view, employment and occupational discrimination can be explained mainly as status and control of economic opportunity phenomena. Whites do not object to physical association with blacks so long as blacks occupy an inferior status. It follows that white workers have resisted the employment or upgrading of black workers both because blacks were regarded as "inferior" people who would reduce the status of their occupations and because white workers seek to monopolize economic opportunities for themselves.

While some aspects of the neoclassical economic model provide valuable insights into employment decisions, especially the assumption that employers seek primarily to maximize profits, our work makes us skeptical of the central construct in the neoclassical system which defines discrimination as a "taste" *for which decision makers are willing to pay*. We likewise doubt that the same model can be used to explain both access to initial employment (what we have called "penetration rates") and occupational upgrading (measured by our index of occupational position). In our view, *job control* is a much more important and broader concept than wages in explaining racial employment and occupational differentials.

It seems very unrealistic to assume that workers would insist on wage differentials between black and white workers in identical jobs, especially if they are unionized. Wage differentials for perfect substitutes would weaken collective bargaining and would provide the employer with a powerful incentive to substitute black workers for whites, greatly reducing the latter's ability to sustain wage differentials. It is our view that white workers are more likely to seek to exclude black workers entirely than to insist on wage differentials. This is a more realistic explanation for employment segregation than Arrow's attempt to explain away the convexity in indifference maps in order to make the neoclassical price-wage theory model conform with reality.

The concept of wage differentials for perfect substitutes is central to neoclassical discrimination theory, partly because of the way discrimination is defined in order to make it fit the neoclassical wage theory mold. But such differentials are relatively unimportant if we consider only different wages for workers in the same firms who are perfect substitutes except for race. The main way in which racial wage differentials are perpetuated is by misclassifying black workers as "helpers" or "laborers" when they are actually working as journeymen. It seems to us that this reflects status considerations more than it does a taste for discrimination for which the employer is willing to pay or for which white workers and foremen demand payment.

The neoclassical formulation also gives inadequate attention to the importance of supplies of black labor. Blacks have been able to acquire some jobs by being able to supply the employer's labor requirements entirely, which explains in part why industries characterized by small (competitive) firms often have larger proportions of black workers than larger "monopolistic" firms.

Moreover, the actions of white workers seem primarily to be functions of:

1. Their estimate of the employer's reaction to their resistance to the hiring of blacks in "their" jobs
2. Black workers' ability to replace whites if the latter boycott employers
3. The desirability of the jobs in question
4. White workers' estimates of governmental or community reactions to their discriminatory practices
5. The bargaining power of white workers vis-à-vis employers

White workers' bargaining power is determined mainly by their ability to inflect costs on the employer or to withhold benefits from employer, which in turn depends upon such factors as labor skill levels, personnel costs of replacement, the availability of substitute workers, the strategic location of the discriminating whites in the production process, and community reactions to discrimination by white workers.

For example, if the jobs in question are highly desirable, if there are many blacks who can readily occupy them, and if the white workers expect the employer to be firm in a decision to hire blacks, then white workers will rarely resist the employment of blacks, quit their jobs, or demand wage differentials. Regardless of their attitudes, white workers ordinarily will accept occupational or job integration rather than sacrifice good jobs. On the other hand, white workers often resist integration if they believe that their resistance will cause the employer to refrain from hiring blacks–which is more likely to happen if there are limited supplies of black workers qualified to replace whites.

We doubt very much that employers' motives are ordinarily based to any significant degree on "tastes for discrimination" or on the ratio of black to white workers. We believe, moreover, that large corporate employers have very limited status concerns in hiring workers. Status and "tastes for discrimination" probably are more important for small employers who have strong personal identifications with their enterprises and with their workers. Since blacks apparently are more likely to be employed in these firms than in larger ones, it must be mainly because small employers can meet their labor requirements with all-black work forces or because blacks can be relegated to low-status occupations for which dependable supplies of whites are not available. These supply considerations sometimes cause employers to prefer blacks for low-status occupations.

In addition to their feeling that blacks are "better suited" than whites for low-status jobs, the main way in which employers make decisions that affect employment is the extent to which they assign probabilities that blacks or whites are likely to meet the qualifications for (*a*) those jobs for which workers are hired from the open market or (*b*) upgrading within a firm. Since whites have higher education levels and have more experience in skilled and white-collar jobs, employers expect to minimize their recruiting and training costs by hiring workers recommended by existing employees, thus perpetuating the exclusion of blacks from all-white work forces. However, as labor markets tighten and the supplies of white labor decline, employers are forced to increase their recruiting costs by tapping nontraditional supplies and using more expensive screening methods to ascertain employee qualifications.

It appears, then, that employers assign priorities to different kinds of workers for various categories of jobs. Blacks are at the front of the queue for undesirable jobs because they provide a more dependable supply and because many employers have stereotyped them as "better suited" for these jobs. Conversely, blacks are at the end of the line for better jobs for much the same reasons and because adequate supplies of whites are available for these jobs. As noted earlier, blacks are prevented from being employed in particular occupations by overt discrimination, but institutional discrimination causes them to have inadequate education and training for jobs with few blacks in them; there has therefore been a tendency for blacks to prepare mainly for jobs traditionally available to them.

Thus, employer discrimination is better understood in a social rather than an isolated individual context. Although isolated economic tendencies, as outlined in the neoclassical models, define *theoretical* tendencies drawn from restrictive assumptions, they are not necessarily predictive of *actual* behavior, because economic tendencies can be counteracted by social forces. In making employment decisions which maximize profits, employers must therefore consider the reactions of customers, unions, present employees, government agencies, black organizations, and the public, all of which can influence costs, revenues, and ability to operate.

For example, neoclassical theorists postulate greater discrimination by monopolistic than competitive firms. They reason that competition will force employers to hire workers on the basis of their productivity, rather than on the basis of such irrelevant factors as race. Our studies suggest some important limitations to this line of reasoning. In the first place, the neoclassical theory ordinarily assumes full employment, which would lessen the ability of employers to hire all their workers from a given race. Moreover, the neoclassical analysis ignores the effects of consumer or labor market boycotts by one race or the other, which offset the marginal gains the employer might realize from hiring an integrated work force.

The traditional neoclassical model also assumes information about employee qualifications to be costless, whereas in reality employers incur personnel costs in order to recruit and adapt workers to their particular needs, though this assumption has been modified in Arrow's analysis outlined earlier. The neoclassical model tends to ignore the workers' inadequate knowledge of job opportunities and the specificity of particular nontransferable job requirements, which cause wages and employment to be imperfectly responsive to market forces. As noted earlier, the neoclassical model is likely to give inadequate attention to supply problems by assuming that units of labor are perfect substitutes, whereas different racial groups in fact have different amounts of human resource investment in the form of education, training, and experience.

The neoclassical model is therefore likely to produce misleading policy conclusions, principally because it exaggerates the importance of market forces in overcoming discrimination. We agree that market forces *tend* to eliminate racial discrimination but think that this tendency may never change employment patterns because it is counteracted by important forces not included in the neoclassical model. (It is also argued in chapter 1 that the institutional forces associated with industrialization also *tend* to reduce discrimination.)

Since they ignore the influence of group strategy, neoclassical economists are likely to consider monopolists to be more discriminatory than competitive and therefore advocate measures to improve product market competition as effective means of increasing black employment. Indeed, some studies have shown a high correlation between product market concentration rates and some measure of discrimination. However, there are formidable inferential problems with this approach.

The first is that there tends to be a high correlation between product market concentration ratios and industry skill and educational requirements. Since the black population has lower skill and educational attainments, any industry with high skill and educational requirements would have a low probability of having many blacks, even without overt discrimination.

Since competitive industries tend to be low-wage, labor-intensive operations, it is not surprising to find heavy concentrations of black workers in some of them. However, blacks have had very limited employment opportunities in such competitive industries as agriculture. Even in competitive manufacturing industries, such as textiles, blacks had limited employment opportunities until it became difficult for employers to find adequate supplies of white workers and until the federal government adopted a campaign to get blacks hired (Northrup et al., 1971*a*, *b*). The neoclassical model ignores the fact that large monopolistic firms might form more conspicuous targets for groups seeking to increase black employment opportunities.

Strategies to change industry employment patterns must also consider many aspects of company and industry structure that probably are more important than product market competition. For example, such consumer-oriented industries as retail merchants are vulnerable to consumer boycotts by blacks, especially those firms that sell a large proportion of their output to blacks and operate on such low profit margins that a small loss in sales threatens a company's survival. In such cases, companies wishing to hire blacks are helped by laws that require all employers to practice nondiscriminatory hiring because this reduces the alternatives available to white workers and customers who might boycott a particular employer.

On the other hand, consumer boycotts are less effective against companies producing capital goods or those oriented toward raw materials. For example, the study of black employment in Birmingham by Rungeling and Ignatin demonstrates that U.S. Steel's Birmingham affiliate, TCI, was relatively impervious to black pressures for equality. However, the company was more responsive to threats by the federal government to cancel contracts with the parent company of U.S. Steel and all its affiliates unless they complied with the antidiscrimination provisions of their contracts. The Birmingham study also indicates the importance of the extent to which a company's interests coincide with those of a particular community. U.S. Steel apparently had little interest in the economic development of Birmingham because Alabama's main value to that company was as a source of raw materials. As a consequence, Birmingham's racial disputes were basically ignored by the company, which made little attempt to promote racial harmony there.

On the other hand, our studies in Memphis and Atlanta demonstrate the significance of power structures whose basic economic interests were inextricably bound to community economic development. In Memphis a black boycott hurt downtown merchants and led to the emergence of white leaders whose interests required racial harmony. Significantly, during the late 1960s and early 1970s, when commercial interests became stronger relative to the steel industry in Birmingham, leaders emerged who were concerned with the city's image and who moved to prevent racial unrest. In Atlanta the importance of the black vote and the presence of a moderately strong and active black community influenced race relations in that city.

We also differ from the neoclassical economists in our concept of the importance of attitudes in influencing discrimination. If discrimination is defined as specific overt acts by decision makers, based on prejudices, it is important to measure discrimination and the "attitudes" or "tastes" by which it is presumed to be caused. Public policy designed to overcome this kind of discrimination is therefore limited to efforts to educate whites to reduce their prejudices and demonstrate their self-interest in merit employment and to enforce antitrust laws to limit employment discretion not based on merit.

In our conceptual framework, on the other hand, institutionalized behavior patterns are much more significant than specific overt acts of discrimination. Changing these institutional forms requires attention to fundamental structures and institutions rather than to attitudes. Furthermore, we are persuaded that attitudes are more likely to be influenced by institutional arrangements than vice versa. In other words, the operational constraints which confront union leaders and employers are more important than attitudes as determinants of discrimination. If the context is conducive to such action, a bigoted employer will hire and promote blacks and a bigoted union leader will promote the interests of black workers as members. On the other hand, in a different context, an "egalitarian" (in terms of attitudes) employer or union leader will permit, practice, or perpetuate unequal hiring and occupational upgrading. Once the contextual situation requires blacks to be hired, attitudes are likely to change to reinforce and rationalize the conduct that whites are forced to adopt.

However, we do not mean to imply that attitudes are unimportant. We are persuaded that attitudes are of marginal significance in determining black employment patterns in specific situations. Attitudes determine actions in the context within which decision makers operate. It therefore becomes important to try to influence those attitudes in order to promote social change. However, it is more important to change the context by increasing the supplies of skilled and educated black labor and preventing overt discrimination (whether or not *attitudes* change immediately in those situations). Finally, attitudes are important in the sense that they influence public policy, which in turn influences the employment situation.

Our main argument, then, is that discrimination does not necessarily result directly from the attitudes of individual decision makers. As a result, we think public policy should be directed toward changing the context within which people operate as well as toward changing their attitudes and tastes. Consequently, we are more interested in determining what kinds of things need to be done to improve black employment opportunities than we are in the highly technical and difficult analytical task of isolating the impact of racial prejudice on black employment patterns. We think institutional discrimination is so pervasive that it influences such "productivity" factors as education, on-the-job training, and skills training, making it difficult to pinpoint these factors in the total constellation of forces determining black employment patterns.

White Workers and Unions

A behavioral model such as we propose must include some conceptual framework concerning the factors likely to influence the behavior of white workers and unions. Prevailing racial prejudice is one important factor, but, as we have argued, it does not necessarily determine conduct. White workers are concerned about race as it influences the respect people have for their jobs. If blacks are considered to be "inferior," whites will tend, for this reason, to resist the inclusion of blacks on "their" jobs. However, whether whites succeed in resisting the employment of blacks depends upon the whites' ability to bring pressure to bear on the employer. If whites are in sufficient supply to fill particular occupations, in the absence of countervailing powers, employers will find it profitable to hire only whites. However, if blacks are in sufficient supply to meet the employer's labor requirements, they might be used to weaken white unions or to undermine the wage structures established by whites. In the latter case the employer will not necessarily pay the black workers a different wage, but their presence tends to moderate wages pressures unless blacks and whites form a united bargaining front.

Similarly, the white workers' bargaining power would be weakened even if blacks are in "helper" or other mislabeled occupational categories while really performing the same jobs as whites. Bigoted whites are not likely to quit good jobs because of their racist attitudes, nor are they likely to demand wage differentials to compensate for their prejudices. Even assuming that they have adequate knowledge of alternatives, prejudiced whites are likely to stay on their jobs if moving is costly in terms of loss of seniority, good wages, and the advantages of specialized nontransferable job skills in places where they have worked.

White workers naturally tend to maximize job control and will use the unions they control to preserve and ration job opportunities. Similarly, there are few examples where blacks have used unions they control to bar whites from some jobs, although black power in the larger community has not been strong enough to give blacks control of very many "good" jobs. Consequently, the union does not create job discrimination, but it might be used to perpetuate the exclusion of blacks from certain jobs or to strengthen job segregation within plants.

Race enters into the union operating procedures in a variety of ways. Different kinds of unions have different motives and procedures and therefore will react differently to the presence of black workers or potential workers. If there are no black workers in an industry or trade, unions are motivated by monopoly and status considerations to keep them out. Whether these unions are able to bar blacks depends mainly on their control of entry into the occupation. Craft unions, for example, ordinarily have considerable control of the supply of labor. The three main job-control instruments of craft unions are control of (*a*) training, (*b*) entry into the trade and union, and (*c*) job referrals. In order for blacks to penetrate these crafts and unions, they must ordinarily either threaten the unions' control instruments or inflict monetary losses on unions. Because of their entrenched powers, the craft unions' racial practices are likely to be changed less by direct threats than by appeals which offer to help preserve basic union control processes in exchange for the admission of blacks. Apprenticeship outreach programs have been moderately successful where they follow the above pattern. However, these programs have been more successful outside the South than in some southern cities because there have been stronger threats to the unions' control procedures in the North than in the South.

In cases where there are supplies of black workers who can replace striking or boycotting whites, unions ordinarily have not been successful in excluding blacks. Union conditions would clearly be undermined by exclusion unless black competitors could be relegated to nonunion positions or otherwise restricted so that they could not compete directly with union members. However, some unions, such as the Brotherhood of Locomotive Firemen, have allowed their race biases to weaken the union by refusing to organize large numbers of black competitors. In this case, however, the union attempted to have black firemen removed from their jobs. In the case of such unions as the carpenters and bricklayers, on the other hand, blacks could not be excluded in the South, but they could be segregated and ordinarily were before World War II.

Industrial unions generally have adopted different procedures mainly because they confronted different situations, not because their members had any more or less racial prejudice than craftworkers, although job status considerations seem to have been weaker in the case of industrial unions. But the main difference between craft and industrial unions is that the latter have little direct influence over hiring. In order to organize their jurisdictions, industrial unions must therefore appeal to the workers hired by the employer. Thus, if blacks have been hired in competition with white workers, the union's ability to organize and its bargaining strength will depend on its ability to attract blacks.

The growth of industrial union membership, and black participation in those unions, was augmented by events during the 1930s. As was demonstrated in chapter 1 black workers' power to change union racial practices was strengthened when the Railway Labor and National Labor Relations acts established government-supervised elections to determine whether unions would be given representation rights.

The legal developments gave industrial unions motives for catering to black workers in order to gain their support in representation elections and in order to avoid prosecution by courts, the National Labor Relations Board, and other government antidiscrimination agencies. But there were other motives as well, because the industrial unions formed during and after the New Deal had broad political and social objectives which required them to form political alliances with black leaders.

The political objectives have carried over to the AFL-CIO, mainly a political organization. Since federations and national unions have broader political objectives than the locals, the motive for racial equality increases as we move from the local to the national level. Moreover, national craft unions also have stronger motives to take in blacks than do their locals because the national's power depends to some extent upon the size of its membership, whereas the local often conceives its power to depend more narrowly upon control of labor supplies in local labor markets.

Although the racial practices of unions will depend upon union structure (local, national, federation, craft, or industrial) and the impact of blacks on the union's ability to carry out its primary objectives through its usual job-control procedures, there are many counteracting forces impinging on the racial practices of a local union. Local leaders interested in keeping their jobs must consider their relations with the white membership, with the black membership, and with employers. If blacks are organized into effective political forces within unions, or if there are many blacks in jurisdictions the union is trying to organize, the union's leaders will be more responsive to black interests. If there are few or no blacks and the local's white members are either racists or have strong interests in restricting job opportunities to white members and their relatives, they will resist the admission of blacks.

Yet there are forces tending to overcome white control of job opportunities, including more problack attitudes in the larger community, government measures to increase black employment opportunities, pressures on the local from its national union organization (making the power relation between national and local unions and between the national and the AFL-CIO or other unions important linkages in the power-transmission channels influencing local union racial practices), and the power and organization of the black workers outside the union. The blacks outside craft unions derive their power mainly from the extent to which they can threaten the wage rates and job-control procedures of discriminating white union members and their leaders; this in turn depends, primarily, on the number of blacks in a labor market who possess the necessary skills to compete with white union members and, secondarily, on the extent to which the black community and antidiscrimination forces are organized to overcome white resistance to the admission of blacks. Even if civil rights forces are well organized to achieve this objective, they will have limited impact unless they produce black applicants for employment, upgrading, apprenticeship, or journeyman status who meet the qualifications imposed by unions and employers, or unless they successfully challenge the standards and specifications themselves. These considerations make it obvious that an effective strategy to overcome local union resistance ordinarily will require considerable attention to local labor market conditions and the control mechanisms used by the local union to regulate labor supplies and control jobs.

These specific and immediate forces affecting black employment patterns are influenced by such general factors as the relative amount and quality of education available to blacks, race relations in the larger community, the age and sex composition of the black work force, alternative income sources available to black workers and their families, housing patterns and transportation costs relative to the location of jobs, the physical and emotional health of blacks relative to whites, whether an industry is growing or declining in terms of employment, black and white migration patterns, the structure of industry in terms of its customers (blacks, whites, other employers, or government), general business conditions, skill requirements and job structures within industry, the black community's relative accessibility to job information, and the processes through which employers and unions recruit and train workers for jobs.

Summary

While all these factors are important determinants of black employment patterns, some are more important and measurable than others. We started this study with the conviction that general business conditions were very important because tight labor markets would facilitate the employment and upgrading of blacks. However, we refined this view because experience has made it clear that tight labor markets–which characterized most of the SMSAs we studied–were necessary but not sufficient causes of change. Moreover, there is a difference between a labor market where unemployment is declining and one where unemployment is low and stable. Our studies also caused us to conclude that concerted efforts to change institutional arrangements can make it possible for black employment to increase in a particular category even when white employment is falling, as was the case between 1966 and 1969 in many of the cities we studied. Thus, we should keep in mind that we are dealing with patterns caused by a complex constellation of forces rather than single, "most important" causes.

We also refined our thinking about the importance of education. The extent to which education is a significant variable in black employment has been debated. Some observers have argued that education is not important, because blacks seem to gain very little with increasing education, and indeed blacks with higher levels of education are discriminated against relatively more than those with lower levels of education (Thurow, 1969, pp. 76–80).

However, we found education to be a much more complicated variable than this sample analysis would imply. For one thing, the importance of education was in a state of dynamic flux during the 1960s as employers and unions formalized their entry requirements in response to civil rights forces and as broadening job opportunities increased black motives to acquire education and rising incomes increased their ability to do so. Moreover, the relative quality of black education also undoubtedly rose as a result of continued urbanization of the black population and the racial ferment following World War II. Nevertheless, in using education as a variable to explain black employment patterns, we face the problem of discounting for the relative quality of black education. Our evidence is fairly uniform that the educational attainment gap between blacks and whites increases with the level of education.

Another measurement problem with respect to education involves establishing the relationship between education and productivity (which is highly correlated with income) (Levitan et al., 1972). We suspect that education and other factors influencing black job opportunities strongly affect the kinds of jobs blacks are likely to get. Lifetime income-earning abilities are influenced very strongly by the kinds of job ladders people get on, because experience and on-the-job training opportunities vary with different kinds of jobs. Education tends to be used as a screening device for jobs with higher levels of return per year of experience.

In the past blacks have been barred from jobs with upward occupational mobility regardless of their level of education. If these jobs are opened up to blacks, as there is some evidence that they have been, then returns to education for younger blacks would be greater than returns to their parents, a trend reinforced by the declining gap in the quality of education. As a consequence, estimates based on returns to average levels of education for blacks would understate the future significance to them of increasing their levels of education.

Conclusion

In order to put our basic conceptual framework in perspective, this chapter has examined a number of empirical and theoretical studies of employment discrimination. Because of its wide acceptability among economists, we examined the neoclassical model in considerable detail and concluded that it provided some useful analytical insights, but, because it forces the problem of racial discrimination into the price-theory mold, the neoclassical model inadequately defines discrimination and does not include enough variables either to provide sufficient understanding of the basic factors influencing black employment patterns or to form the basis for policy prescriptions to promote equal employment opportunities.

We therefore favor behavior models which specify different variables for various kinds of discrimination (overt and institutional) and for different aspects of employment opportunity (employment or penetration rates and upgrading or occupational position).

Employment patterns are products of profit-maximizing decisions made by employers, influenced to varying degrees by actual and anticipated reactions from unions, white employees, customers, government officials, and public opinion. Moreover, since the employment patterns of black women are determined by different factors from those of black men, we have found it useful to specify different models for each sex.

The reactions of white workers, who are influenced by job status and control of job opportunities, are particularly important in understanding racial employment patterns. Sometimes whites use unions to accomplish their objectives, but we have seen that labor organizations vary in their racial practices according to the influence of racial exclusion or admission on their basic objectives. Similarly, company employment practices also vary according to their product market orientations and the nature of their customers.

Thus, racial employment practices are products of prevailing racial institutions as modified or sustained by the power relationships among and between white workers and their organizations, employers, and blacks and their organizations. Public opinion influences employment decisions mainly through laws and regulations concerning discrimination.

These short-run or immediate factors influencing employment decisions in the South take place within a larger context of social institutions influenced by the long-run political, social, and economic trends discussed in all preceding chapters of this book.

References

Arrow, Kenneth. 1971*a*. *Some Models of Racial Discrimination in the Labor Market*. Santa Monica, Calif.: Rand Corporation (February).

———. 1971*b*. "The Theory of Discrimination." Paper presented at a conference on discrimination in labor markets. Princeton University, October 7–8.

Ashenfelter, Orley. 1971. *Racial Discrimination and Trade Unionism*. Working Paper no. 17. Princeton, N.J.: Industrial Relations Section, Princeton University.

Atkinson, Lloyd. 1970. "The Prospect of Equality of Income between White and Black Families under Varying Rates of Unemployment: A Comment." Mimeographed. College Park: Project on the Economics of Discrimination, University of Maryland.

Becker, Gary. 1957. *The Economics of Discrimination*. Chicago: University of Chicago Press.

Bergmann, Barbara. 1970. "Occupational Segregation, Wages, and Profits When Employers Discriminate by Race and Sex." Mimeographed. College Park: Project on the Economics of Discrimination, University of Maryland.

———. 1971. "The Effect on White Incomes of Discrimination in Employment." *Journal of Political Economy* 79, no. 2 (Spring).

Bergmann, Barbara, and Jerolyn Lyle. 1970. "Difference among Metropolitan Areas and Industries in the Occupational Standing of Negroes in the Private Sector." Mimeographed. College Park: Project on the Economics of Discrimination, University of Maryland.

Briggs, Vernon. 1970. "The Negro in American Industry: A Review of Seven Studies." *Journal of Human Resources* (Summer).

Coleman, James S., et al. 1966. *Equality of Educational Opportunity*. Report to the U.S. Office of Education. Washington, D.C.: Government Printing Office.

Gilman, Harry J. 1965. "Economic Discrimination and Unemployment." *American Economic Review* (December).

Ginzberg, Eli. 1956. *The Negro Potential*. New York: Columbia University Press.

Guthrie, Harold W. 1970. "The Prospect of Equality of Incomes between White and Black Families under Varying Rates of Unemployment." *Journal of Human Resources* (Fall).

Hiestand, Dale. 1964. *Economic Growth and Employment Opportunities for Minorities*. New York: Columbia University Press.

Kain, John. 1968. "Housing Segregation, Negro Employment, and Metropolitan Decentralization." *Quarterly Journal of Economics* (May).

Killingsworth, Charles. 1967. "Jobs and Income for Negroes." Paper prepared for a symposium in social science research in race relations. Mimeographed. University of Michigan.

———. 1968. *Jobs and Income for Negroes*. Ann Arbor: Institute of Labor and Industrial Relations, Wayne State University, and University of Michigan and National Manpower Policy Task Force.

Levitan, Sar, et al. 1972. *Human Resources and Labor Markets*. New York: Harper and Row.

McKersie, Robert. 1971. *An Analysis of Minority Employment Pat-*

terns in the Chicago SMSA. Washington, D.C.: Equal Employment Opportunity Commission.

Maddox, James G. 1967. *The Advancing South: Manpower Prospects and Problems*. New York: Twentieth Century Fund.

Marshall, Ray. 1965. *The Negro and Organized Labor*. New York: John Wiley and Sons.

———. 1967. *The Negro Worker*. New York: Random House.

Mooney, Joseph D. 1969. "Housing Segregation, Negro Employment, and Metropolitan Decentralization: An Alternative Perspective." *Quarterly Journal of Economics* (May).

Northrup, Herbert, et al. 1971*a*. *Negro Employment in Basic Industry*. Philadelphia: University of Pennsylvania Press.

———. 1971*b*. *Negro Employment in Southern Industry*. Philadelphia: University of Pennsylvania Press.

Rayack, Elton. 1961. "Discrimination and the Occupational Progress of Negroes." *Review of Economics and Statistics* (May).

Schiller, Bradley. 1970. "Class Discrimination vs. Racial Discrimination." Mimeographed. College Park: Project on the Economics of Discrimination, University of Maryland.

Strauss, Robert. N.d. *Discrimination against Negroes in the Labor Market*. Madison: Institute for Research on Poverty, University of Wisconsin.

Thurow, Lester. 1969. *Poverty and Discrimination*. Washington, D.C.: Brookings Institution.

Tobin, James. 1965. "On Improving the Economic Status of the Negro." *Daedalus* (Fall).

Weiss, Randall. 1970. "The Effect of Education on the Earnings of Blacks and Whites." *Review of Economics and Statistics* (May).

Welch, Finis. 1967. "Labor Market Discrimination: An Interpretation of Income Differences in the Rural South." *Journal of Political Economy*.

About the Authors and the Center for the Study of Human Resources

VIRGIL L. CHRISTIAN, JR., received a Ph.D. in 1955 from the University of Kentucky, where he now is professor of economics. He attended a summer seminar in statistical quality at the University of Wisconsin in 1957, a summer institute in statistics conducted jointly by Iowa State University and the University of Wyoming in 1959, and a Ford Foundation seminar in mathematical models at the University of Chicago in 1964. He has been a frequent consultant to the Legislative Research Commission, Commonwealth of Kentucky, on various taxation problems and on reapportionment of legislative districts. His published research has been principally in the areas of employment and training, with particular emphasis on the economics of discrimination.

CARL C. ERWIN received a Ph.D. in agricultural economics from the University of Illinois in 1952. He worked in agricultural extension education before joining the Department of Economics at the University of Kentucky in 1956. His research interests have been centered on farm problems, with particular concern regarding the impact of technological change in agricultural production on the black population in the rural south.

ROBERT GLOVER has conducted research on employment discrimination and job training since receiving his Ph.D. in economics from the University of Texas at Austin in 1972. His published work includes *Training and Entry into Union Construction* (U.S. Department of Labor, Manpower R & D Monograph 39, 1975), which he coauthored with Ray Marshall and William S. Franklin, and *Minority Enterprise in Construction* (Praeger, 1978). He presently works as acting director of the Center for the Study of Human Resources and assistant professor at the Lyndon B. Johnson School of Public Affairs, the University of Texas at Austin. He also chairs the Federal Committee on Apprenticeship, a tripartite advisory body to the Secretary of Labor composed of representatives from labor, management, and the general public.

RAY MARSHALL is U.S. Secretary of Labor. He is a nationally recognized economist known for his work on labor market discrimination. His previous books include *The Negro and Apprenticeship* (Johns Hopkins University Press, 1967), coauthored with Vernon M. Briggs, Jr.; *The Negro Worker* (Random House, 1967); *The Negro and Organized Labor* (John Wiley and Sons, 1965); and *Employment Discrimination: The Impact of Legal and Administrative Remedies* (Praeger, 1978), coauthored with Charles Knapp, Malcolm Liggett, and Robert Glover. Marshall received his Ph.D. in economics from the University of California at Berkeley in 1954. He is a past president of the Industrial Relations Research Association and the Southern Economic Association.

ADAMANTIOS PEPELASIS is currently deputy governor of the Agricultural Bank of Greece. He holds degrees from the University of Athens, the London School of Economics, and the University of California at Berkeley, where he received the Ph.D. in 1954. He has taught in the United States at three California institutions–the Berkeley and Davis campuses of the University of California system and San Francisco State College–and at the University of Buffalo, New York, and the University of Kentucky. In addition, he has conducted research for the Social Sciences Research Council, at Stanford University, and with the Agricultural Bank of Greece. His research in the area of economic development has been particularly distinguished and has given him a world-wide reputation.

R. LYNN RITTENOURE currently is chairman of the Economics Department at the University of Tulsa. He received a Ph.D. in economics from the University of Texas at Austin in 1970 and was affiliated with the Center for the Study of Human Resources as a research associate until 1973. His publications include *Black Employment in the South: The Case of the Federal Government* (University of Texas Bureau of Business Research, 1976).

DAVID F. ROSS attended Michigan State University, the University of Michigan, and Harvard University, from which he graduated *magna cum laude* in economics in 1950. He received a Ph.D. degree from Harvard in 1956. He has been a member of the faculty at the University of Puerto Rico, Florida State University, Bethany College, Cuttington College in Liberia, and the University of Kentucky. Also, he served as assistant director of the Office of Economic Research, Economics Development Administration of Puerto Rico. In 1971 he became executive editor of *Growth and Change: a Journal of Regional Development*, published by the College of Business and Economics, University of Kentucky.

Initiated in June 1970, the Center for the Study of Human Resources, University of Texas at Austin, is an interdisciplinary research and training center focused on policy issues concerning education and training, labor markets, equal opportunity, and rural development. Whenever possible, research projects are linked to demonstration efforts to field-test.

Key attention is devoted to the following subjects related to human resource development:

1. Economic policy, particularly economic development of lagging regions and unemployed, underemployed, or subemployed people
2. Employment and training programs, including labor market adjustment procedures, job information and projections, the movement of workers between areas, skill training, pre-employment training, and public employment
3. Antidiscrimination programs and policies
4. Education, with special emphasis on the role of education in the preparation for work
5. Health, welfare, and income maintenance, with special emphasis on the use of these activities to support manpower programs

Index